T0219891

Big Data Analytics

Big Data Analytics

Applications in Business and Marketing

Kiran Chaudhary and Mansaf Alam

CRC Press
Taylor & Francis Group
Boca Raton London

CRC Press is an imprint of the
Taylor & Francis Group, an **informa** business

First edition published [2022]
by CRC Press
6000 Broken Sound Parkway NW, Suite 300, Boca Raton, FL 33487–2742

and by CRC Press
4 Park Square, Milton Park, Abingdon, Oxon, OX14 4RN

© 2022 Taylor & Francis Group, LLC

CRC Press is an imprint of Taylor & Francis Group, LLC

Library of Congress Cataloging-in-Publication Data
A catalog record for this book has been requested

ISBN: 978-1-032-00788-5 (hbk)
ISBN: 978-1-032-18766-2 (pbk)
ISBN: 978-1-003-17571-1 (ebk)

DOI: 10.1201/9781003175711

Typeset in Garamond
by Apex CoVantage, LLC

Contents

Preface

Big Data Analytics: Applications in Business and Marketing is a book that focusses on business and marketing analytics. The objective of this book is to explore the concept and applications related to marketing and business. In addition, it also provides future research directions in this domain. It is an emerging field that can be extended to performance management and improved business dynamics understanding for better decision-making. As we know, investment in business and marketing analytics can create value by proper allocation of resources and resource orchestration processes. The use of data analytics tools can be used to diagnose and improve performance. This book is divided into five parts: Introduction, Applications of Business Analytics, Business Intelligence, Analytics for Marketing Decision Making, and Digital marketing. Part I of this book discusses the introduction of data science, big data, data analytics, and so forth. Part II of this book focuses on applications of business analytics that include big data analytics and algorithm, market basket analysis, customer view—variation in shopping patterns, big data analytics for market intelligence, advancements and challenges in business applications of SAR images, and exploring quantum computing to revolutionize big data analytics for various industrial sectors. Part III includes a chapter related to business intelligence featuring an evaluation study of churn prediction models for business intelligence. Part IV is dedicated to analytics for marketing decision-making, including big data analytics for market intelligence, data analytics and consumer behavior, and the responsibility of big data analytics in organization decision-making. Part V of this book covers digital marketing and includes the prediction of marketing by consumer analytics, web analytics for digital marketing, smart retailing, leveraging web analytics for optimizing digital marketing strategies, and so forth. This book includes various topics related to marketing and business analytics, which helps the organization to increase their profits by making better decisions on time with the use of data analytics. This book is meant for students, practitioners, industry professionals, researchers, and faculty working in the field of commerce and marketing, big data analytics, and comprehensive solution to organizational decision-making.

Kiran Chaudhary
Mansaf Alam
New Delhi, India

Preface

Editors

Dr. Kiran Chaudhary is assistant professor in the Department of Commerce, Shivaji College, University of Delhi. She has 12 years of teaching research experience. She has completed a Ph.D. in marketing (commerce) from Kurukshetra University, Kurukshetra, Haryana. Her area of research includes marketing, the Cyber Security Act, big data and social media analytics, machine learning, human resource management, organizational behavior, business and corporate law. She was district topper in M. Com and among the top 10 at Kurukshetra University, recipient of the Radha Krishnan scholarship of Merit in M.com final year (2007), and topper with 88 % marks in financial management in B.Com. She has published a book on probability and statistics. She has also published several research articles in reputed international journals and proceedings of reputed international conferences. She delivered various invited talks and chaired sessions at international conferences.

Dr. Mansaf Alam is associate professor in the Department of Computer Science, Faculty of Natural Sciences, Jamia Millia Islamia, New Delhi-110025, Young Faculty research fellow, DeitY, Govt. of India, and editor-in-chief, *Journal of Applied Information Science*. He has published several research articles in reputed international journals and proceedings of reputed international conferences published by IEEE, Springer, Elsevier Science, and ACM. His area of research includes big data analytics, machine learning and deep learning, cloud computing, cloud database management system (CDBMS), object oriented database system (OODBMS), information retrieval and data mining. He serves as reviewer of various journals of international repute like *Information Science*, published by Elsevier Science. He is also a member of the program committee of various reputed international conferences. He is an editorial board member of some reputed intentional journals in computer sciences. He has published *Digital Logic Design* by PHI, *Concepts of Multimedia* by Arihant and *Internet of Things: Concepts and Applications* by Springer.

Contributors

Preeti Agarwal
Department of Computer Science,
  Faculty of Natural Sciences, Jamia
  Millia Islamia
New Delhi, India

Maharaja Agrasen
Institute of Technology
New Delhi, India

Mansaf Alam
Department of Computer Science,
  Faculty of Natural Sciences, Jamia
  Millia Islamia
New Delhi, India

Shoaib Amin Banday
Department of Electronics and
  Communication Engineering,
  Islamic University of Science and
  Technology
Awantipora, India

Tarun Krishnan Louie Antony
Department of Information Science
  and Engineering, M.S. Ramaiah
  Institute of Technology
Bangalore, India

Ezeifekwuaba Tochukwu Benedict
University of Lagos
Lagos, Nigeria

Lakshita Bhargava
Institute of Technology
New Delhi, India

Sandeep B.L.
Department of Information Science
  and Engineering, M.S. Ramaiah
  Institute of Technology
Bangalore, India

Krishnaveer Abhishek Challa
Andhra University
Andra Pradesh, India

Iffat Sabir Chaudhry
College of Business, Al Ain University
Al Ain, United Arab Emirates

Kiran Chaudhary
Shivaji College, University of Delhi
New Delhi, India

Md Rashid Farooqi
Department of Commerce and
  Management, Maulana Azad
  National Urdu University (Central
  University)
Hyderabad, India

Zameer Fatima
Institute of Technology
New Delhi, India

Siddhartha Ghosh
Mohan Malaviya School of Commerce
and Management Sciences,
Mahatma Gandhi Central
University
Bihar, India

Siddesh G.M.
Department of Information Science
and Engineering, M.S. Ramaiah
Institute of Technology
Bangalore, India

Nabeela Hasan
Department of Computer Science,
Jamia Millia Islamia
Delhi, India

Li Qin Hu
Department of Information
Management, Chengdu Neusoft
University
Chengdu, China

Suraiya Jabin
Department of Computer Science,
Faculty of Natural Sciences, Jamia
Millia Islamia
New Delhi, India

C.C. Jayasundara
University of Kelaniya
Colombo, Sri Lanka

Pankaj Kakati
Department of Mathematics
Jagannath Barooah College
Jorhat, India

Prachi Kaushik
Department of Computer Science,
Faculty of Natural Sciences, Jamia
Millia Islamia
New Delhi, India

Samiya Khan
School of Mathematics and
Computer Science, University of
Wolverhampton
Wolverhampton, United Kingdom

Alok Kumar
Institute of Technology
New Delhi, India

Neeraj Kumar
Department of Business Management,
L.N. Mishra College
Muzaffarpur Bihar, India

Pavnesh Kumar
Mohan Malaviya School of Commerce
and Management Sciences,
Mahatma Gandhi Central
University
Bihar, India

Hong Liu
Department of Human Resource,
Chengdu University of Technology
Chengdu, China

Suzanee Malhotra
Shaheed Bhagat Singh Evening College,
University of Delhi Sheikh Sarai,
New Delhi, India

Venkata Rajasekhar Moturu
Indian Institute of Management
Visakhapatnam, India

Farooq Mughal
School of Management, University of
Bath
Bath, United Kingdom

Ambika N.
St. Francis College
Bangalore, India

Samala Nagaraj
Woxsen University
Hyderabad, India

Srinivas Dinakar Nethi
Indian Institute of Management
Visakhapatnam, India

Ghanshyam Parmar
Constituent College of CVM University:
Natubhai V. Patel College of Pure
and Applied Sciences
Anand, India

Tripti Paul
Indian Institute of Technology (Indian
School of Mines)
Dhanbad, India

Saifur Rahman
Department of Mathematics, Rajiv
Gandhi University
Itangar, India

Sandip Rakshit
American University of Nigeria
Yola, Nigeria

Rumesh Ranjan
Department of Plant Breeding and
Genetics, Punjab Agriculture
University
Punjab, India

S.R. Mani Sekhar
Department of Information Science
and Engineering, M.S. Ramaiah
Institute of Technology
Bangalore, India

Sana Siddiqui
Department of Computer Science,
Jamia Millia Islamia
New Delhi, India

Tihana Škrinjarić
University of Zagreb
Zagreb, Croatia

Sapna Sood
Accenture
Dublin, Ireland

Anushka Tiwari
Department of Computer Science,
Jamia Millia Islamia
New Delhi, India

Muhammad Nawaz Tunio
Alpen Adria University
Klagenfurt, Austria

Amit Yadav
Department of Information and
Software Engineering, Chengdu
Neusoft University
Chengdu, China

Chapter 1

Embrace the Data Analytics Chase: A Journey from Basics to Business

Suzanee Malhotra

Contents

DOI: 10.1201/9781003175711-1

1.1 Overview

The coming age of business has introduced new terminologies in the business dictionary, some of which add 'data science', 'big data', 'analytics', and many more puzzling terms to the list. With the 'data' coming to the center stage of business, data collection, data storage, data processing, and data analytics have all become fields in themselves. Further, novel data keeps on adding to the previous data sets at humungous speeds. With rapid advances at the front of business, companies place data on the same pedestal as the other corporate assets, for it offers the potential and capabilities to derive many important findings. The sections following provide us with the meanings of *data science* and *big data* and a comparison of the two.

1.1.1 Data Science

With the data and data-related processes becoming more and more worthy, data science has become the need of the hour. *Data science* refers to scientific management of data and data-related processes, techniques, and skills used to derive viable information, findings and knowledge from the data belonging to various fields (Dhar 2013). It is a complex term that deals with collection, extraction, purification, manipulation, enumeration, tabulation, combination, examination, interpretation, simulation, visualization, and other such processes applied to data (Provost and Fawcett 2013). The various processes and techniques applied to data are derived from many different disciplines like computer science, mathematics, and statistical analysis (Dhar 2013). But it is not only limited to these disciplines and finds equal and substantial application in the fields of national defense and safety, medical science, architectonics, social science areas, and business management areas like marketing, production, finance, and even training and development (Provost and Fawcett 2013). In simple terms, *data science* is an all-encompassing term for tools and methods to derive insightful information from the data.

1.1.2 Big Data

Big data is often termed as "high volume, high variety and high velocity" data (McAfee and Brynjolfsson 2012). Big data is known as the enormous repository of data garnered by organizations from a variety of sources like smartphones and other multimedia devices, mobile applications, geological location tracking devices, remote sensing and radio-wave reading devices, wireless sensing devices, and other similar sources (Yin and Kaynak 2015). The global research and advisory firm Gartner considers "big data as high-volume, and high velocity or high-variety information assets that demand cost-effective, innovative forms of information processing that enable enhanced insight, decision making, and process automation" (Gartner Inc. 2021). Many organizations add another 'v', that is, *veracity*, to the definition of big data (Yin and Kaynak 2015). Big data represents the important and huge amount of data not amenable to traditional data-processing tools but with the potential to guide businesses to strategic decision-making from the important insights derived from it (Khan et al. 2017). Big data is categorized into structured, unstructured or semistructured types of data sets (McAfee and Brynjolfsson 2012). *Structured data* refers to well-organised and systematic data (like that once stored in DBMS software). The data that is simply stored in the raw version (like analogue data generated from a seismometer) without any systematic order or structure is known as *unstructured data* (Alam 2012b). In between these two lies *semistructured data*, where some part of data is unstructured and some structured (like data stored in XML or HTML formats).

Other types of data sets can be categorised on the basis of the time, viz., historical (or past information data) or current (novel and most-recently collected information data). On the basis of the source of data collection, data sets can be categorised as *first-party data* (collected by the company directly from their consumers), *second-party data* (purchased from another organization) and *third-party data* (the composite data obtained from a market square). Organizations often keep a customized and dedicated software for storage of big data, from which it can be easily put to computation and analysis to discover insightful trends from data in relation to various stakeholders.

1.1.3 Data Science vs. Big Data

With a basic understanding of these two data-revolutionizing ideas, let's explain the boundaries separating these two.

Data science is an extended domain of knowledge, composed of various disciplines like computers, mathematics, and statistics. Contrastingly, *big data* is a varied pool of data from varied sources so huge in volume that it requires special treatment. Big data can be everything and anything, from content choices to ad inclinations, search results or browsing history, purchasing-pattern trends, and much more (Khan et al. 2015). Data science provides a number of ways to deal with big data and compress it into feasible sets for further analysis. Data science is a superset that provides for both theoretical and practical aid to data sorting, cleaning and churning out of the subset big data for the purpose of deriving useful insights from it. If big data is the big Pandora's box waiting to be discovered, then data science is the tool in the hands of an organization to do such honours. Thus, one can say that, if data science is an area of study, then big data is the pool of data to be studied under that area of study.

After explaining these two upcoming concepts of both data science and big data, now let us turn our focus to the understanding of data analytics and its related concepts.

1.2 Data Analytics

Data analytics is the application of algorithmic techniques and methods or code language to big data or sets of it to derive useful and pertinent conclusions from it (Aalst 2016). Thus, when one uses the analytical part of data science on big data or raw data in order to derive meaningful insights and information, it is called *data analytics*. It has gained a lot of attention and practical application across industries for strategic decision-making, theory building, theory testing, and theory disproving. The thrust of data analytics is on the inferential conclusions that are arrived at after computation of analytical algorithms. Data analytics involves manipulation of big data to obtain contextual meanings through which business strategies can be formulated. Organizations use a blend of machine-learning algos, artificial intelligence, and other systems or tools for data-analytics tasks for insightful decision-making, creative strategy planning, serving consumers in the best manner, and improving performance to fire up their revenues by ensuring sustainable bottom lines.

1.2.1 Relationship Among Big Data, Data Science, and Data Analytics

Data, defined as a collection of facts and bits of information, is nothing novel to organizations, but its importance and relevance has acquired a novel pedestal in the current times. With global data generation growing at the speed of zetta and exabytes, it has indeed become an integral part of the business-management domain. Dealing with a mass of data existing in many folds of layers and cutting across many domains is the common link connecting data science, big data, and data analytics. Table 1.1 summarizes the interconnected relationship among big data, data science, and data analytics.

1.2.2 Types of Data Analytics

It is vital to get a clear understanding of the different variants of data analytics available so as to leverage the stack of data for material benefits. The four variants of data analytics are descriptive, diagnostic, predictive, and prescriptive. The data analytics type is given in Figure 1.1. A combined usage of the different variants of data analytics and their corresponding tools and systems adds clarity to the puzzle—where

Table 1.1   Interconnected Relationship among Big Data, Data Science, and Data Analytics

Big Data →	Data Science →	Data Analytics
Big data is humungous in volume, value, and variated data gathered from different sources, requiring further dissection and polishing using data science and data analytics for important inferences to be derived from it.	Data science refers to a multidisciplinary field that involves collection, mining, manipulation, management, storage, and handling of the big data for smooth utilization and analysis of data.	Data analytics is an approach to derive trends and conclusions from the chunks of processed big data as made available after the initial mining and management processes run under the domain of data sciences for revealing intriguing and influential insights amenable to practical application.

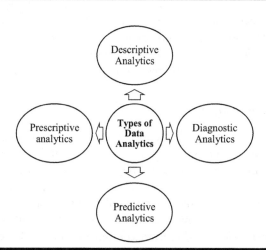

Figure 1.1 Types of Data Analytics.

the firm is standing and the journey to where it can reach by achieving its goals. A discussion regarding the four types is provided in the following paragraphs.

1.2.2.1 Descriptive Analytics

As the name suggests, *descriptive analysis* describes the data in a manner that is orderly, logical, and consistent (Sun, Strang and Firmin 2017). It simply answers the question of 'what the data shows'. It is further used by all the other types of data analytics to make sense of the complete data. Descriptive analytics collates data, performs number crunching on it, and present the results in visual reports. Serving as the primary layer of data analytics, it is most widely used across all fields from healthcare to marketing to banking or finance. The tools and methods applied in the process of descriptive analytics present the data in a summarized form. The data collated from a consumers' mailing records, describing their mail ID, name, and contact details, is an example of it.

1.2.2.2 Diagnostic Analytics

As suggested by the name, *diagnostic analytics* looks into the reasons or causes of any event or happening and supplements the findings of the descriptive analytics (Aalst 2016). It simply answers the question 'why or what led to any specific event?' by delving into the facts to direct the future course of planning. It aims at first diagnosing the problems out of the data sets and then dissecting the reasons behind the problems by using techniques like regression or probability analysis. Such a type of analytics is widely used across fields like medicine to diagnose the cause of the problems, marketing to know the specific reasons behind consumer behavior, or even in the finance area to know the cause behind an investment decision. For example, when diagnostic analytics is applied in the area of human resource, it can provide important details like the reasons behind employee performance or which kind of training and development programs improve employee efficiency.

1.2.2.3 Predictive Analytics

As suggested by the name, *predictive analytics* aims to predict or prognose what could happen in the future (Sun, Strang and Firmin 2017). It simply answers the question 'what events could unfold in future, or what events could flare up?' One of the key features of business is staying ahead of others, and predictive analytics help business firms in maintaining the lead ahead of others by foreseeing what can happen in the future along with some probabilities. Within the available data sets, predictive analytics search for certain patterns or trends for events that could pan out in the future, followed by estimating the probabilities for the events that panned out. It provides predictive insights in areas of retailing and commerce for rolling out products aligned with consumer preferences, stock markets for predicting future stock prices, and even project appraisal areas for forecasting the risks posed. There is no surety of these estimated probabilities fructifying into realities, but still the attained information at hand is better for the business than moving forward in a dark alley.

1.2.2.4 Prescriptive Analytics

As the name suggests, *prescriptive analytics* prescribes a course of action to be adopted by the firm (Sun, Strang and Firmin 2017). It simply answers the question of what the firm should do in the future. Descriptive analytics describes a scenario, diagnostic analytics identifies the important issues of the scenario, predictive analytics predicts what surprises the future holds, but it is the prescriptive analytics that finally guides a business firm through those events. While prescriptive analytics may suggest to grab hold of the strengthening opportunities, the findings may also help a firm to ward-off any danger that it may face by stepping into scenarios that could be threatening to the firm. It can be leveraged for use across fields like business management for budget preparation or inventory management, in healthcare for prescribing suitable treatment, or in construction activities for streamlining operations.

Data analytics has found a place in many fields, from life-saving medicine and surgery (Kaur and Alam 2013) to money-making and finance, from administering government and public works to controlling money supply and banking, from the nation-building education sector (Khan, Shakil and Alam 2016, 2019; Khan et al. 2019; Khanna, Singh and Alam 2016) to entertaining media and hospitality, from automated manufacturing to self-driven cars and trucks, which are a gift of artificial intelligence. Across all the fields, data analytics has made core contributions and is continuing to make further improvements on the road ahead (Syed, Affan and Alam 2019). One such area of utilization of data analytics is the business domain, and business data analytics has become a field of its own. Let us understand the intricacies of the business data analytics in the sections that follow.

1.3 Business Data Analytics

With the clumping of data in each nanosecond, the working of business institutions has drastically seen a reversal. Though 'data' is considered a business asset in current times, what would a clump of data do itself; what benefit would it yield on its own; would the numbers or the bit language of 0s and 1s lead to any amenable change in the existing company position and turnover?

A clear-cut understanding and know-how of the 'whys and why nots' that one wants the data sets to answer can help the business firms to dive for precious pearls. Their discovery can indeed provide mileage to the firms in profitability, revenue generation, and productivity. Business analytics involves the application of varying data analytics tools, techniques, and systems to a big-data pool to derive intriguing insights, simulation models, strategizing decisions, and tactical plans (Christian and Winston 2015). A proper and channelized utilization of analytics in business can help the firms to face the future hiccups in operating the business in the pushing environment. Those firms who miss out on tapping the benefits offered by the analytics at play in business loose tons of add-on value compared to their peers (Amankwah-Amoah and Adomako 2019).

The power of business analytics is not restricted to decision-making only, but many withering industries and firms do seem to apply the power of analytics in industrial, business, and processes reengineering. Due to this, many companies have recently changed their orientation and approach toward data collection, storage, maintenance, and manipulation. From exploration to new discoveries out of big data (Khan, Shakil and Alam 2017), the quantitative tools are applied to make progressive traction in the business growth curve.

Business analytics refers to the deployment of statistical, mathematical, and computing tools (Khan, Shakil and Alam 2018; Kumar et al. 2018; Shakil and Alam 2018), techniques, or systems on the big-data pool for discovering, simulation, examination, extrapolation, interpretation, and communication of the insightful results with the business executives for formidable execution and preparation (LaValle et al. 2011). Business data analytics offer plenty of real-world solutions across multiple business domains. Using the power of question and intuition, a perfect know-how of computing and statistics leveraged along with trending technologies provides solutions to many hard-hitting issues and problems.

1.3.1 Applications of Data Analytics in Business

With daily additions to the existing data pile, the use of data analytics in the business domain is cutting across thresholds, offering novel opportunities to be grabbed and threats to be warded off for the business firms. The correct approach used by business firms to exploit the merits of data analytics can affect the strengths and weaknesses of the firms in competitive markets. An index list of business-data analytics is presented in Table 1.2, which presents the contributions of analytics in the world of business, showcasing the exponential relevance of analytics in this sector more than ever before.

The wide applications of big data analytics (Alam and Shakil 2016; Khan, Shakil and Alam 2018; Malhotra et al. 2017) are capable of making critical contributions to many different fields and arenas, offering potential competitive edges to move forward. Along with the 'buzz' of the concepts like 'data science', 'big data',

Table 1.2 Applications of Data Analytics in Business

Production and Inventory Management	• In product development for gaining knowledge about consumer needs and wants, preferences, and the latest trends • In supply chain management for keeping flow of inbound logistics • In inventory management for maintaining economic order quantity, just-in-time purchases, and ABC analysis of stock items • In production process for seeking productive efficiency gains from the resources put to use

Sales and Operations Management	• In retail-sales management for product shelf display and replenishment, running special discount sales and loyalty programs • In outbound logistics to ensure proper physical distribution to different business locations • In warehouse and storage management for maintaining proper upkeep and ready-to-serve features
Price Setting and Optimization	• In price determination of goods and services, for analysis of the indicators like factor input costs, competitors' price-lists, price elasticity trends, etc. • In tax and duty adjustments regarding different duties, levies and taxes, computations, and calculations • In determining features like discounts, rebates, special prices or coupons • In optimization of input costs and overhead costs for maintaining sustainable profitability
Finance and Investment	• In the stock market to track stock performance, future trend, and company's future earning potential • In capital budgeting decisions for making investment decisions, dividend decisions, or determining the valuation of a firm • In investment banking for the tasks of lead book running, arriving at mergers, and amalgamations decisions • In credit rating generation, financial fraud detection or prevention, portfolio creation, management or diversification
Marketing Research	• In segmenting, targeting, and positioning strategy formulating • For the search-engine optimization process, to return the best and relevant results from search queries run in real time • In advertising from the idea conceptualization to content creation and designing of banners or billboards or directing the advertisement • In creating a recommendation system in this era of ecommerce so that products or services reach the appropriate and targeted audiences • In consumer-relationship building activities by maintaining close links and contacts with consumers, for personalized marketing activities for brand loyalty, and to constantly better the business in providing memorable consumer experiences

(Continued)

Table 1.2 (Continued)

Human Resource Management	• In recruitment and selection for conducting background checks, screening candidates, and calling eligible candidates for interviews • In training and development schemes for building and polishing the skills that employees lack or for the infusion of new skills as per trending needs • In compensation management for successful motivation, retention, and satisfaction of employees by giving them a good mix of both pecuniary and nonpecuniary motives • In performance appraisal for seeking information regarding employee promotion and transfers, career development, and attrition rate

'data analytics', and 'business data analytics', other terminologies like 'data mining', 'data warehouse', and 'data visualization' have come to the fore. Let us explain them now.

1.4 Data Mining, Data Warehouse Management, and Data Visualization

1.4.1 Data Mining

Every diamond, before gleaming on a beautiful finger, requires polishing. In a similar analogy, data needs to be polished and refined before yielding intriguing insights. This useful service is what data mining does. Data mining is one of the first steps of the systematic process of big data analytics. It is described as the process of drawing out the data from varied raw data sources like databases (Alam 2012a), email or spam filtering, or consumer surveys (Tan, Steinbach and Kumar 2014). The tasks of extraction, transformation, and loading of data (ETL) are key composites of the data-mining process (Ge et al. 2017). These simple tasks help to deduce usable data sets in a proper format for further data analysis and maintenance of a data repository. Data mining is one of the most integral but strenuous tasks in the whole data analytics process.

1.4.2 Data Warehouse Management

Maintenance of a data repository is essential for proper and well-managed data storage (Shakil et al. 2018). It is termed *data management* or *data warehouse management* in the process of data analytics (Santoso and Yulia 2017). Data warehouse management involves a well-planned and structured database designed (Malhotra et al. 2018) to have straightforward and simplified access to data for data manipulation or future reference (Agapito, Zucco and Cannataro 2020). The simplistic form of the maintained data warehouse is known as a data mart (Mbala and Poll 2020).

1.4.3 Data Visualization

It's always said a picture explains better than a thousand words. This is so in the case of data analytics, where data presentation or data visualization is capable of independently summarizing tones of data in visually appealing forms to important stakeholders (Ge et al. 2017). Effective and reasonable data visualization forms or charts can narrate the core of the data meaning and give important insights to all the decision-making executives (Tan, Steinbach and Kumar 2014). It involves usage of charticle graphs or captivating diagrams or simple tabular forms to represent all forms of data types, aiding in quicker data-analytics understanding.

1.5 Insights in Action: Gains from Insights Generated out of Data Analytics

In this digital age where consumers keep on expressing their preferences at a click or tap, each of their clicks or taps speaks volumes about useful insights. That is to say, every tap or click reflects usable information for the business firms and thus becomes potential data for business analytics. It can yield important information like the picture of the segmented or target market or how to position the brand message in a specific segment or target market. Even the consumer likes, comments, or reviews can serve as usable data sources. By tapping the data regarding a consumer's likes or comments, the marketer can metaform an understanding regarding the demographic or psychographic picture of them and use the generated insights to hone future consumer experiences or pass on the insightful knowledge to other advertisers for better consumer connect.

The latest Apple iPhone 12 provides the vivid application of data analytics into an actionable product development. Sensing that the age-old competitor like Samsung and upcoming rivals like Realme, Oppo, and Vivo were capturing a larger market share on the grounds of improved camera features with the added advantage of night-mode for dim-light pictures, Apple looked at the consumer data along with churning the data regarding demographic, psychographic, and behavioral segmentation to deliver the most advanced version of the iPhone loaded with features like a fast bionic processing chip, fabulous retina XDR display, protective ceramic shield, perfect Dolby vision for video recording, and advanced night mode for all cameras. It indeed indicates the power of data analytics, which help the business firms in bettering their products and services to cut through the competition.

Two important helping hands in the growth and prevalence of big data and data analytics are machine learning and artificial intelligence, which are discussed in the sections ahead.

1.6 Machine Learning and Artificial Intelligence

In a 2020 Netflix Korean drama called *Start-up*, the lead couple were depicted having a conversation regarding the meaning of 'machine learning'. The female lead had no clue about it, and the male lead drew an analogy from the characters of 'Tarzan' and 'Jane' from the famous Disney film *Tarzan*, where Tarzan, with no previous human encounter (especially from the opposite sex), being in a jungle, learns by and by what things make Jane happy. Similarly, the lead hero explained that, in machine learning, the computer learns from the data by and by to perform operations and present results, making its users happy.

Machine learning is defined as "the machine's ability to keep improving its performance without humans having to explain exactly how to accomplish all the tasks it's given" (Brynjolfsson and Mcafee 2017, 2). Thus, when a machine learns to perform some functions on its own, barring the need for overt programming, to meliorate the user experience, it is referred to as machine learning (Canhoto and Clear 2020; Kibria et al. 2018). In machine learning, an attempt is made to understand the computer algorithms (Alam, Sethi and Shakil 2015) that further let the computer programs automatically improve via continuous experiences (Mitchell 1997).

One practical application of machine learning, utilized by the music-streaming apps like Spotify or Gaana.com, is corresponding the user's music preferences with the music composition details, like the singer or genre information, to automatize likely recommendations for the user in the future (Le 2018). Similarly, in the medical field machine learning can automatize the x-ray machines with respect to the patterns emerging out of the x-ray images for aiding some medical analysis (Iriondo 2020).

Machine learning is of three types, viz., supervised (where the data analysis groups the output under already labelled patterns), unsupervised (where the data analysis groups the output under novel patterns in an unlabelled manner) and reinforcement (where the data analysis happens by constantly taking cues from the environment while constantly learning to extrapolate for new outputs) (Fumo 2017). With the abilities and advances offered by machine learning, it has really become a 'dazzlingly magical buzzword' in the business domain (Stanford, Iriondo and Shukla 2020).

A cinematic delight of director Steven Spielberg, *A.I. Artificial Intelligence* beautifully puts forth the meaning and domain of Artificial Intelligence, popularly dubbed as AI, where an 11-year-old boy, appearing so real with real love-like emotions, happens to be a robot. His journey leads to discovery of a new meaning for audiences at large. Five decades back, with the inception of chess-playing computer programs, AI came to the forefront (Brynjolfsson and Mcafee 2017).

However, recently it has acquired a new meaning with changing times and technology (Iriondo 2020).

The term 'artificial intelligence' means a human-made manner of doing or understanding things and carrying out operations in a system (Kibria et al. 2018). Thus, when human-like intelligence is added to machines or computers for performing functions or activities, it is termed artificial intelligence or AI (Canhoto and Clear 2020; Iriondo 2020). Andrew Moore, once dean at Carnegie Mellon University, has considered AI as "the science and engineering of making computers behave in ways that, until recently, we thought required human intelligence" (High 2017, 4).

Business firms are now actively using both machine learning and AI to collect consumer data to strive to improve their brand experiences in the future (Canhoto and Clear 2020). While machine learning is a step toward AI (Mitchell 1997), the domain of AI is far- and wide-ranging (Kibria et al. 2018). By studying the patterns of big-data sets, new trends and subtle details can be explored for actuating strategies (Brynjolfsson and Mcafee 2017).

The recent gadgets like Siri and Alexa, coupled with human-like skills, are revolutionizing the AI industry, which further pulls the strings for app development and content creation. Siri and Alexa have now become human-like personal assistants aiding the humans with providing data for brand building (Brynjolfsson and Mcafee 2017; Iriondo 2020).

While AI makes a computer do smart work solving multiplex issues with human-like intelligence (Kibria et al. 2018), machine learning analyses the data patterns to automatize the functions, boosting efficiency and effectiveness (Han et al. 2017). AI runs on the key theme of spontaneity, and machine learning broadly runs on premeditated algorithms. However, both serve as important decision tools for business strategy formulation. One can certainly agree that, with the continuing technological pace, sometime in the future today's revered Siri and Alexa may become obsolete like chess-playing programs, and many new things further are waiting to be unfolded in the tech-savvy future (High 2017; Iriondo 2020).

1.7 Course of the Book

With the changing times, 'analytics' is occupying the center stage in the business world. The key actors playing an influential role for the business firms to embrace these changing times are 'big data', 'data science', and 'data analytics'. This book provides a route into these domains, with a special focus from a marketing perspective. The book focusses on exploring these data-centered concepts and their application from marketing, business, and research angles. The Linkages among Big Data, Data Science, and Data Analytics is given in Figure 1.2.

Initial parts of the book provide a conceptual understanding of the contemporary business problems encountered by organizations, big-data analytics and related algorithms, the data mining process, and others. From the conceptual, progress is

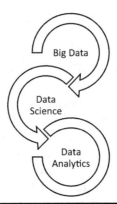

Figure 1.2 Linkages among Big Data, Data Science, and Data Analytics.

made toward the erupting complexities surfacing in the globalization era and how the big-data management approach of businesses can provide unconventional aid in the decision-making of the business world. This is followed by a discussion for the role of big data in contributing intelligent inputs for project life cycle management, decision support systems, and performance management and monitoring. The roles of big-data intelligence and analytics in strategic decisions like supply-chain management, planning, and organizing are further discussed.

Then the course of discussion trends toward the helping hand of analytics lent in the marketing domain specifically. The marketing intelligence analysis derived from the data analytics used in different marketing decisions and strategies like designing marketing mix, value delivery, product life cycle decisions, understanding consumer behavior and decision-making, and making strategic product and service decisions are discussed is length and in depth. The application of analytics in the digital and online marketing domain is covered next. Then the patterns emerging from online marketing, predicting trends from consumer analytics, web-analytics trends, and the usage of marketing intelligence for optimization of marketing efforts is discussed for deriving useful insights, coupled with smart retailing and advertising trends.

So, brace yourself, readers, for we are going to take you all through an insightful and intriguing journey driven by the knowledge and understanding of the buzz of the hour – 'data analytics' in the marketing and business world.

References

Aalst, Will van der. 2016. *Process Mining: Data Science in Action*. Heidelberg: Springer.

Agapito, Giuseppe, Chiara Zucco, and Mario Cannataro. 2020. "COVID-warehouse: A Data Warehouse of Italian COVID-19, Pollution, and Climate Data." *International Journal of Environmental Research and Public Health* 17, no. 5596, 1–22.

Alam, Mansaf. 2012a. "Cloud Algebra for Cloud Database Management System." *The Second International Conference on Computational Science, Engineering and Information Technology (CCSEIT-2012)*. Coimbatore, India: ACM, 26–28.

Alam, Mansaf. 2012b. "Cloud Algebra for Handling Unstructured Data in Cloud Database Management System." *International Journal on Cloud Computing: Services and Architecture (IJCCSA)* 2, no. 6, 2231–5853 [Online]; 2231–6663 [Print]. https://doi.org/10.5121/ijccsa.2012.2603

Alam, Mansaf, Shuchi Sethi, and Kashish Ara Shakil. 2015. "Distributed Machine Learning Based Biocloud Prototype." *International Journal of Applied Engineering Research* 10, no. 17, 37578–37583.

Alam, Mansaf, and Kashish Ara Shakil. 2016. "Big Data Analytics in Cloud Environment Using Hadoop." *International Conferences on Mathematics, Physics & Allied Sciences.* Goa, India: ICMPAS.

Albright, S. Christian, and Wayne L. Winston. 2015. *Business Analytics: Data Analysis and Decision Making*. Stamford, CT: Cengage.

Amankwah-Amoah, Joseph, and Samuel Adomako. 2019. "Big Data Analytics and Business Failures in Data-Rich Environments: An Organizing Framework." *Computers in Industry* 105, 204–212.

Brynjolfsson, Erik, and Andrew Mcafee. 2017. "The Business of Artificial Intelligence." *Harvard Business Review* 7, 3–11.

Canhoto, Ana Isabel, and Fintan Clear. 2020. "Artificial Intelligence and Machine Learning as Business Tools: A Framework for Diagnosing Value Destruction Potential." *Business Horizons* 63, no. 2, 183–193.

Dhar, Vasant. 2013. "Data Science and Prediction." *Communications of the ACM* 56, no. 12, 64–73.

Fumo, David. 2017. "Types of Machine Learning Algorithms You Should Know." *Towards Data Science*, June 15. Accessed December 28, 2020. https://towardsdatascience.com/types-of-machine-learning-algorithms-you-should-know-953a08248861.

Gartner Inc. 2021. *Gartner Glossary, Information Technology*. Accessed January 28, 2021. www.gartner.com/en/information-technology/glossary/big data.

Ge, Zhiqiang, Zhihuan Song, Steven X. Ding, and Biao Huang. 2017. "Data Mining and Analytics in the Process Industry: The Role of Machine Learning." *Ieee Access* 5, 20590–20616.

Han, Shuangfeng, I. Chih-Lin, Gang Li, Sen Wang, and Qi Sun. 2017. "Big Data Enabled Mobile Network Design for 5G and Beyond." *IEEE Communications Magazine* 55 no. 9, 150–157.

High, Peter. 2017. "Carnegie Mellon Dean of Computer Science on the Future of AI." *Forbes*, October 30. Accessed December 28, 2020. www.forbes.com/sites/peter-high/2017/10/30/carnegie-mellon-dean-of-computer-science-on-the-future-of-ai/?sh=4d9a1a8c2197.

Iriondo, Roberto. 2020. "Machine Learning (ML) vs. Artificial Intelligence (AI)—Crucial Differences." *Medium*, November 12. Accessed December 28, 2020. https://medium.com/towards-artificial-intelligence/differences-between-ai-and-machine-learning-and-why-it-matters-1255b182fc6.

Kaur, Aankita, and Mansaf Alam. 2013. "Role of Knowledge Engineering in the Development of a Hybrid Knowledge Based Medical Information System for Atrial Fibrillation." *American Journal of Industrial and Business Management* 3, no. 1, 36–41. https://doi.org/10.4236/ajibm.

Khan, Imran, Shane Kazim Naqvi, Mansaf Alam, and S.N.A. Rizvi. 2015. "Data Model for Big Data in Cloud Environment." *2015 2nd International Conference on Computing for Sustainable Global Development (INDIACom)*. New Delhi, India: IEEE, 582–585.

Khan, Samiya, Xiufeng Liu, Kashish Ara Shakil, and Mansaf Alam. 2017. "A Survey on Scholarly Data: From Big Data Perspective." *Information Processing & Management* 53, no. 4, 923–944.

Khan, Samiya, Xiufeng Liu, Kashish Ara Shakil, and Mansaf Alam. 2019. "Big Data Technology—Enabled Analytical Solution for Quality Assessment of Higher Education Systems." *International Journal of Advanced Computer Science and Applications (IJACSA)* 10, no. 6, 292–304. https://doi.org/10.14569/IJACSA.2019.0100640.

Khan, Samiya, Kashish Ara Shakil, and Mansaf Alam. 2016. "Educational Intelligence: Applying Cloud-based Big Data Analytics to the Indian Education Sector." *2016 2nd International Conference on Contemporary Computing and Informatics (IC3I)*. Noida, India: IEEE, 29–34.

Khan, Samiya, Kashish Ara Shakil, and Mansaf Alam. 2017. "Big Data Computing Using Cloud-Based Technologies: Challenges and Future Perspectives." In: Mahmoud Elkhodr, Qusay F. Hassan, and Seyed Shahrestani (eds.), *Networks of the Future: Architectures, Technologies and Implementations*. London: Chapman and Hall.

Khan, Samiya, Kashish Ara Shakil, and Mansaf Alam. 2018. "Cloud-Based Big Data Analytics—A Survey of Current Research and Future Directions." In: V.B. Aggarwal, Vasudha Bhatnagar, and Durgesh Kumar Mishra (eds.), *Big Data Analytics*. *Advances in Intelligent Systems and Computing 654*. Singapore: Springer. https://doi.org/10.1007/978-981-10-6620-7_57.

Khan, Samiya, Kashish Ara Shakil, and Mansaf Alam. 2019. "PABED—A Tool for Big Education Data Analysis." *2019 20th IEEE International Conference on Industrial Technology (ICIT 2019)*, Melbourne, Australia: IEEE, 794–799.

Khanna, Leena, Shailendra Narayan Singh, and Mansaf Alam. 2016. "Educational Data Mining and Its Role in Determining Factors Affecting Students' Academic Performance: A Systematic Review." *2016 1st India International Conference on Information Processing (IICIP)*. Delhi, India: IEEE, 1–7.

Kibria, Mirza Golam, Kien Nguyen, Gabriel Porto Villardi, Ou Zhao, Kentaro Ishizu, and Fumihide Kojima. 2018. "Big Data Analytics, Machine Learning, and Artificial Intelligence in Next-generation Wireless Networks." *IEEE Access* 6, 32328–32338.

Kumar, Vinod, Rajendra Kumar, Santosh Kumar Pandey, and Mansaf Alam. 2018. "Fully Homomorphic Encryption Scheme with Probabilistic Encryption Based on Euler's Theorem and Application in Cloud Computing." In: V.B. Aggarwal, Vasudha Bhatnagar, and Durgesh Kumar Mishra (eds.), *Big Data Analytics*. *Advances in Intelligent Systems and Computing 654*. Singapore: Springer. https://doi.org/10.1007/978-981-10-6620-7_58.

LaValle, Steve, Eric Lesser, Rebecca Shockley, Michael S. Hopkins, and Nina Kruschwitz. 2011. "Big Data, Analytics and the Path from Insights to Value." *MIT Sloan Management Review* 52, no. 2, 21–32.

Le, James. 2018. "Spotify's 'This Is' Playlists: The Ultimate Song Analysis for 50 Mainstream Artists." *Towards Data Science*, July 11. Accessed December 28, 2020. https://towardsdatascience.com/spotifys-this-is-playlists-the-ultimate-song-analysis-for-50-mainstream-artists-c569e41f8118.

Malhotra, Shweta, Mohammad Najmud Doja, Bashir Alam, and Mansaf Alam. 2017. "Bigdata Analysis and Comparison of Bigdata Analytic Approaches." *2017 International Conference on Computing, Communication and Automation (ICCCA)*. Noida, India: IEEE, 309–314.

Malhotra, Shweta, Mohammad Najmud Doja, Bashir Alam, and Mansaf Alam. 2018. "Generalized Query Processing Mechanism in Cloud Database Management System." In: V.B. Aggarwal, Vasudha Bhatnagar, and Durgesh Kumar Mishra (eds.), *Big Data Analytics. Advances in Intelligent Systems and Computing 654*. Singapore: Springer. https://doi.org/10.1007/978-981-10-6620-7_61.

Mbala, Isaac Nkongolo, and John Andrew van der Poll. Nov. 16–17, 2020. "Towards a Formal Modelling of Data Warehouse Systems Design." *18th JOHANNESBURG International Conference on Science, Engineering, Technology & Waste Management (SETWM-20)*. Johannesburg, SA: EARET, 323–329.

McAfee, Andrew, and Erik Brynjolfsson. 2012. "Big Data: The Management Revolution." *Harvard Business Review* 90, no. 10, 60–68.

Mitchell, Tom M. 1997. "Does Machine Learning Really Work?" *AI Magazine* 18, no. 3, 11–20.

Provost, Foster, and Tom Fawcett. 2013. *Data Science for Business: What You Need to Know About Data Mining and Data-analytic Thinking*. Sebastopol, CA: O'Reilly.

Santoso, Leo Willyanto, and Yulia. 2017. "Data Warehouse with Big Data Technology for Higher Education." *Procedia Computer Science* 124, 93–99.

Shakil, Kashish Ara, and Mansaf Alam. 2018. "Cloud Computing in Bioinformatics and Big Data Analytics: Current Status and Future Research." In: V.B. Aggarwal, Vasudha Bhatnagar, and Durgesh Kumar Mishra (eds.), *Big Data Analytics. Advances in Intelligent Systems and Computing 654*. Singapore: Springer. https://doi.org/10.1007/978-981-10-6620-7_60.

Shakil, Kashish Ara, Mansaf Alam, Shabih Shakeel, Ari Ora, and Samiya Khan. 2018. "Exploiting Data Reduction Principles in Cloud-based Data Management for Cryo-image Data." *ICCMB '18: Proceedings of the 2018 International Conference on Computers in Management and Business*. Oxford: Association for Computing Machinery, New York, NY, 61–66. https://doi.org/10.1145/3232174.3232177.

Stanford, Stacy, Roberto Iriondo, and Pratik Shukla. 2020. "Best Public Datasets for Machine Learning and Data Science." *Medium*, August 7. Accessed December 28, 2020. https://medium.com/towards-artificial-intelligence/best-datasets-for-machine-learning-data-science-computer-vision-nlp-ai-c9541058cf4f.

Sun, Zhaohao, Kenneth Strang, and Sally Firmin. 2017. "Business Analytics-based Enterprise Information Systems." *Journal of Computer Information Systems* 57, no. 2, 169–178.

Syed, Arshad Ali, Mohammad Affan, and Mansaf Alam. 2019. "A Study of Efficient Energy Management Techniques for Cloud Computing Environment." *9th International Conference on Cloud Computing, Data Science & Engineering (Confluence)*. Noida, India: IEEE, 13–18. https://doi.org/10.1109/CONFLUENCE.2019.8776977.

Tan, Pang-Ning, Michael Steinbach, and Vipin Kumar. 2014. *Introduction to Data Mining*. Harlow: Pearson.

Yin, Shen, and Okyay Kaynak. 2015. "Big Data for Modern Industry: Challenges and Trends [point of view]." *Proceedings of the IEEE* 103, no. 2, 143–146.

Chapter 2

Big Data Analytics and Algorithms

Alok Kumar, Lakshita Bhargava, and Zameer Fatima

Contents

DOI: 10.1201/9781003175711-2

2.1 Introduction

There is no denying the fact that the digital era is on the horizon, and it is here to stay. In this digital era, a shift is occurring from an industry-based to an information-based economy, which has caused a large amount of data to be accumulated with a mindboggling increase every single day. It is estimated that by 2025 we will be generating 463 exabytes of data every day. This staggering amount of data available is both a boon and a curse for humanity. Improper handling of data can lead to breaches of privacy, an increase in fraud, data loss, and much more. If handled properly, a tremendous growth and enhancement in technology can be achieved. The traditional methods of handling and analyzing data like storing data in traditional relational databases usually perform very poorly in handling big data, the reason being the sheer size of the data. This is where the power of big-data analytics comes into full swing.

The key highlight and main contributions of the chapter include

- The main idea behind writing this chapter is to provide a detailed and structured overview of big-data analytics along with various tools and technology used in the process.
- The chapter provides a clear picture of what big-data analytics is and why it is an extremely important and dominant technology in the current digital era.
- We have also discussed different techniques of big-data analytics along with their relevance in different scenarios.
- A later section of the chapter focuses on some of the most popular and cutting-edge algorithms being used in the process of big-data analytics.
- The chapter concludes with a final section discussing the shortcomings of current data analytics techniques, along with a brief discussion of upcoming technologies that can bridge the gaps present in current techniques.

2.2 Big Data Analytics

Big-data analytics in very simple terms is the process of finding meaningful patterns in a large seemingly unorganized amount of data. The primary goal of big-data analysis is always to provide insights into the source that is responsible for the generation of data. These insights can be extremely valuable for companies to understand the behavior of their customers and how well their product is working in the market. Big-data analytics is also extensively used for revealing product groupings as well as products that are more likely to be purchased together. A mindboggling real-world example of this is the 'diaper-beer' product association found by Walmart upon analyzing its consumer's data. The finding suggested that working men tend to purchase beers for themselves and diapers for their kids together when coming back home from work on Friday night. This led Walmart to put these items together, which saw an increase in the sales of both the items. This finding gives a clear demonstration of the power of big-data analytics for finding product associations, as by using classical product-association techniques it is nearly impossible to find such a bizarre correlation. To get a better understanding of how the process of big-data analytics works in the real world, let's take an example of how an ecommerce company can leverage the power of big-data analytics to increase the sales of their product. In this example, we would consider the broad analysis of two categories of data, data generated by the users in the course of purchasing a product and data generated in after-sales customer service. Big-data analytics techniques like market-basket analysis, customer-product analysis, etc. can be used in the first kind of dataset to find associations like product–product association, customer–product association, or customer–customer association. These findings can be used by the company to improve its product-recommendation system as well as product placement on its portal. Similarly, the results obtained after analysis of after-sales data like customer care phone calls, complaint emails, etc. can be used for training customer-care personnel or even in the development and improvement of smart chatbots. These factors combined can increase the overall customer satisfaction, which can boost the sales number and also help in new-customer acquisition. A surface-level picture of the process is provided in Figure 2.1. Big-data analytics also have found widespread application in the field of medical science. Various data-mining and analytics techniques have been used in a variety of medical applications like disease prediction, genetic programming, patient data management, etc. [1–3]. Data analytics can also be used in educational sectors to analyze students; data and generate better frameworks for enhancing their education [4–5].

2.3 Categories of Big Data Analytics

Big-data analytics is usually classified into four main categories as shown in Figure 2.2. In this section, we will be looking into each of these categories in detail as a separate subsection.

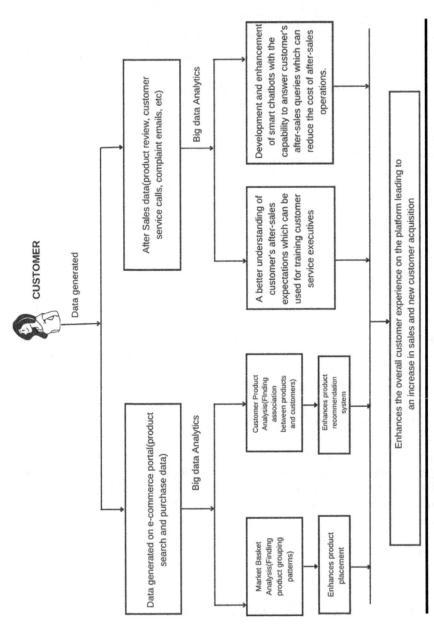

Figure 2.1 Levering Big-Data Analytics in An Ecommerce Company.

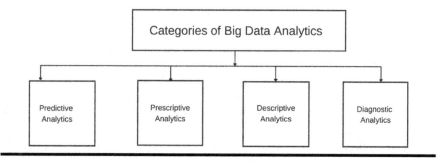

Figure 2.2 Categories of Big-Data Analytics.

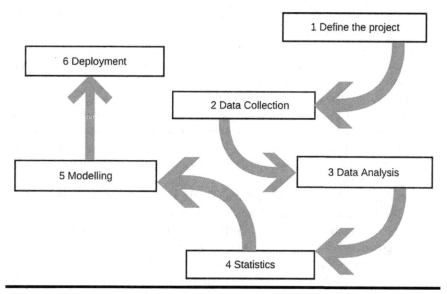

Figure 2.3 Process of Predictive Analytics.

2.3.1 Predictive Analytics

Predictive analytics is a variation of big +-data analytics that is used to make predictions based on the analysis of current data. In predictive analytics, usually historical and transactional data are used to identify risks and opportunities for the future. Predictive analytics empowers organizations in providing a concrete base on which they can plan their future actions. This allows them to make decisions that are more accurate and fruitful compared to the ones taken based on pure assumptions or manual analysis of data. This helps them in becoming proactive and forward-looking organizations. Predictive analytics can even be extended further to include a set of probable decisions that can be made based on the analytics obtained during the process. The whole process of predictive analytics can be broken down into a set of steps as shown in Figure 2.3.

Steps involved in predictive analytics process:

1. Define the project—The first and one of the most important steps in the process of predictive analytics is defining the project. This step consists of identifying different variables like scope and the outcome as well as identifying the dataset on which predictive analytics needs to be executed. This step is extremely crucial as it lays down the foundation for the whole process of data analytics.
2. Data collection—Data is the most fundamental piece of every data-analytics process; it's the same when it comes to predictive analytics. In the data-collection stage organizations collect various types of data through which analytics can take place. The decision to determine the type of data that need to be collected usually depends on the desired outcome of the process established during the project definition stage.
3. Data analysis—The data analysis stage comprises cleaning, transforming, and inspecting data. It is in this stage that patterns, correlations, and useful information about the data are found.
4. Statistics—This is a kind of intermediate stage in which the hypotheses and assumptions behind the model architecture are validated using some existing statistical methods. This step is very crucial as it helps in pointing out any flaws in the logic and highlights inaccuracies that may plague the actual model if unnoticed.
5. Modeling—This stage involves developing the model with the ability to automatically make predictions based on information derived during the data-analytics stage. To improve the accuracy of the model, usually a self-learning module is integrated, which helps in increasing the accuracy of the model over time.
6. Deployment—In the deployment stage, the model is finally deployed on a production-grade server, where it can automatically make decisions and send automated decision reports based on that. It can also be exposed in the form of an application programming interface (API), which can be leveraged by other modules while abstracting the actual complicated logic.
7. Monitoring—Once the deployment is done it is advisable to monitor the model and verify the predictions done by the model on actual results. This could help in enhancing the model and rectifying any minor or major issues that could cripple the performance of the model.

Predictive analytics is being used extensively to tackle a wide variety of problems ranging from simple problems like predicting consumers' behavior on the ecommerce platforms to highly sophisticated ones like predicting the chance of occurrence of a disease in a person based on their medical records. With the advancement in the field of data analytics, the accuracy of predictive analytics models has increased exponentially over the decade, which has enabled their uses in the field of medical science. Maryam et al. have discussed various predictive analytics techniques for predicting

Drug Target Interactions(DTIs) based on analysis of standard datasets [6]. Shakil et al. have proposed a method for predicting dengue disease outbreaks using a predictive analytics tool Weka [1].

2.3.2 Prescriptive Analytics

Prescriptive analytics is a branch of data analytics that helps in determining the best possible course of action that can be taken based on a particular scenario. Prescriptive analytics unlike predictive analytics doesn't predict a direct outcome but rather provides a strategy to find the most optimal solution for a given scenario. Out of all the forms of business analytics, predictive analytics is the most sophisticated type of business analytics and is capable of bringing the highest amount of intelligence and value to businesses [7].

2.3.2.1 How Prescriptive Analytics Works

Prescriptive analytics usually relies on advanced techniques of artificial intelligence, like machine learning and deep learning, to learn and advance from the data it acquires, working as an autonomous system without the requirement of any human intervention. Prescriptive-analytics models also have the capability to adjust their results automatically as new data sets become available.

2.3.2.2 Examples of Prescriptive Analytics

The power of prescriptive analytics can be leveraged by any data-intensive business and government agency. A space agency can use prescriptive analytics to determine whether constructing a new launch site can endanger a species of lizards living nearby. This analysis can help in making the decision to relocate of the particular species to some other location or to change the location of the launch site itself.

2.3.2.3 Benefits of Prescriptive Analytics

Prescriptive analytics is one of the most efficient and powerful tools available in the arsenal of an organization's business intelligence. Prescriptive analytics provides an organization the ability to:

1. Discover the path to success—Prescriptive-analytics models can combine data and operations to provide a road map of what to do and how to do it most efficiently with minimum error.
2. Minimize the time required for planning—The outcome generated by prescriptive-analytics models helps in reducing the time and effort required by the data team of the organization to plan a solution, which enables them to quickly design and deploy an efficient solution

3. Minimize human interventions and errors—Prescriptive-analytics models are usually fully automated and require very few human interventions, which makes them highly reliable and less prone to error compared to the manual analysis done by data scientists.

2.3.3 Descriptive Analytics

Descriptive analytics answers the question of what has happened. The process of descriptive analytics uses a large amount of data to find what has happened in a business for a given period and also how it differs from another comparable period. Descriptive analytics is one of the most basic forms of analytics used by any organization for getting an overview of what has happened in the business. Using descriptive analytics on historic data, decision-makers within the organization can get a complete view of the trend on which they can base their business strategy. It also helps in identifying the strengths and weaknesses lying within an organization. Being an elementary form of analytics technique, it is usually used in conjunction with other advanced techniques like predictive and prescriptive analysis to generate meaningful results.

2.3.4 Diagnostic Analytics

The branch of diagnostic analytics comprises a set of tools and techniques that are used for finding the answer to the question of why certain things happened. Diagnostic analytics takes a deep dive into the data and tries to find valuable hidden insights. Diagnostic analytics is usually the first step in the process of business analytics in an organization. Diagnostic analytics, unlike predictive or prescriptive analytics, doesn't generate any new outcome; rather, it provides the reasoning behind already known results. Techniques like data discovery, data mining, drill-down, etc. are used in the process of diagnostic analytics.

2.3.4.1 Benefits of diagnostic analytics

Diagnostic analytics allows analysists to translate complex data into meaningful visualizations and insights that can be taken advantage of by everyone. Diagnostic analytics also provides insight behind the occurrence of a certain result. This insight can be used to generate predictive- or prescriptive-analytics models.

A comparison of all these four analytics processes along with the critical question answered by each one of them is shown in Table 2.1 and Figure 2.4 respectively.

2.4 Big Data Analytics Algorithms

In the current digital era, data is the new gold. Every organization nowadays understands the importance of having a stockpile of data at its disposal. Companies like Google, Microsoft, and Facebook are dominating the modern era, and a big credit

Table 2.1 Comparison of Different Categories of Data Analytics

Category of classification	Predictive	Prescriptive	Descriptive	Diagnostic
Source of data	Uses historical data	Uses historical data	Uses historical data	Uses historical data
Data manipulation	Fills in gaps in available data	Estimates outcomes based on variables	Reconfigures data into easy-to-read format	Identifies anomalies
Role of analytics	Creates data models	Offers suggestions about outcomes	Describes the state of business operation	Highlights data trends
Technique used	Forecasts potential future outcomes	Uses algorithms, machine learning, and AI	Learns from the past	Investigates underlying issues
Critical question answered	Answers 'What might happen?'	Answers 'If, then questions'	Answer 'What questions'	Answer 'Why questions'

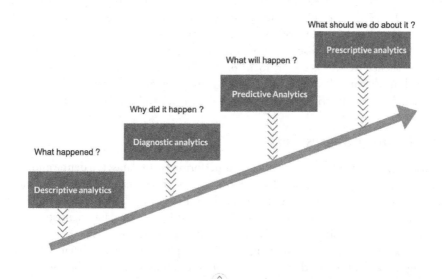

Figure 2.4 Critical Questions Answered by Different Analytics Techniques.

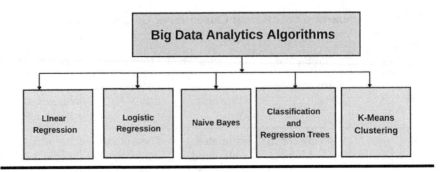

Figure 2.5 Big-Data Analytics Algorithms.

for that goes to the mammoth data stores they have at their disposal. Having such huge data stores at their disposal has enabled these companies to push the boundaries of technological advancement in a way that was never seen before. A burning example that exhibits the power of data and what can be achieved through its proper analytics is Google Maps. Built on top of data pipelines containing a huge amount of dynamic and diverse data collected by Google from multiple sources, it is a piece of technology that seems like something straight from the future.

But having data alone is not sufficient. Data on its own is useless and becomes meaningful only when proper analysis of that data is done. With an unprecedented increase in the amount of data generated in the last couple of years, it has become more necessary now than ever to have fast and efficient data-analytics algorithms at our disposal as the classical methods of data analysis using graphs or charts are simply not enough to keep up with this huge amount of data otherwise also known as Big Data. To solve this problem, data scientists all over the world have developed and are in the process of developing new advanced algorithms for analyzing big data efficiently. To discuss all of these algorithms is beyond the scope of this chapter, hence we will keep our focus on the five most popular big-data analytics algorithms that usually form the basis of the majority of high-performance analytics models. These algorithms are shown in Figure 2.5 and discussed afterward.

2.4.1 Linear Regression

Linear regression is a kind of statistical test performed on a dataset to define and find the relation between considered variables [8]. Linear regression is one of the most popular and frequently used statistical analysis algorithms. Being a very simple yet extremely powerful algorithm for data analysis, it is used by data scientists extensively for designing simple as well as complicated analytical models.

Linear regression, as the name suggests, is a simple linear equation that combines the input values (x) and then generates the solution as a predicted output (y). In the linear-regression model, a scale factor is assigned to each of the input values or independent variables, which is also known as a coefficient and is symbolized using the Greek letter Beta (β). An extra coefficient, also known as intercept or bias coefficient, is added to the equation, which provides an additional degree of freedom to the line. If the linear-regression equation contains a single dependent variable (y) and a single independent variable (x), it is known as *univariate regression* and is represented by equation 2–1:

$$y = \beta_1 * x + \beta_0 \qquad (2\text{–}1)$$

y = dependent variable
x = independent variable
β_1 = scale factor
β_0 = bias coefficient

The regression model with more than one independent variable is known as *multivariate regression*. In a multivariate-regression model, an attempt is made to account for the variation of independent variables in the dependent variable synchronically [9]. The equation of multivariate regression is an extension of univariate regression and is represented in equation 2–2:

$$y = \beta_0 + \beta_1 * x_1 + \cdots + \beta_n * x_n + \varepsilon \qquad (2\text{–}2)$$

y = dependent variable
x = independent variable
$(\beta_1 - \beta_n)$ = scale factor
β_0 = bias coefficient
ε = error

2.4.1.1 Preparing a Linear-Regression Model

Preparing a linear-regression model, also known as model training, is the process of estimating the coefficients of the equation to find the best-fitting line for our dataset. There are several methods for training a linear-regression model. In this section, we will be discussing three of the most commonly used methods among them.

1. Simple Linear Regression—Simple linear regression is a technique for training linear-regression models when there is only one input—or, better to say, only one independent variable—in the equation. In the method of simple linear regression, model statistical properties from the data like mean, standard deviation, correlations, and covariance are calculated, which are used for estimating the coefficients and hence finding the best-fitting line.

2. Least Square—The method of least square is used when there are multiple dependent variables and an estimation of the values of the coefficients is required. This procedure seeks to attenuate the sum of the squared residuals. The method suggests that, for a given regression curve, we can calculate the space from each datum to the regression curve, square it, and determine the sum of all of the squared errors together. This is often the value that the method of least squares needs to attenuate.

3. Gradient descent—The method of gradient descent is used in the scenario when there are one or more inputs and there is a requirement for optimizing the value of the coefficient, which is done by an iterative minimization of the error of the model on training data. The algorithm starts by assigning random values to every coefficient. Calculating the sum of squared errors for all pairs of input and output values is the next step in the process of gradient descent. A learning rate is associated, which acts as a multiplier with which the value of coefficients are updated with the goal of minimizing the error. This process gets terminated when either minimum-squared sum has been achieved or any further improvement is not feasible.

The variation of gradient descent using a rectilinear-regression model is more commonly used as it is relatively straightforward to understand. This algorithm finds application in the scenario when the dataset is large and hence won't fit into the memory.

2.4.1.2 Applications of Linear Regression

Linear regression is a simple yet very sophisticated algorithm that finds application in a wide variety of fields. Roy et al. have proposed a *Lasso Linear Regression Model* for stock-market forecasting [9]. Zameer et al. have used a linear-regression-based model for predicting crude-oil consumption [10]. In general, linear-regression models are quite good in performing predictive data analytics.

2.4.2 Logistic Regression

The technique of *logistic regression* in big data analytics is used when the variable to be considered is dichotomous (binary). The basis of logistic regression, just like all other regression, is a predictive analysis. Logistic regression is employed to elucidate data and to explain the connection between one dependent binary variable and one or more nominal, ordinal, interval, or ratio-level independent variables.

Logistic regression works on the concept of logit—the natural logarithms of an odds ratio [11]. This type of regression model works quite well when the dependent variable is categorical. Some examples of real-world problems where the dependent variable can be categorical are predicting if the email is spam (1) or not (0) or if a tumor is malignant (1) or safe (0). Logistic regression is a component of a bigger class of algorithms referred to as the generalized linear model (GLM). In 1972,

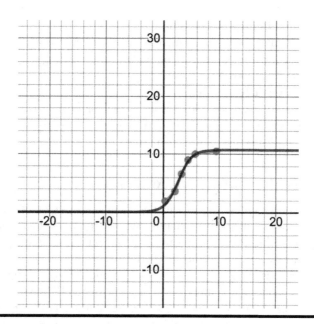

Figure 2.6 A Sample Logistic-Regression Plot.

Nelder and Wedderburn proposed this model in an attempt to supply a way of using rectilinear regression with the issues that weren't directly fitted to the application of rectilinear regression. They proposed a category of various models (linear regression, ANOVA, Poisson regression, etc.), including logistic regression as a special case. Equation 2–3 represents a general equation of logistic regression.

$$loglog\left\{1-p\right\}=\beta_0+\beta_1 * x \qquad (2\text{--}3)$$

(p/1-p) = odd ratio
x = independent variable
β_1 = *scale factor*
β_0 = *bias coefficient*

In this equation $\left\{1-p\right\}$ is the odds ratio. The positive log of an odds ratio usually translates into a probability of success greater than 50%. A sample plot of logistic regression is shown in Figure 2.6.

2.4.2.1 Types of Logistic Regression

1. Binary Logistic Regression
   In binary logistic regression, a categorical response can only have two possible outcomes. Example: Spam or Not email.

2. **Multinomial Logistic Regression**
   In multinomial logistic regression, dependent (target) variables can have three or more categories without ordering. Example: predicting which food is preferred more (Veg, Non-Veg, Vegan).
3. **Ordinal Logistic Regression**
   Ordinal logistic regression is a subset of multinomial logistic regression in which dependent (target) variables can have three or more categories but in a defined order. Example: movie rating from 1–5.

2.4.2.2 Applications of Logistic Regression

Logistic regression is a simple yet efficient algorithm that finds application in a wide variety of fields. Due to its predictive nature, logistic regression finds application in fields ranging from education to healthcare. Ramosaco et al. have developed a logistic-regression-based model to study students' performance levels [12]. Alzen et al. have proposed another logistic-regression-based model to find the relationship between the learning assistant model and failure rates in introductory STEM courses [13].

Although linear regression and logistic regression are both regression-based models, they do share a lot of differences. These differences are shown in Table 2.2.

Table 2.2   Difference between Linear and Logistic Regression

Linear Regression	Logistic Regression
Linear regression is used to predict the continuous dependent variable using a given set of independent variables.	Logistic regression is used to predict the categorical dependent variable using a given set of independent variables.
Linear regression is used for solving the regression problem.	Logistic regression is used for solving classification problems.
In linear regression, we predict the value of continuous variables.	In logistic regression, we predict the values of categorical variables.
In linear regression, we find the best-fitting line, by which we can easily predict the output.	In logistic regression, we find the S-curve by which we can classify the samples.
The least-square estimation method is used for the estimation of accuracy.	The maximum-likelihood estimation method is used for the estimation of accuracy.
The output of linear regression must be a continuous value, such as price, age, etc.	The output of logistic regression must be a categorical value such as 0 or 1, Yes or No, etc.

Linear Regression	Logistic Regression
In linear regression, it is required that the relationship between the dependent variable and independent variable be linear.	In logistic regression, it is not required to have the linear relationship between the dependent and independent variable.
In linear regression, there may be collinearity between the independent variables.	In logistic regression, there should not be collinearity between the independent variables.

2.4.3 Naive Bayes Classifiers

Naive Bayes classifiers are a set of classification algorithms supported by Bayes' theorem. It's not one algorithm but a family of algorithms where all of them share a standard principle, i.e. every pair of features being classified is independent of every other.

Naive Bayes uses the probabilistic approach for constructing classifiers. These classifiers can simplify learning by assuming that features are independent of given class [14]. Naive Bayes classification is a subset of Bayesian decision theory. It's called *naive* because the formulation makes some naive assumptions [15].

The main assumption that Naive Bayes classifiers make is that the value of a specific feature is independent of the value of the other feature. Despite having an oversimplified assumption, Naive Bayes classifiers tend to perform well even in complex real-world scenarios. The main advantage that Naive Bayes classifiers have over other classification algorithms is the requirement of a little amount of training data for estimating the parameters necessary for classification, which is used for an incremental training of the classifier.

2.4.3.1 Equation of the Naive Bayes Classifiers

To understand the equation of Naive Bayes classifiers we need to understand Bayes' theorem, which is the fundamental theorem on which Naive Bayes classifiers work.

Bayes' theorem

Bayes' theorem finds the probability of the occurrence of an event, given the probability of another event that has already occurred. Bayes theorem is stated mathematically as shown in equation 2–4:

$$P\left(\frac{A}{B}\right) = \frac{P\left(\frac{B}{A}\right) * P(A)}{P(B)} \qquad (2\text{–}4)$$

P(A) = Probability of occurrence of event A
P(B) = Probability of occurrence of event B
P(A/B) = Probability of A given B
P(B/A) = Probability of B given A

Bayes' theorem can be extended to find equations of various Naive Bayes classifiers.

2.4.3.2 Application of Naive Bayes Classifiers

Naive Bayes classifiers, despite having certain limitations and assumptions, work quite well for solving classification problems. Karthika and Sairam propose a classification methodology utilizing the Naive Bayesian classification algorithm for the classification of persons into different classes based on various attributes representing their educational qualification [16]. Qin et al. research classifying multilabel data based on Naive Bayes classifiers, which can be extended to multilabel learning [17].

2.4.4 Classification and Regression Trees

Classification and regression trees (CART) is a term coined by Leo Breiman to allude to the decision tree class of algorithms that are used to solve the classification and regression predictive analytics problems.

Traditionally, this calculation is alluded to as 'decision trees'; however, in certain programming languages like R they are alluded to by the more present-day term CART. The CART algorithms give an establishment for some other significant algorithms like bagged decision-tree algorithms, random-forest algorithms, and boosted decision-tree algorithms.

2.4.4.1 Representation of CART Model

The CART model can be represented as a binary tree. Each node in the tree represents a single input variable (x) and a split point theorem variable, and the leaf node is represented using an output variable (y), which is utilized for forecasting.

For example, suppose a dataset having two input variables (x) of height in centimeter and weight of a person in kilogram the output variable (y) will tell whether the sex of the person is male or female. Figure 2.7 represents a very simple binary decision tree model.

A straightforward way for making predictions using the CART model is with the help of its binary tree representation. The traversal of the tree starts with the evaluation of a specific input starting with the root node of the tree. Each input variable in the CART model can be thought of as a dimension in an n-dimensional space. The decision tree in this model splits this plane into rectangles for two input

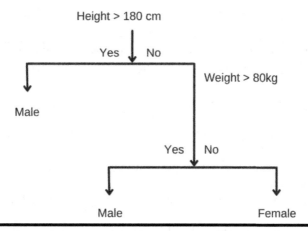

Figure 2.7 Representation of Binary Decision-Tree Model.

variables or into hyperrectangles for higher inputs. The input data gets filtered through the tree and gets placed in one of the rectangles, whereas the prediction made by the model is the output value for the same rectangle; this gives us some idea about the type of decisions that a CART model is capable of making, e.g. boxy decision boundaries.

2.4.4.2 Application of Classification and Regression Trees

Pham et al. have used a classification and regression tree-based model for predicting the rainfall-induced shallow landslides in the state of India based on a dataset of 430 historic landslide locations [18]. Pouliakis et al. have done a study on CART-based models to estimate the risk for cervical intraepithelial neoplasia [19]. Iliev et al. have proposed a CART-based model for modeling the laser output power of a copper bromide vapor laser [20].

2.4.5 K-Means Clustering

K-means clustering is a very simple yet popular data-analytics algorithm. It is an unsupervised algorithm as it capable of drawing conclusions from datasets having only input variables without the requirement of having known or labeled outcomes. The goal of the K-means algorithm is very basic: just group similar data points and reveal the pattern present in the dataset. K-means tries to find a predefined number (k) of the cluster in the dataset. A cluster in very simple terms can be thought of as a group of similar data points. The prerequisite of the algorithm is the target number *k*, which denotes the number of centroids required by us. A centroid can either be a real or an imaginary point that represents the center of one single cluster. Each information point is designated for every one of the groups by reducing the in-cluster sum of squares. The K-means algorithm distinguishes the predefined number of centroids and afterward allots each data point to the nearest cluster, with the goal being to keep the centroids as tiny as could be expected. The 'means' in the K-means alludes to the aggregation of the information or, say, finding the centroid.

2.4.5.1 How K-Means Clustering Works

For handling the learning information, the K-means algorithm in data analytics begins with a set of randomly selected centroids; these are utilized as the starting point for each cluster and afterward perform iterative calculations to improve the places of the centroids.

It stops making and optimizing cluster when either of the conditions is met:

- The centroids have stabilized and the algorithm can proceed further, i.e. the clustering has been successful.
- The predefined number of iterations has been reached.

2.4.5.2 The K-Means Clustering Algorithm

The K-means clustering algorithm follows the approach of expectation-maximization. The expectation step is assigning the data point to the closet cluster. The maximization step is finding the centroid of each of these clusters. The final goal of the K-means algorithm is to minimize the value of squared error function given as:

$$J(V) = \sum_{i=1}^{c}\sum_{j=1}^{c_i}\left(\left\|x_i - v_j\right\|\right)^2$$

$\left|x_i - v_j\right|$ is the Euclidean distance between x_i and v_j

2.4.5.3 Application of K-Means Clustering Algorithms

Being a high performing, unsupervised learning algorithm, K-means finds application in a wide variety of fields. Due to its popularity, researchers have created different hybrid versions of this algorithm that are being used extensively in numerous fields. Youguo & Haiyan have developed a clustering algorithm on top of K-means clustering, which provides greater dependence to choose the initial focal point [21]. Shakil and Alam have devised a method for data management in the cloud-based environment on the basis of the K-means clustering algorithm [22]. Alam and Kishwar have categorized various clustering techniques that have been applied to web search results [23]. Alam and Kishwar have proposed an algorithm for web-search clustering based on K-means and a heuristic search [24].

2.5 Conclusion and Future Scope

In this chapter, we looked into the basics of data analytics along with its application in the real world. We also looked into various categories of data analytics along with some of the most commonly used data-analytics algorithms as well as their applications to the real-world scenario. Apart from the algorithms discussed in this chapter, data scientists all over the world have been working on designing faster and more efficient algorithms. The idea of using neural-network-based algorithms has been also proposed by data scientists [25, 32]. With the rise of quantum computing in the last couple of years, scientists are also looking forward to the possibility of leveraging the power of quantum computers in big-data analytics [26]. Cloud-based big-data analytics is also becoming quite popular as it can leverage the power of cloud computing for big-data analytics [27–31]. With these new technological advancements on the horizon, it can be safely assumed that the future of big-data analytics is going to be bright and exciting.

References

1. Shakil, K. A., Anis, S., & Alam, M. (2015). Dengue disease prediction using weka data mining tool. *arXiv preprint arXiv:1502.05167.*
2. Khan, M. W., & Alam, M. (2012). A survey of application: Genomics and genetic programming, a new frontier. *Genomics, 100*(2), 65–71.
3. Shakil, K. A., Zareen, F. J., Alam, M., & Jabin, S. (2020). BAMHealthCloud: A biometric authentication and data management system for healthcare data in cloud. *Journal of King Saud University-Computer and Information Sciences, 32*(1), 57–64.
4. Khanna, L., Singh, S. N., & Alam, M. (2016, August). Educational data mining and its role in determining factors affecting students academic performance: A systematic review. In *2016 1st India International Conference on Information Processing (IICIP)* (pp. 1–7). New York: IEEE.
5. Shakil, K. A., Sethi, S., & Alam, M. (2015, March). An effective framework for managing university data using a cloud based environment. In *2015 2nd International Conference on Computing for Sustainable Global Development (INDIACom)* (pp. 1262–1266). New York: IEEE.
6. Bagherian, M., Sabeti, E., Wang, K., Sartor, M. A., Nikolovska-Coleska, Z., & Najarian, Z. (2021). Machine learning approaches and databases for prediction of drug—target interaction: a survey paper. *Briefings in Bioinformatics, 22*(1), 247–269. https://doi.org/10.1093/bib/bbz157
7. Šikšnys, L., Pedersen, T. B., Liu, L., & Özsu, M. (2016). Prescriptive analytics. *Encyclopedia of Database Systems,* 1–2.
8. Kaya Uyanık, G., & Güler, N. (2013). A study on multiple linear regression analysis. *Procedia—Social and Behavioral Sciences, 106,* 234–240. https://doi.org/10.1016/j.sbspro.2013.12.027.
9. Roy, S. S., Mittal, D., Basu, A., & Abraham, A. (2015). Stock market forecasting using LASSO linear regression model. In: Abraham, A., Krömer, P., &

Snasel, V. (eds.), *Afro-European Conference for Industrial Advancement. Advances in Intelligent Systems and Computing*, vol. 334. Cham: Springer. https://doi.org/10.1007/978-3-319-13572-4_31.

10. Fatima, Z., Kumar, A., Bhargava, L., & Saxena, A. (2019). Crude oil consumption forecasting using classical and machine learning methods. *International Journal of Knowledge Based Computer Systems*, *7*(1), 10–18.

11. Peng, J., Lee, K., & Ingersoll, G. (2002). An introduction to logistic regression analysis and reporting. *Journal of Educational Research*, *96*, 3–14. https://doi.org/10.1080/00220670209598786.

12. Ramosaco, M., Hasani, V., & Dumi, A. (2015). Application of logistic regression in the study of students' performance level (Case Study of Vlora University). *Journal of Educational and Social Research*, *5*(3). https://doi.org/10.5901/jesr.2015.v5n3p239.

13. Alzen, J. L., Langdon, L. S., & Otero, V. K. (2018). A logistic regression investigation of the relationship between the Learning Assistant model and failure rates in introductory STEM courses. *International Journal of STEM Education*, *5*, Article number 56. https://doi.org/10.1186/s40594-018-0152-1.

14. Rish, I. (2001). An empirical study of the naïve bayes classifier. *IJCAI 2001 Work Empir Methods Artif Intell*, *3*.

15. Kaviani, P., & Dhotre, S. (2017). Short survey on naive bayes algorithm. *International Journal of Advance Research in Computer Science and Management*, *4*.

16. Karthika, S., & Sairam, N. (2015). A naïve bayesian classifier for educational qualification. *Indian Journal of Science and Technology*, *8*. https://doi.org/10.17485/ijst/2015/v8i16/62055.

17. Qin, F., Tang, X., & Cheng, Z. (2012). Application and research of multi_label Naïve Bayes Classifier. In *Proceedings of the 10th World Congress on Intelligent Control and Automation* (pp. 764–768). New York: IEEE. https://doi.org/10.1109/WCICA.2012.6357980.

18. Pham, B. T., Tien Bui, D., & Prakash, I. (2018). Application of classification and regression trees for spatial prediction of rainfall-induced shallow landslides in the Uttarakhand Area (India) using GIS. In: Mal, S., Singh, R., & Huggel, C. (eds.), *Climate Change, Extreme Events and Disaster Risk Reduction. Sustainable Development Goals Series*. Cham: Springer. https://doi.org/10.1007/978-3-319-56469-2_11.

19. Pouliakis, A., Karakitsou, E., Chrelias, C., Pappas, A., Panayiotides, I., Valasoulis, G., Kyrgiou, M., Paraskevaidis, E., Karakitsos, P. (2015). The application of classification and regression trees for the triage of women for referral to colposcopy and the estimation of risk for cervical intraepithelial neoplasia: A study based on 1625 cases with incomplete data from molecular tests. *BioMed Research International*, *2015*, Article ID 914740, 10 p. https://doi.org/10.1155/2015/914740.

20. Iliev, I. P., Voynikova, D. S., & Gocheva-Ilieva, S. G. (2013). Application of the classification and regression trees for modeling the laser output power of a copper bromide vapor laser. *Mathematical Problems in Engineering*, *2013*, Article ID 654845, 10 p. https://doi.org/10.1155/2013/654845.

21. Li, Y., & Wu, H. (2012). A clustering method based on K-means algorithm. *Physics Procedia*, *25*, 1104–1109. https://doi.org/10.1016/j.phpro.2012.03.206.

22. Shakil, K. A., & Alam, M. (2014). Data management in cloud based environment using k-median clustering technique. *International Journal of Computer Applications*, *3*, 8–13.

23. Alam, M., & Sadaf, K. (2013). A review on clustering of web search result. In: *Advances in Computing and Information Technology* (pp. 153–159). Berlin, Heidelberg: Springer.

24. Alam, M., & Sadaf, K. (2015). Web search result clustering based on heuristic search and K-means. *arXiv preprint arXiv:1508.02552.*

25. Mamatha, C., Reddy, P., Kumar, M. A., & Kumar, S. (2017). Analysis of big data with neural network. *International Journal of Civil Engineering and Technology, 8,* 211–215.

26. Shaikh, T. (2016). Quantum computing in big data analytics: A survey. *Conference: 2016 IEEE International Conference on Computer and Information Technology (CIT)* (pp. 112–115). https://doi.org/10.1109/CIT.2016.79.

27. Khan, S., Shakil, K. A., & Alam, M. (2017). Cloud based big data analytics: A survey of current research and future directions. *Big Data Analytics*, Print ISBN: 978-981-10-6619-1, Electronic ISBN: 978-981-10-6620-7, (pp. 629–640). Springer.

28. Alam, M. (2012). Cloud algebra for cloud database management system. *The Second International Conference on Computational Science, Engineering and Information Technology (CCSEIT-2012)*, October 26–28, Coimbatore, India, Proceeding published by ACM.

29. Alam, M. (2012). Cloud algebra for handling unstructured data in cloud database management system. *International Journal on Cloud Computing: Services and Architecture (IJCCSA)*, 2(6), ISSN: 2231–5853 [Online]; 2231–6663 [Print]. https://doi.org/10.5121/ijccsa.2012.2603, Taiwan.

30. Alam, M., & Shakil, K. (2013). Cloud database management system architecture. *UACEE International Journal of Computer Science and its Applications([ISSN 2250–3765), 3,* 27–31.

31. Alam, B., Doja, M. N., Alam, M., & Malhotra, S. (2013). 5-layered architecture of cloud database management system. *AASRI Procedia Journal, 5,* 194–199, ISSN: 2212–6716, Elsevier.

32. Alam, M., Shakil, K. A., Mohd. Javed, S., & Ambreen, M. A. (2014). Detect and filter traffic attack through cloud trace back and neural network. *The 2014 International Conference of Data Mining and Knowledge Engineering (ICDMKE), Imperial College, London, UK, 2–4 July.* Hong Kong: IAENG.

Chapter 3

Market Basket Analysis: An Effective Data-Mining Technique for Anticipating Consumer Purchase Behavior

Contents

DOI: 10.1201/9781003175711-3

3.1 Introduction

In the dynamic market landscape of the 21st century, marketers have been trying for quite some time to get a detailed insight into product affinity and customer buying behavior. This is when the concept of market-basket analysis (MBA) comes into the picture (Blattberg, Kim, & Neslin, 2008). A number of research studies have been carried out to explore MBA and its relevance for marketers. According to Cavique (2007), a *market basket* refers to the itemset bought together by a customer on one visit to a store. MBA is a pivotal tool that assists in implementing cross-selling strategic approaches by marketers and businesses. This approach scrutinizes the commodities and products that customers tend to purchase together. This process sheds light on crucial information that untimely helps marketers and businesses to determine what products to promote together or cross-sell (Blattberg, Kim, & Neslin, 2008).

3.1.1 An Insight into the Market-Basket Analysis Approach

In technology-driven times, new kinds of technologies are being used by marketers to optimally use data and information and sustainably exist in the market setting. According to Nengsih (2015), association rules are among the most useful data-mining techniques used to identify the relationship between one item and another (Nengsih, 2015).

Data mining has been identified as an important step depicted as the retrieval pattern relating to a large crude data set. The innovative technique is implemented to unveil any important knowledge or information found in the data. In the 21st century's technology-driven times, the approach is considered a major step in knowledge retrieval in the database (Kurniawan et al., 2018). In huge databases, the association rule concept comes into play, which helps locate relationships and associations in a huge series of data items. In the MBA concept, association rules are explored intensively to find the products purchased together with other commodities. The generation of an association rule is considered vital in the analytical process as it involves discovering frequent items purchased (Sahnoun et al., 2018). MBA is a data-mining technique used to explore the system of association among various products. This analytical approach is considered valuable in the business landscape as the probable percentage relating to combined commodities relation gives useful knowledge, which ultimately helps make important business decisions (Nengsih, 2015).

Videla-Cavieres and Ríos (2014) have stated that MBA is one of the most applied techniques used while working on transactional data in the market setting. This analytical concept is a part of the plethora of data-mining techniques available today. The fundamental purpose of the MBA approach is to get a customer to spend more money based on two distinctive principles. The first principle involves up-selling, which relates to purchasing a large quantity of the same commodities or adding new warranties or features. The second principle revolves around cross-selling, which involves adding different commodities and items from diverse product categories (Videla-Cavieres & Ríos, 2014). The analysis process encompasses a set of statistically infinite computations considered high relevance in the business domain. They help business managers get a detailed insight into the customers. This tool ultimately helps them to serve the market audience in a better way. The MBA approach sheds light on the combination of products and commodities purchased together. The relationship ultimately determined helps increase a business entity's profitability by adopting suitable strategies such as recommendations, promotions, cross-selling strategies, etc. The analytical approach is based on the theory that customers who purchase a specific product or group of products are more likely to purchase another particular product or group of products. The Market Basket Analysis is shown in Figure 3.1.

For example, if a customer buys cookies and cake in a quick-serve restaurant, they are more likely to purchase a beverage than someone who didn't purchase cookies from the restaurant. Such a correlation is considered valuable in case it is stronger than the cookies and the beverage without the cake (Grosvenor, 2020). The analytical methodology creates value for marketers by locating relationships and establishing patterns across diverse purchases. The relationship that is modelled by the analysis is in the form of a conditional algorithm. According to Monteserin and Armentano (2018), 'the conventional market basket analytical approach fundamentally looks for combining items that typically co-occur

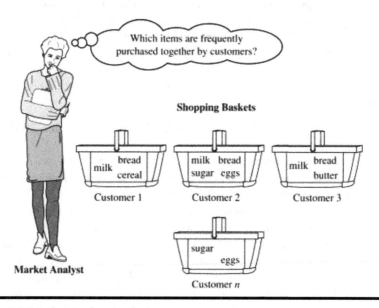

Figure 3.1 Market Basket Analysis

Source: Han, Kamber, & Pei (2012)

in transactions'. Kaur and Kang (2016) have pointed out that a diverse range of algorithms can be used to perform MBA. But the existing algorithms are capable of working on static data and cannot capture the fluctuations and changes in the data with evolving time.

3.2 Application of Market-Basket Analysis

MBA, which is also referred to as *affinity analysis* or *association rule learning*, is highly important in diverse fields and disciplines. Some of the areas where it has created high value in recent times include marketing, education, bioinformatics, and many more. According to Kaur and Kang (2016), the application of MBA in the marketing domain is considered to be very useful, which empowers the business entities. The authors have stated that the analytical tool provides useful information to retailers and businesses, which helps to understand the customers' buying behavior in the market setting. Thus, the innovative analytical model's application helps marketers in the dynamic and unpredictable business landscape to make appropriate decisions that improve the business entities' profitability and performance.

Originally, MBA was applied in supermarkets and the transaction data in a particular market setting.

> The analytical model has derived its name from the fact that customers in the supermarket place the purchased items and commodities in their shopping cart or market basket. But in the prevailing times, the application of the market basket analytical concept is not limited to supermarkets. Instead, it can be applied to any industry and sector that involves selling a broad range of items such as banking institutions, direct marketers, and cataloguers and to new sales channels, especially the internet.
>
> **(Blattberg, Kim, & Neslin, 2008)**

Several studies have been carried out exploring how the MBA tool is deployed in retail contexts, supermarkets, or multiple store settings. Chen et al. (2005) have conducted a study to examine MBA in multiple store settings. The method has been used to discover customer buying patterns by extracting the cooccurrences from the stores' transaction database. But, while performing the analysis, a number of barriers could arise that could restrict the ability to capture important assumptions. For example, in the study, one assumption that acts as a barrier is that it is believed that the commodities under consideration are on the stores' shelf at all times. In order to make optimum use of the analytical tool in the multistore setting, it is necessary to address several elements that could act as obstacles.

For instance, the buying pattern's temporal nature needs to be considered, as it could act as an issue while using MBA. Temporal rules have come into existence to overcome the weaknesses associated with the static association rules that consider that patterns remain consistent over time or locate patterns at a specific point in time. It is necessary to address the issue while applying the analytical method or one may generate biased results (Chen et al., 2005, p. 2).

3.3 Role of Market-Basket Analysis in the Business Setting

Studies indicate that the MBA model's application sheds light on marketers' rich and useful information. In his work, Li has suggested that the analytical model is of high relevance for manufacturers as it helps them position their commodities and goods in the market setting. The role of MBA in the business setting is important as it captures valuable quantity and time information that helps produce insightful results (Blattberg, Kim, & Neslin, 2008). The usefulness of the MBA approach is considered an integral component of the analytical system in diverse business settings such as retail entities. The analysis that revolves around technology plays a cardinal role as it helps marketers operating in the ever-evolving business setting to make a diverse range of strategic decisions. Some of the decisions like ascertainment of the placement of commodities and designing suitable sales promotions for diverse customer segments improve customer satisfaction. Hence, the analytical process can help strengthen a business's profit (Annie & Kumar, 2012).

Case study—When a customer visits a supermarket, the first thing she does is grab a shopping cart. While moving up and down the aisles, she would pick up specific commodities and items and place them in her shopping cart. A majority of the items that have been placed might correspond to the shopping list she had made before her shopping. But there is also a possibility that her shopping cart contains other items that she has picked up spontaneously. When she checks out with the store's cashier, the cart contents are logged into the system. This process helps the supermarket see if it can find any pattern or association in the product selection from one shopper to another. This scenario demonstrates how the MBA process is adopted in the supermarket setting to derive useful information about customers surrounding their purchasing behavior (Zhu & Davidson, 2007). According to Loshin (2012), the analytical process looks for relationships relating to objects that 'go together' within a business context. In the real-life setting, the MBA approach goes way beyond the scenario involving the supermarket. This approach can be applied in any context that involves collecting items to identify affinities that could be exploited in some way (Loshin, 2012).

3.4 Use of Market-Basket Analysis in the Business Context

In the business setting, the MBA model's typical input is the 'point-of-sales' (POS) transaction data. This transaction takes place at the end of the customer level. The analytical tool is designed to extract a diverse range of interesting and useful product associations from the transactional data points. The output that is ultimately generated by using the tool comprises a set of product association rules. For instance, if customers purchase product X, they also tend to purchase product Y. In such a scenario, MBA fundamentally eases the managerial efforts and automates the process for ascertaining which products and commodities are purchased together by the customers. Thus, the analytical model's application lets the transaction data speak for itself and thus helps arrive at the association between diverse goods and commodities (Blattberg, Kim, & Neslin, 2008, p. 2).

The concept of MBA is regarded as of cardinal importance in the business landscape of the 21st century, which can have a major influence on diverse strategic elements. The affinities that are arrived at by using the analytical approach can help make decisions pertaining to diverse areas such as product placement, physical shelf sorting and exhibition, and exploiting cross-sell, up-sell, and bundling opportunities for customer retention by anticipating customer purchase behavior.

- **Product placement**—The application of MBA helps retailers and marketers find associations between diverse products. By assessing customers' purchases and locating patterns, businesses can identify the most likely products to be purchased together in the store. Based on the information, they arrange or place the products in close proximity to encourage them to purchase both the commodities in the store (Cavique, 2007).
- **Physical shelf sorting and exhibition**—An alternate use for product placement in the store is to separate the commodities that are typically bought together or at the same time. This step is taken to encourage the customers to wander around the store and make impulsive purchases while buying what they intend to purchase. For example, shampoos and conditioners could be placed in different sections in a store so that customers would move around the store looking for both of these items and impulsively buy other products as well.
- **Exploiting cross-sell, up-sell, and bundling opportunities**—The affinity grouping relating to a diverse range of products could be used by businesses to indicate that customers might be predisposed to purchase the grouped items at the same time. It enables the presentation of the commodities for the cross-selling purpose.
- **Anticipating customer purchase behavior**—When a customer gets in touch with a business entity for serving a relationship, it is likely for the business representative to utilize the MBA approach. The approach is to arrive at

the right kinds of incentives that can create value for the customer, and the business can retain them. The analytical process helps to derive information from past purchase decisions and anticipate their future buying behavior so that their needs can be fulfilled by the business entity (Cavique, 2007).

3.5 Use of Market-Basket Analysis to Get Insight into Customers

Market baskets arise when customers, on their shopping trips, include products and commodities from a broad range of frequently chosen categories in an independent manner. Boztuğ and Reutterer (2008) have stated that, to get a detailed insight such as the buying behavior of the market audience, explanatory models can be used relating to multicategory choice behavior. But, because of the presence of analytical restrictions, it is not possible to apply multicategory choice models in all kinds of categories (Boztuğ & Reutterer, 2008). MBA acts as an instrument that helps business entities demystify customers' behavior in the market landscape. The tool uncovers the association and relationships between different products and commodities by looking for combinations of the items frequently in customer transactions. It can be stated that MBA enables retailers and marketers to recognize the relationship between the products purchased by customers when they shop. According to Vindevogel, Van den Poel, and Wets (2005), MBA is generally promoted as a means that helps obtain product associations on which the promotional strategy of a retailer is based. Former researchers have provided arguments that associated or related commodities with a high level of interest could be effectively promoted by discounting just one of the two products (Vindevogel, Van den Poel, & Wets, 2005). A simple example that can be used to explain the concept involves bread, jam, and eggs. When a customer is buying bread and jam and sees that a discount is provided on eggs, he will likely be encouraged to spend more to buy eggs. Studies that have been carried out relating to the MBA concept shed light on its importance in the prevailing market setting. For instance, Han has stated in his research study that MBA involves frequent itemset mining. This process helps discover and explore associations among diverse items in humongous relational or transactional data sets. In technology-driven times, companies have access to huge volumes of raw data. The MBA is one of the key techniques that comes into play and helps marketers derive useful meaning relating to product complements, correlations, and associations (Han, Kamber, & Pei, 2012).

According to Videla-Cavieres and Ríos (2014), the MBA model is highly important in the real-life market domain. It gives insight into the customers by shedding light on their buying patterns (Videla-Cavieres & Ríos, 2014). But the analytical tool can further help departmental stores and retail chains sell their products by relying on transactional data generated by sales and customer spending. The study team has used the graph-mining technique to perform MBA and extract useful information involving millions of commodity sales transactions. The analysis conducted by using the tool is useful for business undertakings, but it is also useful for customers. The tool creates value for business entities by helping in decision-making and implementing suitable strategies such as cross-selling or up-selling approaches to improve profitability.

On the other hand, MBA is useful for the market audience. It helps them identify the optimum price of a broad range of commodities and products in the market setting. For example, when a business used a bundling strategy or discounting strategy based on the analytical approach, customers could purchase to save money. According to Aguinis and Joo (2013), the concept of MBA originated in marketing to identify the relationship between a group of products, items, or commodities (Aguinis, Forcum, & Joo, 2013). The association that is arrived at by using the analytical tool plays a cardinal role in shaping many business entities' decisions and strategies in the business landscape. Thus, it impacts the customers as well, based on the patterns identified from their purchasing behavior and spending habits.

3.6 The Anticipation of Customer Purchase Behavior

The customer is known to be kind. They are the chief stakeholders that influence any business's survival and sustainability in the highly dynamic and competitive market landscape. Business entities across diverse industries are always looking to get an in-depth insight into their customers' buying behavior and purchasing decisions. The MBA concept plays a key role that assists in anticipation of customer purchase behavior.

The increase in the internet concept has given rise to entirely new avenues for recording, compiling and analyzing business-related data. MBA is considered to be one of the most useful tools that help convert raw data into useful information and translate actionable metrics (Blattberg, Kim, & Neslin, 2008). The MBA tool is considered to be of cardinal importance in the business and marketing landscape as it enables retailers to get detailed insight into the market audience's purchasing behavior. Businesses can use a diverse range of algorithms that help carry out the MBA. The result of the analysis ultimately helps them make appropriate decisions aligned with the customers' buying behavior. In a large retailing context, the analytical procedure is extremely valuable and useful as these retail organizations deal with many items. Thus, the MBA process comes into the picture and explores the association between the products selected or purchased by the customers (Cavique, 2007).

In the highly competitive business landscape, making predictions in the business setting has become a necessary procedure that helps firms to be prepared to adapt to the evolving market context. The MBA technique comes into the picture and helps business organizations make predictions about customers' future purchasing behavior. According to Kumar and Gore, shopping-basket evaluation is highly appealing for retailers (Gangurde, Kumar, & Gore, 2017). Such an analysis is backed by sophisticated technologies that make it possible for business entities across diverse industries and sectors to capture the customers' information and what they purchase in the market setting. The authors have highlighted that the analytical process is precious in the study as it helps business undertakings capture patterns. This allows the retailers to adjust their promotional strategies, marketing strategies, and store setting, which ultimately helps to serve the customers better by making predictions about how they are likely to behave in the future (Gangurde, Kumar, & Gore, 2017). The idea of the MBA approach is simple. It is based on the idea that the customers in the market context who buy particular products or commodities are highly likely to buy another product. Various studies have captured the implication of the analysis of the business processes and operations of retailers. According to Musalem, Aburto, and Bosch (2018), the MBA application helps understand the interdependencies between different product categories (Musalem, Aburto, & Bosch, 2018). The study's findings have highlighted that the processing of the raw data from a retail store or supermarket creates value for the respective business by uncovering the products or product categories that are generally jointly bought by the customers while shopping. The insight into the product interrelationships ultimately helps companies make decisions pertaining to diverse marketing and business strategies. The sales turnover can be increased by making estimations about the market audience's buying behavior. The analysis has direct and significant implications in the practical business setting as retailers can manage their product categories by identifying, acknowledging, and leveraging the interconnectedness among diverse product categories (Musalem, Aburto, & Bosch, 2018). For example, if customers purchase notebooks and pens together, a business might find the association between them by applying the MBA approach. The company could further use the insight, and it could introduce a discount on pens so that the customers would be encouraged to purchase pens while buying notebooks when they come to the store to shop in the future. Aguinis, Forcum, and Joo (2013) have identified in their study that, in marketing, the market basket analytical tool could generate valuable knowledge for marketers that is both relevant and actionable. Thus, in the business landscape, the insight into customer behavior in the near future backed by existing data helps bridge the divide between science and practice (Aguinis, Forcum, & Joo, 2013).

3.7 Implementation of Suitable Strategizes Based on Market-Basket Analysis

A diverse range of studies has pointed out that the MBA process results help businesses make important decisions and devise appropriate strategies and tactics. According to Pande and Abdel-Aty (2009), the MBA methodology is used by retailers and marketers to identify the offerings that are purchased together. The captured transactions shed light on the interdependence among diverse offerings of a business that is further used in the decision-making process and strategic formulation function (Pande & Abdel-Aty, 2009). Some of the chief strategic steps taken by marketers and businesses based on the MBA approach include customizing the promotional strategies, identifying the sales influencers, and arranging the stock-keeping units' display.

■ **Promotional strategies**

The promotional strategy adopted by a business entity plays a cardinal role in influencing the market audience to make confident purchase decisions. For example, the MBA process is considered useful in the online market setting (Blattberg, Kim, & Neslin, 2008). This is because it helps the retailers to examine the buying behavior of the online customers in detail. Thus, the assessment helps make estimations and predictions relating to what the customers might purchase in the future. For instance, if a customer likes barbecues, he is likely to buy meat and barbecue sauce during the weekends. Thus, the insight can help retailers customize special offers based on the needs of individual customers.

■ **Recognizing sales influencers**

All the commodities that exist in a retail store have some degree of affinity with other items. The affinity could be weak or strong. The market analysis approach can help marketers and retailers to study the purchasing trend relating to a specific set of stock-keeping units. For instance, a couple of stock-keeping units could reveal a strong affinity for a specific period, and sales could suddenly reduce because of the existence of a diverse range of factors. Factors include introducing a new brand, the increase in the price of a particular stock-keeping unit, or the unavailability of specific stock-keeping units. Thus the insight could help marketers to comprehend the impact of diverse activities that influence sales.

■ **Better display of stock-keeping units**

The MBA tool can help identify the commodities and goods with some degree of association and relationships, even if they belong to different categories. The information captured by using the analytical process is considered useful for retailers so that products with high affinity can be placed close to one another (Blattberg, Kim, & Neslin, 2008). Such a placing strategy can help marketers to boost the level of sales turnover. For example, when chips are placed close to cold drinks, there is a high possibility that the customers will purchase both the food items. This strategy can help to improve the sales of a business.

3.8 Advantages of Using Market-Basket Analysis for Marketers

The outcome arrived at by a marketer by using MBA comprises a set of association rules. These rules are considered highly valuable for business entities in the dynamic business landscape. They shed light on the association and relationships between different products, items, commodities, and product categories. Marketers and businesses can use the analytical approach insights through the association rules to strengthen the efficiency of their marketing strategic approaches and tactics. The analysis carried out using MBA helps marketers learn how commodities or services are bought at the same time or in a specific sequential order (Blattberg, Kim, & Neslin, 2008). Thus, the association rules derived from the analysis are considered beneficial, valuable, and actionable for the business entities that deal with diverse products and services. Some of the most common categories of businesses that can benefit from applying the MBA process in their respective business landscapes include financial institutions such as credit card firms, retailers, direct marketers, catalog marketers, internet merchants, etc. In the retail business landscape, the MBA approach is considered a cardinal element because it involves a substantial stock-keeping unit (SKU). An Aberdeen Group survey conducted in recent times has revealed that 38% of the retailers who took part in the poll utilized MBA in their respective business contexts. They considered that the tool had a positive impact on their overall business. In the uncertain and dynamic business landscape of the 21st century, the application of MBA is a top necessity that can help business entities get a competitive advantage in their field of operation. The assessment of market basket data sheds light on critical aspects. It provides valuable information that business firms can use to make crucial decisions that influence their business performance in the market domain (Blattberg, Kim, & Neslin, 2008). The broad range of association rules generated by using the analytical tool could help make different decisions that could impact the business at varying levels. For instance, the association rules from the MBA could be applied by a supermarket or a retail chain to manage the shelf space. Therefore, the business would stock the associated commodities close to one another so that customers would not forget to purchase both the products and would be encouraged to buy both the offerings.

The analysis can also be used by businesses to formulate suitable promotional and marketing strategies that are in sync with the target-market audience's previous buying behavior. The insight from historic customer purchasing behavior and buying pattern could be used as the foundation based on which bundling strategies or cross-selling strategic approaches could be designed (Blattberg, Kim, & Neslin, 2008). In addition to this, the analytical model, along with the temporal components, could be of high value for marketers while choosing cross-sectional commodities. For instance, MBA performance can help marketers identify the customers who bought property insurance within nine months of purchase of a property availing a home loan. Thus, such a scenario can help an insurance business to identify the opportunity relating to cross-selling. Therefore, an insurance salesperson's scope is to get in touch with the customers who have purchased property recently on a home-loan basis.

3.9 Summary

The MBA approach is a proper data-mining technique that anticipates customers' purchasing behavior. This innovative analytical process works by following the association rule concept and locating the relationships among a diverse range of commodities, items, and products in the market setting. From the insight into the association based on the transactional data on the customers' end, marketers and businesses can derive meaning from historical data and find relevant patterns relating to the customers' buying behavior and purchasing habits. Based on the information arrived at by using MBA, marketers can formulate suitable strategic approaches and business decisions that align with the customers' buying behavior pattern.

References

Aguinis, H., Forcum, L. E., & Joo, H. (2013). Using market basket analysis in management research. *Journal of Management, 39*(7), 1799–1824.

Annie, L. C. M., & Kumar, A. D. (2012). Market basket analysis for a supermarket based on frequent itemset mining. *International Journal of Computer Science Issues (IJCSI), 9*(5), 257.

Blattberg, R. C., Kim, B. D., & Neslin, S. A. (2008). Market basket analysis. In *Database Marketing* (pp. 339–351). Springer, New York, NY.

Boztuğ, Y., & Reutterer, T. (2008). A combined approach for segment-specific market basket analysis. *European Journal of Operational Research, 187*(1), 294–312.

Cavique, L. (2007). A scalable algorithm for the market basket analysis. *Journal of Retailing and Consumer Services, 14*(6), 400–407.

Chen, Y. L., Tang, K., Shen, R. J., & Hu, Y. H. (2005). Market basket analysis in a multiple store environment. *Decision Support Systems, 40*(2), 339–354.

Gangurde, R., Kumar, B., & Gore, S. D. (2017). Building prediction model using market basket analysis. *The International Journal of Innovative Research in Computer and Communication Engineering, 5*(2), 1302–1309.

Grosvenor, M. (2020). *Market Basket Analysis 101: Anticipating Customer Behavior—Smartbridge.* Retrieved 9 December 2020, from https://smartbridge.com/market-basket-analysis-101/

Han, J., Kamber, M., & Pei, J. (2012). 6-mining frequent patterns, associations, and correlations: Basic concepts and methods. *Data Mining (Third Edition), The Morgan Kaufmann Series in Data Management Systems,* 243–278.

Kaur, M., & Kang, S. (2016). Market basket analysis: Identify the changing trends of market data using association rule mining. *Procedia Computer Science, 85*(Cms), 78–85.

Kurniawan, F., Umayah, B., Hammad, J., Nugroho, S. M. S., & Hariadi, M. (2018). Market basket analysis to identify customer behaviours by way of transaction data. *Knowledge Engineering and Data Science, 1*(1), 20.

Loshin, D. (2012). *Business Intelligence: The Savvy Manager's Guide.* USA: Newnes.

Monteserin, A., & Armentano, M. G. (2018). Influence-based approach to market basket analysis. *Information Systems, 78,* 214–224.

Musalem, A., Aburto, L., & Bosch, M. (2018). Market basket analysis insights to support category management. *European Journal of Marketing, 52*, 1550–1573.

Nengsih, W. (2015, May). A comparative study on market basket analysis and apriori association technique. In *2015 3rd International Conference on Information and Communication Technology (ICoICT)* (pp. 461–464). Nusa Dua, Bali, Indonesia: IEEE.

Pande, A., & Abdel-Aty, M. (2009). Market basket analysis of crash data from large jurisdictions and its potential as a decision support tool. *Safety Science, 47*(1), 145–154.

Sahnoun, S., Boutahala, M., Tiar, C., & Kahoul, A. (2018). Adsorption of tartrazine from an aqueous solution by octadecyl trimethyl ammonium bromide-modified bentonite: Kinetics and isotherm modeling. *Comptes Rendus Chimie, 21*(3–4), 391–398.

Videla-Cavieres, I. F., & Ríos, S. A. (2014). Extending market basket analysis with graph mining techniques: A real case. *Expert Systems with Applications, 41*(4), 1928–1936.

Vindevogel, B., Van den Poel, D., & Wets, G. (2005). Why promotion strategies based on market basket analysis do not work. *Expert Systems with Applications, 28*(3), 583–590.

Zhu, X., & Davidson, I. (2007). *Knowledge Discovery and Data Mining: Challenges and Realities* (p. 118). Hershey: Information Science Reference.

Chapter 4

Customer View— Variation in Shopping Patterns

Ambika N

Contents

4.1 Introduction

Information (Mehdi Khosrow-Pour D.B.A., 2021) investigation is also known as data analytics (Holmlund et al., 2020) (Runkler, 2012). It is learning to examine rudimentary evidence to make judgments about those facts. A significant number of the measures and sequences of facts are scrutinized and computerized into motorized revolution and calculations that work underdone is material for humanoid operation. Information examination actions can discover designs and quantities missing in the bulk of the facts. These records would then be able to be used to progress sequences to expand the universal efficiency of a profession or agenda. Information examination can do substantially more than call attention to blockages. Gaming administrations use evidence examination to set award timetables

DOI: 10.1201/9781003175711-4

for actors that keep most of the players lively in the game. Gratified administrations use a significant amount of like-evidence inspection to keep you ticking, inspecting, or putting together material to get an extra opinion or another snap. Information investigation is divided into four vital categories. Enlightening verification renders what has happened in the timeframe. Has the number of appearances departed? Do dealings havetheir footing for the present period compared to the previous? Demonstrative investigation zeros in addition to ones happened. It considers more arranged content introduced and estimated. Did the environmental condition affect larger dealings? The visionary investigation relocates to the ones that are likely going to happen in the adjacent condition. The dealings of the previous contribution have to be analyzed. What amount of environmental condition framework foresees a hotter season this period? Descriptive investigation recommends a strategy. On the off chance, work estimation is based on the pentad environmental condition framework. It is higher than 58%, and hence we should add a right move to the distillery and rent an additional container to expand production.

Businesses aim to satisfy their customers. They put in a lot of effort to bring satisfaction to their clients. In most of the cases, a business is customercentric. They use different kinds of approaches to convince their customers and provide them assurance of their doings. The trust built in their clients helps their trade grow bigger and bring them good profits. These satisfied clients can also influence their correspondence about their experience with the purchased products. Diverse people make their choices on preferences and needs. The proposal is a case study analyzing the age of the person with respect to the shopping patterns (Falk & Colin Campbell, 1997).

4.2 Literature Survey

Many case studies and surveys were conducted by authors to interpret the customer satisfaction with respect to different kinds of products. The section is a summary of the same. The architecture (Deaton & Gabriel, 1997) was designed to disclose the marketing of the client. The system includes verifying the client by evaluating his identity number. The client data is entered into a computer. The client's distinct numbers along with his dealings are created. The computer accepts the unique number feed and stores the dealings in the processing unit. The component verifies the number feed against the database records. On evaluation, the system acknowledges with the verification status. The data is regularly updated. This database is utilized to surge the market value of the goods sold at the outlet.

To identify the things in a field, the creators (Zhou, Shangguan, Zheng, Yang, & Liu, 2017) apply a Gaussian model-based modification discovery scheme for importance of foundation location in picture handling. They provide differences in emotional changes in the stage floods of each attachment. It consolidates the outcomes from numerous connections. The shop driller recognizes hot things by identifying and checking the client's activities. A client notices it by turning it from the sideview to the front view. A client investigates a thing by selecting it from the dress rack. The two activities show various degrees of interest in things. Clients frequently pivot an appealing thing for its underlying appearance and choose it for a nearer and more itemized examination when they show more interest. The Shop driller performs division on the stage readings to distinguish whether a select/pivot activity happens.

A blended strategy approach (Terblanche, 2018) composed of subjective and quantitative research is a part of the investigation. It has survey improvement, inspecting, information assortment, and measurable evaluation of the information. The six elements are estimated during in-store client shopping encounters. It is exposed to an assessment by a showcasing research specialist and senior showcasing scholastics to guarantee content legitimacy of the survey and things for an investigation on in-store client shopping encounters. An arbitrary email address of clients of a specific retailer is with the information provider. An online survey post on a college site is with the online information assortment. The IBM Statistical Package for the Social Sciences programming program directs an exploratory factor investigation. It distinguishes the factor design of the in-store client spending involvement. The in-store client shop practice model was then exposed to a corroborative factor examination to test the estimation model.

The aftereffects of the primary investigation (Barari, Ross, & Surachartkumtonkun, 2020) affirm the applied model of client experience annihilation. Results show that organization disappointment in web-based shopping prompts incongruence among the expected population. It is a viable and intellectual objective accomplishment. It gives the clients full emotional and psychological experience obliteration information assembly employing an online overview. A pilot survey is given to 30 members to test the nature of the poll. The Qualtrics stage is a plan of exploring poll in Amazon Mechanical Turk. It disseminates the survey among US respondents. The discoveries demonstrate that organizations consider the significance of disappointment. It prompts clients' negative encounters and responses. Albeit's positive experience is the organizational accomplishment of having an online setting. The after effects have examination show administration disappointment. It causes both emotional and intellectual devastation. An exploration control check result shows that the likelihood of administration achievement is high and fundamentally higher than five.

The suggestion (Blackhurst & Upton, 2011) is trade-related method. The algorithm is loaded into the client's system. The work connects to the client's system. The procedure invigilates the client's position with respect to period. The algorithm jolts down the travelling history of the client. The regularity of the client is analyzed by the system. Other facilities provided by the architecture include availability of different offers related to the item, contesting items, and hoarding regarding the item. The system transmits the related promos by analyzing the customer's doings. Some of the factors considered include the purchase history and the client's appeal.

Tobii Pro compact appreciation-following glasses verified the judgment develop-ments of the members and their visual field (Grewal, Ahlbom, Beitelspacher, Noble, & Nordfält, 2018). Eye-following precisely catches what buyers do in the store. It is appropriate to inspect the doings of components that may occur during purchasers from completing their shopping trips as proficiently as expected. The test executives are present at the passage of each store at various times of the week. All buyers pass-ing by the passageway give their interest in an exploratory study. It offers a coupon as remuneration. The members additionally needed to react to a short survey with things identified with their segment data. The member's doings are given to test executives. It has duplicates of receipts. Now, members expressed their satisfaction with the store visit. The crude recordings comprise over 90 periods of film. It was physically implied by the assessment heads, utilizing a broad coding grid, which estimates what the cli-ent takes a gander at and for how long. Coding eminence authorizations of data are given by an extra scientist. It uses rationale authorizations in the implicit information and pictorial examination. These are considered as vital. The excellence watches con-cern cell phone utilization that is uncovered with no errors during coding.

The current creation (Dharssi & Mckay, 2015) gives a framework to following and grouping things being added to and taken out from a shopping repository. An essential microchip inside a movement identification gadget gets information from a motion sensor. An auxiliary microchip inside a picture receives a sign from the vital chip. It catches an image of the object. It gets a gathered shading picture of the thing. It dissects the image to distinguish the object. It makes a record of the object in the shopping container. It includes the character of everything in the shopping repository. One or both movement recognition gadgets and picture gadgets join to and structure part of the store. The location gadget and picture gadget that are not connected don't frame a piece of the container but are presented in the repository. The essential microchip and the auxiliary chip are safely associated with informa-tion sharing over the web. In another viewpoint, the vital chip and the optional microchip associate with information sharing over an intranet.

Frameworks and strategies (Todasco, 2017) for giving client shopping help incor-porate a framework supplier gadget. It first gets client area data from signal gadgets at a shipper's actual area. The principal client area is the data gathering during a shopping meeting a first client gadget. The framework supplier gadget examines the primary client area data to decide a shipper's actual area territory. It is the vendor's actual area in which the client is not available in the shopping meet. The framework supplier gadget at this point chooses the main component from a majority of items. It is related to the vendor's actual area in an information base. It is in the dealer's original area territory. The framework supplier gadget gives an item suggestion to the principal component. It is about the organization of the primary client gadget.

The objective of the study (Machleit & Eroglu, 2000) is to produce a descriptive account. It consisted of the character and kind of emotional responses. The primary sample was from 401 college students at a western university. The second knowledge assortment concerned college students from two different universities, a western and a southern. The secondary flow of knowledge assortment is in the replication functions for insuring looking happenings. Increasing the range of looking practices was deemed particularly fascinating in assessing and comparing the three feeling scales. For the last set of knowledge, the sample consisted entirely of grown-up respondents. Two different daycare clubs and a residential district parenting/social cluster were part of the task. The daycare clubs and also the parenting cluster got $2.00 for every form.

The planned selection paradigm (Mosteller, Donthu, & Eroglu, 2014) is stock-still within the stimulus—organism—response structure. It posts the info conferred influences with its knowledge and process by the individual, poignant activity and attitudinal responses. During this study, online noise functions as the informational provocations conferred to shoppers. The analysis on looking circumstances is the exploitation of the structure that shows the shoppers the method for environmental motives that affect their activity intent and responses, like payment (Shobha, 2020). The study aims to increase the interactionist perspective in an internet atmosphere. It interrogates the connections between the features of online product info and also the sensory activity constructs. The criterion highlights sensory activity tools as an issue inside the patron. It is formed by the client's thoughts of the conferred information. That ultimately influences perceived shopping outcomes. It represents three accurately shaped kinds of product info attributes. The acknowledgment refers to buyers' perceived quality of and settlement with their product selection call. The privilege of the process is the physical alternative of information. It indicates sensory activity facility, whereas the benefit is within the subconscious interprets and abstract fluency. The experiment manipulated info intensity by varying the number of attributes conferred per difference. These thresholds support the numerous variations detected during a previous study.

Different locations were assigned to disseminate reviews and ordered interviewers to administer examinations to handily designated guests. The regime (Yuksel, 2004) of the survey distribution lasted about a month and had 3,500 surveys. The choice of questions created the tactic of the convenience of sampling subject. The guest's sample was throughout late August and early September. It will comprise a large kind of sociodemographic background of respondents. Out of 3,500, 729 usable questionnaires came, which represents a response rate of twenty-one. Of the total, 139 domestic guests came with available questionnaires, and 590 of the questionnaires completed by international guests were appropriate for the analysis. The comparatively low rate of useful forms might be thanks to the expanse of the form and restricted time of guests for fillingin the form. It had been tough to recruit tourists. Its main motivations are unit enjoyment and relaxation.

The multi-way methodology (Shangguan, Zhou, Zheng, Yang, Liu, & Han, 2015) has an impact on the stage elements. The request has three volunteers stroll to and fro along trails 01 and 02 for 10min. More than 20,000 stage analyses records are considered from 48 backscatter join. We arbitrarily picked five labels and investigate their worldly elements. Shopdriller first parts the stage pattern into different stage frameworks. Each edge comprises m × d pixels. In the wake of parting stage patterns into outlines, Shop-driller breaks down pixel esteems in each casing linebyline. Pixel esteems do not have foundation conveyance view as frontal area. The reasoning is that, since clients stop for some time before well-known things, the LOS (line-of-sight links) joins between these labels, and receiving wires will stay hindered for quite a while. Such an edge-based technique prunes labels having LOS joins that are inadvertently hindered by clients. It is fundamental to have a precise Gaussian model for each identifier. The boundaries of Gaussian prototypical figures are applicable when there are not many or no clients in the shop. At that point image estimations of the foundation, parts embedded into the model, and the model boundaries get refreshed.

The recommendations (Fornell, 1992) that advance from the ideal-point model and the exchanging boundary impact propose that consumer loyalty ought to be lower in industries where rehash purchasers face high exchanging costs and where the business offers a homogeneous item to a heterogeneous market. It is a proportion of execution. A few authors even believe consumer (Chaudhary, Alam, Al-Rakhami, & Gumaei, 2021) loyalty to be the best indicator of an organization's future benefits. An instant percentage of exchanging obstructions is hard to get. All expenses related to abandoning one provider for another establish exchanging boundaries. The idea of those boundaries can be different in various enterprises. Any endeavor to quantify every one of them would be a staggering assignment. All things being equal, the supposition is that reasons for dependability other than consumer (Chaudhry, Chandhiok, &Dewan, 2011) loyalty, grumbling administration, and exchanging obstructions are unimportant. Three rules direct the demonstration exertion. The proposal of Tse and Wilton offers a hypothetical. Wilton offers theory and observational aid for remembering the speedy effect of superficial completion for fulfilment. It recommends that it might have a more grounded impact than assumptions in deciding fulfilment. Hirschman's recommendation recognizes three vital results of changes in satisfaction/disappointment: leave, voice, and unwaveringness. If the connection between voice and dependability is positive, the association's protest is practical and deliberate; it transforms complainants into faithful clients. If it is negative, an expanding number of protests make the firm more impervious to client complaints, and complainants are bound to look for different providers.

Five theories (Anderson, 1998) are considered in the examination. The first portrays thatlow fulfillment clients ought to participate in more noteworthy verbal exchange than high-fulfillment clients. The subsequent one: word of mouth ought to be higher for amazingly fulfilled or disappointed clients comparative with those encountering more moderate degrees of fulfillment. The third one is word of mouth movement. It will increase a prominent rate of disappointment increments as fulfillment increments. The fourth theory: the degree of consumer loyalty ought to be higher, and the degree of informal exchange ought to be lower in the United States, instead of Sweden. By and large, it is stable across the two countries.

This investigation (Oh, 1999) gathered information from clients at two lavish lodgings situated in a northeastern US city. An aggregate of 3,451 visitors were reached over a four-week study period. During the examination of time frame, all visitors are in the wake of barring such extraordinary client as welcomed explorers and global gathering voyagers who were accepted to cause reaction inclination for the reasons for the current research. Of the 3,451 visitors reached, 550 took an interest in the investigation, bringing about a reaction pace of 15.9%. The 550 respondents delivered a sum of 545 usable reaction sets. All factors depended on the self-report. The room rates are paid by the subjects and communicated in dollar value and is a substitute proportion of the real cost. They were guestroom tidiness, registration speed, educated workers, neatness of hall territories, guestroom quietness, security and wellbeing, representation cordiality, and guestroom things ready to rock 'n' roll. One regulated survey chose guestroom with the objective visitor's complete name and room number showing up on the envelope. The lodgings' safety faculty conveyed the survey somewhere in the range of 7:00 and 9:00 p.m. consistently during the four-week study period. In the inns' front work area, the board helps to keep away from potential 'two-fold conveyances' and guaranteeing that the subjects had remained at the lodging, at any rate, one night before they got the poll. No follow-up is due to situational troubles emerging from this on-location study. Subjects restored their finished review to either the lodging's primary entryway front counter or the front counter situated on an alternate floor in the inn. All topics were the motivating force of a 30-minute significant distance calling card when they restored the study.

Consumer loyalty (Anderson & Fornell, 2000) has three forerunners: seen quality, seen worth, and client assumptions. Seen quality or execution, the served market's assessment of ongoing utilization experience, is required to have an immediate and positive effect on consumer loyalty. The second determinant of consumer loyalty is esteem or the apparent degree of item quality comparative with the cost paid. Adding superficial worth joins cost data into the model and expands the outcomes across offerings, enterprises, and areas. The third cause, the attended shop's conventions, addresses both the served market's earlier utilization practice with the contribution as well as nonexperimental data accessible through sources, for example, promoting and verbal, and a conjecture of the provider's capacity to convey excellence later on. Clients approach to assess items and administrations that they have bought and utilized. A direct synopsis of what clients say in their reactions to the inquiries may have a specific shortsighted allure. Such a methodology will miss the mark concerning some other rule. The most genuine of these is the skewness of the recurrence circulations. Clients tend lopsidedly to utilize the high scores on a scale to communicate fulfilment. Skewness tends to use a genuinely high number of scale classifications and a different marker approach.

The administration (Trevinal & Stenger, 2014) highlights heterogeneity within the conceptualization of the expertise. Six classes were treated equally within the literature. The psychological feature and affection states charges, figures, and rituals fully fledged by the customers are widely documented. The social side has the sensor physical side solely for offline expertise. The pragmatic aspects of the practice measure are assumed within the literature. The flow is barely thoughtabout within the online consumer expertise literature. It drives the United States to style associate degree integrative abstract framework. It conceptualizes the web-looking expertise supported in four dimensions. It is the offline circumstance that the shopping experience is deep-seated with a physical angle within the context. It visits the time/duration of the expertise. Second, states and metaphorical associations may additionally be a part of the shopping experience. They constitute the associate degree ideologic dimension of the shopping experience related to the flexibility of the web-looking setting to associate and build an unreal world. It is a practice-based or functional dimension. It is thought about victimization aspects that provide measure and doubtless essential components of the shopping experience. The acts and gestures associated with the utilization of tools. The appropriation of settings is routines. Finally, the social dimension is necessary for ancient-looking expertise, maybe half the package of the shopping experience.

The sensational searching exercises (Ofir & Simonson, 2007) are sometimes been studied by examining shoppers' emotional bonding before and once the searching exercise. It aims to increase read by evaluating shoppers' responses with the searching trial before, throughout, and during the searching method, to receive a comprehensive image of the emotional shifts shoppers undergo throughout the searching activity. They tend to expect to urge an additional refined image. The emotions amend throughout the searching. A three-step analysis methodology was used. They use the internet to spot shoppers in United Nations agency as compulsive shoppers. They convey a digital descriptive anthropology study of human activity with shoppers' victimization of their portable phones. They conduct individualized examination with the determined shoppers to listen to them depict their feelings committed to the searching act and their emotions toward searching in their personal textual matter. The trio course complemented one another and yielded the United States. with the flexibility to assure and confirm effect across the various styles of information gathered. The consequence display for ambitious shoppers undergoes an Association in Nursing passionate rollercoaster method throughout the searching method. The initiate committed the feeling to finding a cut price. A cutprice outlines a decent deal or a state of affairs within which the shoppers understand they get intellectual contentment from their acquisition. If ambitious shoppers build a cutprice, they experience pride, emotional state, and destination accomplishment. They succeed to search out a cutprice; they experience frustration, depression and defeat. These feelings shift backward and forward during the searching act. The biggest dissatisfaction for these shoppers comes if they assume they managed to search out a cutprice and notice that it was not one, after all. However, this frustration may be upset if another cut price is found. These findings expand on previous literature by showing that the emotions shoppers undergo throughout the searching method aren't preponderantly negative or actual before or during the searching method. Instead, shoppers move up Associate in Nursing down on an emotional time throughout the searching. They feel pride and satisfaction once searching if they manage to search out a cutprice.

At the principal stage (Sudman, 1980) shopping focuses on multistage region likelihood testing strategies that evolve. At the subsequent stage, care is required in picking data at malls. Testing is preliminary at passageways. It examines inside the focus an area. It is conceivable and requires extra data when the customer showed up at the middle. Restricting the example to a solitary noncentral area prompts huge likely predispositions. Time inspects by methods for likelihood strategies. The organization of customers will fluctuate considerably based on time of day and day of the week. The information is weighed by the number of excursions and attributions. Controlling for sex in the determination cycle is generally preliminary. It amends for differential participation yet is probably not going to have significant sway, without help from anyone else, on other example predispositions.

Examination of the general assessment on Sunday shopping (Bethlehem, 2015) has three reviews. An eye-to-eye review in the retail plazas is a study from an agent's online board. It is an online overview of self-determination. The three reviews were led and utilized a similar poll. Their results were different. Expecting the board study gauges are nearest to genuine populace esteem, the self-choice review and the retail outlet study should be awful surveys. Numerous regions in the Netherlands have a supposed resident board. The board vitally gathers information given the board is a delegate of the populace. It is conceivable if individuals are enlisted for the board by methods for likelihood examining. One path for districts to accomplish this is to choose an arbitrary example from the populace register. It welcomes the chosen individuals to turn into an individual from the board. The exertion evades nonresponse in the enlistment measure. It very well may be shrewd to direct a weighting change strategy to address for a potential absence of representation. A weighting change method applies to the aftereffects of the self-determination review. In the wake of weighting, there were still enormous contrasts between the appraisals of the self-choice overview and the board study.

4.3 Research Methodology

The case study is conducted to understand the needs of the customer. Their age and their wants are evaluated to realize their requirements and what they look for. The clients look into lot of aspects to do their shopping. They pick up their products based on the offers given by dealers. The data is collected from varying age groups. Based on their age, people make their choices. The study interprets the patters they follow. A large part of the population opts to shop for clothing (Francis & Burns, 1992): 32% compared to other products. This is followed by shopping for footwear (Collazzo, 1988): 16%. Figure 4.1 represents the different products opted to shop for by the customers.

I have used quantitative research methodology and heterogeneity sampling in this work. The problem focuses to analyze the different shopping patterns of various customers falling in different age groups. The data is collected among various ages of people irrespective of the gender. The individual makes a choice with the product based on several options like brand, discounts offered, quantity and price offered. They follow a particular interval in shopping. The data is collected from the

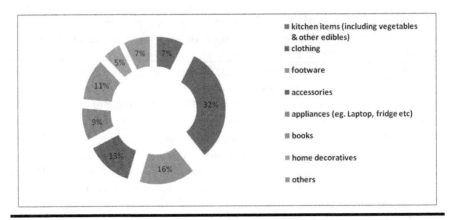

Figure 4.1 Summary of different set of groups opting for various products.

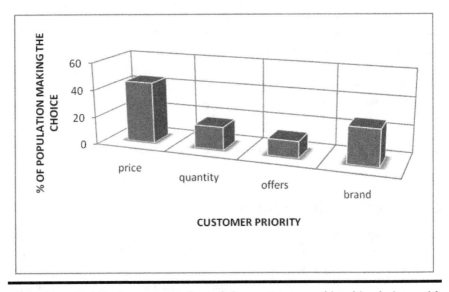

Figure 4.2 Graphical representation of the customer making his choices with respect to various available options.

available population. To draw out conclusions from the data collected, the populace is divided into different age groups, frequency they opt to shop, the priority they make, and various products chosen by them.

If one lowers the price, the quantity (Cude & Walker, 1984) increases. The clients look for quantity, discounts (Carpenter, 2008), price of the product (Lichtenstein, Ridgway, & Netemeyer, 1993), and brand to shop. Most of the customers are concerned about the price of the product (44.7%). 26.3% look for brand (Park & Lennon, 2009) of the product. Figure 4.2 represents the priority given by the customers. Figure 4.3 provides the frequency with which the customers opt to shop for the essentials. Table 4.1 provides the group mean for product shopping, and Table 4.2 displays the calculated ANOVA.

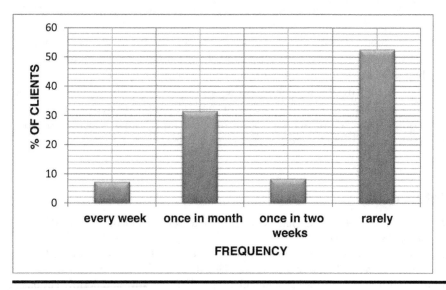

Figure 4.3 Frequency the customers do their shopping.

Table 4.1 Calculation of Group Mean with Respect to Product Shopping

	20–25	*26–35*	*36–50*	*Above 50*
size	55	10	8	2
group mean	29.81	13	12.5	15

Table 4.2 Statistical Computation to Find ANOVA

	Sum of squares (SS)	*Degrees of Freedom (df)*	*Mean squares (MS)*	*F-value*
SSB	8239.96	K=4	MSB=2746	
SSE	475586.4	N-K=51	MSE=9325.22	0.29447
SST	483826.4			

4.4 Conclusion

For traditional purchasing within the ancient shop, you should leave home. You either walk or take a ride to the shop or store to shop for what you needs. It permits one to envision the product before paying the cash. One may get the appropriate product that they like. It is a necessary virtue for individuals shopping for the style stuff like fashion garments and shoes. It ought to confirm the garments or shoe area unit with the right color or size. This virtue of ancient-looking makes sure the deal may be a safe one. Traditional looking makes certain one may get the merchandise. It is often terribly helpful in looking at the urgentlyneeded daily requirements like shampoos and tissues. Today's trend is for most of the populace to go for online purchasing. This method cuts down their time. The study is analyzing the essentials the customer looks into before buying a product.

References

Anderson, E. W. (1998). Customer satisfaction and word of mouth. *Journal of Service Research*, 1(1), 5–17.

Anderson, E. W., & Fornell, C. (2000). Foundations of the American customer satisfaction index. *Total Quality Management*, 11(7), 869–882.

Barari, M., Ross, M., & Surachartkumtonkun, J. (2020). Negative and positive customer shopping experience in an online context. *Journal of Retailing and Consumer Services*, 53, 1–9.

Bethlehem, J. (2015, December). Essay: Sunday shopping-the case of three surveys. *Survey Research Methods*, 9(3), 221–230.

Blackhurst, J., & Upton, M. W. (2011). Patent No. 13/152,052. U.S.

Carpenter, J. M. (2008). Consumer shopping value, satisfaction and loyalty in discount retailing. *Journal of Retailing and Consumer Services*, 15(5), 358–363.

Chaudhary, K., Alam, M., Al-Rakhami, M. S., & Gumaei, A. (2021). Machine learning based mathematical modelling for prediction of social media consumer behaviour using big data analytics. *Journal of Big Data*, 8, Article No. 73.

Chaudhry, K., Chandhiok, T., & Dewan, P. (2011). Consumer protection and consumerism in India. *ZENITH-International Journal of Multidisciplinary Research*, 1(1), 83–94.

Collazzo, C. (1988). A 1986–1987 study of consumer problems in shopping for footwear, with emphasis on size and fit. *Journal of Testing and Evaluation*, 16(4), 421–424.

Cude, B., & Walker, R. (1984). Quantity surcharges: Are they important in choosing a shopping strategy? *Journal of Consumer Affairs*, 18(2), 287–295.

Deaton, D. W., & Gabriel, R. G. (1997). Patent No. 5,621,812. Washington, DC: U.S.

Dharssi, F. T., & Mckay, A. (2015). Patent No. 14/385,713. U.S.

Falk, P., & Colin Campbell, E. (1997.). *The shopping experience*. New York: Sage.

Fornell, C. (1992). A national customer satisfaction barometer: The Swedish experience. *Journal of Marketing*, 56(1), 6–21.

Francis, S., & Burns, L. D. (1992). Effect of consumer socialization on clothing shopping attitudes, clothing acquisition, and clothing satisfaction. *Clothing and Textiles Research Journal*, 10(4), 35–39.

Grewal, D., Ahlbom, C. P., Beitelspacher, L., Noble, S. M., & Nordfält, J. (2018). In-store mobile phone use and customer shopping behavior: Evidence from the field. *Journal of Marketing*, 102–126.

Holmlund, M., Van Vaerenbergh, Y., Ciuchita, R., Ravald, A., Sarantopoulos, P., Ordenes, F. V., & Zaki, M. (2020). Customer experience management in the age of big data analytics: A strategic framework. *Journal of Business Research*, 356–365.

Lichtenstein, D. R., Ridgway, N. M., & Netemeyer, R. G. (1993). Price perceptions and consumer shopping behavior: A field study. *Journal of Marketing Research*, 30(2), 234–245.

Machleit, K. A., & Eroglu, S. A. (2000). Describing and measuring emotional response to shopping experience. *Journal of Business Research*, 49(2), 101–111.

Mehdi Khosrow-Pour D. B. A., e. (2021). *Encyclopedia of information science and technology*, Fifth Edition (3 Volumes). Hershey: IGI Publications.

Mosteller, J., Donthu, N., & Eroglu, S. (2014). The fluent online shopping experience. *Journal of Business Research*, 67(11), 2486–2493.

Ofir, C., & Simonson, I. (2007). The effect of stating expectations on customer satisfaction and shopping experience. *Journal of Marketing Research*, 44(1), 164–174.

Oh, H. (1999). Service quality, customer satisfaction, and customer value: A holistic perspective. *International Journal of Hospitality Management*, 18(1), 67–82.

Park, M., & Lennon, S. J. (2009). Brand name and promotion in online shopping contexts. *Journal of Fashion Marketing and Management: An International Journal*, 149–160.

Runkler, T. A. (2012). *Data analytics*. Wiesbaden: Springer. https://doi.org/10.1007/978-3-658-14075-5.

Shangguan, L., Zhou, Z., Zheng, X., Yang, L., Liu, Y., & Han, J. (2015). ShopMiner: Mining customer shopping behavior in physical clothing stores with COTS RFID devices. In *13th ACM conference on embedded networked sensor systems* (pp. 113–125). Seoul South Korea: ACM.

Shobha, B. G. (2020). digital payments-analysis of its present status in India. *International Journal of Creative Research Thoughts (IJCRT)*, 8(7), 4071–4081.

Sudman, S. (1980). Improving the quality of shopping center sampling. *Journal of Marketing Research*, 17(4), 423–431.

Terblanche, N. S. (2018). Revisiting the supermarket in-store customer shopping experience. *Journal of Retailing and Consumer Services*, 40, 48–59.

Todasco, M. (2017). Patent No. 9,760,927. Washington, DC: U.S.

Trevinal, A. M., & Stenger, T. (2014). Toward a conceptualization of the online shopping experience. *Journal of Retailing and Consumer Services*, 21(3), 314–326.

Yuksel, A. (2004). Shopping experience evaluation: A case of domestic and international visitors. *Tourism Management*, 25(6), 751–759.

Zhou, Z., Shangguan, L., Zheng, X., Yang, L., & Liu, Y. (2017). Design and implementation of an RFID-based customer shopping behavior mining system. *IEEE/ACM Transactions on Networking*, 25(4), 2405–2418.

Chapter 5

Big Data Analytics for Market Intelligence

Md. Rashid Farooqi, Anushka Tiwari, Sana Siddiqui, Neeraj Kumar, and Naiyar Iqbal

Contents

DOI: 10.1201/9781003175711-5

5.1 Introduction

The whole traditional business and marketing has become more digital. Traditional methods or strategies are being replaced with data-supported strategies and campaigns focused upon computation. Big data acts as a tool to accelerate the growth of business and marketing (Sun & Yearwood, 2014). The present era is one of big data (Chen & Zhang, 2014). Big data and its accompanying technology, big-data analytics, have brought new revolution to the area of research, innovation, and development as well as in business and management (Alam et al., 2013). Big-data analytics services have produced big market change (Ahmad & Alam, 2014) in order to facilitate big-data-driven conclusions for corporations and individuals to reach our desired output from business. It has come to be a conventional market adopted in a big way through corporate industries, organizations, and geographical regions (Gandomi & Haider, 2015). Market intelligence has received wide attention in academics, and research development has received attention in business and commerce management (Delen & Demirkan, 2013) over the past two decades. This is not only supposed to be an important technology for enhancing the performance of a business but also an implement for growing ecommerce and eservices. (Turban et al., 2011). However, market intelligence came across new opportunities and challenges due to dramatic development of big data and big-data analytics. It has come to be one of the important research frontiers (Chen & Zhang 2014). This has become a serious matter for business, ecommerce, eservices, and information systems—that is, the manner in which the big data can be used to enhance market intelligence. Big data is the great game-changing chance for business and marketing since the internet went conventional just about twenty years ago. Nowadays, businesses have become very complex organizations facing an overwhelming amount of data complexity within the firm, fast change in consumer behavior, and increased competitive pressure. The new emerging technology as well as quick accretion channels and platforms have been created. A multiplex nature simultaneous with technology and the explosion of data allowed for an unparalleled array of insight into customer requirements and behaviors. A few companies are earning big-data promises in reality. In fact, those firms that use big data analytics are effectively showing much productivity and profit rising 5 to 6% higher than those of their peers (www forbes.com 2013). Those who are using big data analytics are effectively show a much better rate of productivity and profitability. The industry is embarking on cutting-edge technology such as artificial intelligence, robotics, the Internet of Things, and 3D printing. These digital technologies are redefining business and marketing and are driving forces of attaining core competence and competitive advantage apart from designing and successfully implementing every element of strategic intent. In recent times, we have witnessed some very innovative and disruptive business models emerge based on artificial intelligence and big data. These web-based businesses have prudently used digital technologies to establish new benchmarks in all components of business. Value chain and experiential marketing resulted in new standards of customer expectation and satisfaction and thus redefined a new name of the game (Chaudhary & Kumar, 2016).

Evolution of internet technology made a revolution in the game of marketing, and many traditional strategies of business and marketing received the threat of dagger edge from artificial intelligence (AI), machine learning (ML), big data, and cloud computing (Kaur, 2017). With the advent of artificial intelligence, digital marketing has become a game changer in the business world. AI and big data have become indispensable in the paradigm shift of new relationships among stakeholders and strengthen the business process by aligning resource planning and organizational structure (Kaur, 2017). Big data is an indispensable tool for knowledge accumulation and crucial decision-making in the modern knowledge-based industry (Tan & Zhan, 2017).

Contrary to popular belief, the main concern of big data is not colossal cache of data, but it is more associated with ingress, analysis, and clout of the intended information in real time to align with real-world reconnaissance and managerial advantage (Mawed & Aal-Hajj, 2017). Organizations can be highly benefited by big data techniques through tracking down the information flow, analyzing voluminous data, planning and executing their action plan according to idiosyncratic and customized information at a fair pace, and sharing needed data with claimants (Xu et al., 2016). Big data assists business in collecting, processing, and utilizing varied forms of information resources. Data is refined and sieved with trailblazing, revolutionary, and reckoning rigorous analytics of customers are processed into customer insights, which is supposed to be highly beneficial for right business decisions. At a functional level, various departments specifically marketing can be highly advantageous in the big-data ecosystem to embark on effective knowledge sharing and decision-making (Tan & Zhan, 2017).

5.2 Literature Review

The aim of this chapter is to share a basic analysis of the accessible literature on big-data analytics in terms of business intelligence sectors. Accordingly, various multiple big datasets tools, and methodology of big data analytics which can implements on paper are discussed, and their applications and chances in business terms are successfully supplied in different decision domains that are depicted. The literature was chosen based on its novelty and discussion of significant topics associated with big-data analytics in the field of business and marketing intelligence sectors in order to give out the purpose of our research in the present time. This is the main reason that big-data analytics are nowadays being focused upon business and marketing research topics. Because of details of the review processes of the journals, our chapter mainly focused on the big-data analytics, its tool and applications as well as methodology in business intelligence (Elgendy & Elragal, 2014). Although big data analytics is very famous researched in educational sectors, various industrial sectors, and this new technology gives an idea were mostly discussed in industrial area papers. Therefore, business and marketing analytics solutions are being advanced all over organizations in order to gain profit from big-data analytics solutions in these fields. In fact, maximum implementations are not yet very successful in gaining effective profits in areas like integrated marketing and business big-data analytical solutions. Moreover, analytical methods are also applied to a small dimension of data, and challenges concerning the huge size of data have lately risen, such as integrating a wide number of various different sources that are very helpful to deal with both structured and unstructured data, as well as performance issues. Although, big data analytics has also embedded within this study. However, it is basically highlighted to major hub of the study is to appreciate that how Big Data is being managed and handle new marketing challenges and complexities of today's business.

5.3 Basics of Big Data Analytics

The basic definition of "big data" is difficult to nail down because people use it with different purposes in business and marketing area like vendors, practitioners, and business professionals. Generally, we can say that big data have following purposes:

■ Large datasets.
■ The large data sets are helping in terms of classification of using computer strategies and technologies in the field of business and marketing (MOBINSPIRE.com).

In this circumstance we can say that the large dataset is a dataset that has a huge amount of data that is logical to process or storage with established tooling or a single computer system. it is a meaning full that is a common scale of big datasets is continuously shifting and may differ remarkable from organization to organization. The comate and types of business intelligence media can differ from each other. The richest media like pictures, video, and audio recordings are included in the text files, structured logs, etc. Moreover, the conventional data processing systems have expected data that is in the pipeline that has remarkable format and its organization in a big data system that is often accepted and collects the data near to the raw state. Successfully, any types of transformations or changes that take place in raw data it will always store in memory at the processing time.

5.3.1 Methodology and Tools of Big Data Analytics

Due to progression of big data analytical technology and its effective growth in various sectors of multiple different data in and out position of organizations regularly, we have need for faster and more accurate direction to analyze these data. The method

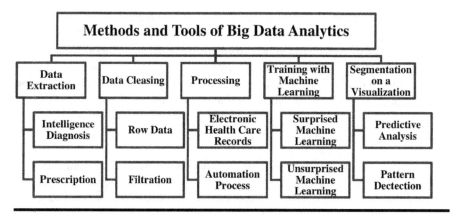

Figure 5.1 Methods and tools of big data analytics.

Source: (MobInspire.com)

and tools of big data analytics is given in Figure 5.1. These data sets are completely unable to be easily analyzed if or longer time with conventional data management and helpful to analysis the techniques and infrastructures in business intelligence sectors. Although its growing area has basic needs for new and accurate tools and methods which is calculated as well as specialized for big data analytics in the business and marketing sectors in present time because of its architectures or methodology for storing and managing of these data. According to the appearing of big data analytics has remarkable on each step-in business intelligence system from the data itself and storage for the cleaning and to the final take out as well as its decision systems.

There are few basic methodologies and tools are available that are very helpful for big data in business, marketing, and sales in present times. These are following types:

These data sets can be surveyed for a long time with traditional data management and also help in analyzing the techniques and infrastructures with big data in business intelligence sectors.

5.3.1.1 Data Extraction

Big data analytics in business and marketing intelligence usually require the extraction of data from many different resources. Although these resources are somewhere different from each other and have become dependent on the project, various plate forms like social media as well as search engine queries are the most usable resources of data nowadays. Although banking sectors are also used for transaction records that help in the fraud detection cases, and if we talk about healthcare sectors, they also use this data regarding patients' medical history, it becomes helpful in training the software for intelligent diagnosis of multiple diseases cases as well as prescription in present time.

These sectors are very helpful for providing the video on demand (VOD) services, which are helpful in acquiring these all data about users' online activities. These data become successful for providers to help in determining the consumer's choices of the relevant video content. These sectors often profit from their own enterprise data to make corporate decisions in present era. So, we can say that data extraction is the initial stage in the fields of big data analytical process to flow in a data lake.

5.3.1.2 Data Cleansing

A data lake is like a container in which we can store raw data. The aim of data cleansing is to give an accurate and apportioned filter of data that is helpful in ensuring that invalid data, relatable older, and unmatchable data become filters and then steps of big data procedures take place.

Data related to business analytics often apply on those sources from which we have acquired that dataset. For example, we need electronic healthcare records (EHR) to train the software for automatic performance of any patients of prescription and diagnosis. Data currency show how an updated dataset is in business and marketing sectors. Data has become a requirement nowadays because the decades-old EHR would be unable to give accurate information about prevalence of any disease in a particular region. Placing the validity filters and developing phase are the most important and crucial for the data-cleansing phase. So, cleansing of data is one of the most important things in processing big data analytics.

5.3.1.3 Preprocessing

This stage is basically involved in structures of data into unique and accurate formatting and their types. Data required are deposited from different resources into the data lake that is mainly unstructured datasets. There are not any different datasets involved in their terms of types and sizes of the data. Many data analysts consider data cleansing of data as a part of this phase. Moreover, data cleansing is another individual phase because of the number of tasks embedded in it.

Therefore, the cleansing of data is changed with the normalization and accurate techniques in business and marketing sectors and transformation changes the data into accurate readable forms for the big data algorithms. So, if the data has a big range, it is easy to change the values into handed equivalents in present time and it becomes more useful in business and marketing intelligence sectors. This transformation process is basically performed again once the data mining is complete to turn the data back into its original forms.

5.3.1.4 Training with Machine Learning

This is very useful when it is implemented in a variety of cases, case forming. This is important between big data analytics methods and technologies in the field of business and marketing. Machine learning basically leverages training of various software that help in detection of patterns and help in identification of objects in industrial fields. Moreover, machine learning technique is important when the project involves solving one of these tasks in business and marketing intelligence sectors. Machine learning has basically two types: supervised and unsupervised (Iqbal & Islam, 2016).

5.3.1.4.1 Supervised Machine Learning

This is the perspective when the software is basically trained by the help of human artificial intelligence engineers. Data engineers handle certain bounds so that the result can't proceed to the range of logical pattern. Supervised machine learning is one of the terms when the big data engineer's despite to the performance of the functions like categorization as well as regression. Categorization is the function that helps in identification of the various objects and software are basically trained for the unique performance and this recognition pattern basically decision. For example, if an object is shown in a frame, is this image an apple or not? This system helps in creating a basic probability that is based on the training that is provided for it, making it an important step in processing pipelines of big data, and regression is performed when we decide to create a pattern in a dataset.

5.3.1.4.2 Unsupervised Machine Learning

Unsupervised machine learning signifies the area where there are not any limitations and the results are unusual in these methods. This machine learning process basically gives more accurate terms of identification process because it is not bound by any limitation of any outcomes.

In this method clustering is one of the important usable cases of unsupervised machine learning. This technique has basically segmented data into various groups of identical instances in machine learning. Data of the same group are more identical to each other than those of data that belong to another group. It has a usually big range of variables for clustering processes in business and marketing intelligence. Association is another instance that has implements to verify the relations in between the large-scale databases in the fields of business and marketing (Alam & Maurya, 2014).

Most of the dataset projects are required for a refined learning that belongs to that technique where the software systems are helpful in improving the results through award-based training.

5.3.1.5 Segmentation and Visualization

The results of machine learning are helpful in founding the different groups of data of the technique that we use in the present day. All these various groups somewhere are run through the more filterable data at a time, if it is needed. The stage of segmentation is the nurture of dataset used to perform the predictive and accurate analysis and it helps in the pattern detection in the fields of business and marketing. One remarkable example is the pattern detection and identification of frauds in financial transaction sectors. These segmentation results are somewhere an essential part that take the form of the relational databases. At this point, data researchers are capable of visualization of the outcomes in big data analytics. Datasets after become a big data processing that is helpful in visualization through charts and graphs, as well as in the form of tables. The outcomes of visualization of any data sets of data are published on an executive informative system that would be helpful in leadership to make strategic and cooperative planning in business and marketing systems (Elgendy & Elragal, 2014).

5.4 Big Data and Market Intelligence

This part will exhibit marketing and business intelligence and their relationship with big data sets. Marketing and business intelligence is the practice of collecting data associated with marketing efforts of a firm, then analyzing those data effects accurately to guide the decision-making process of a campaign (Turban et al., 2011). Market and business intelligence is defined as providing valuable knowledge and information to decision makers by leveraging a different type of data analytics sets. Marketing and business intelligence is a framework consisting of theories, concepts, and methods to enhance marketing and business decision-making by using a fact-based support system. The first definition highlights knowledge as information for decision makers. The second definition stresses upon a gathering of information about technologies, and the last definition's emphasis is upon a set of methods, concepts, and theories to enhance business decision making. The principal tools for this include software for database reporting and query such as SAP (ERP etc. for multidimensional analysis of data mining, predictive analysis, text mining, web mining etc. It is certainly a new term by any means. Basically, the prospectus of marketing and business intelligence refers to developing insight and knowledge obtained from data for the purpose of marketing decision-making. Data mining is helpful in accomplishing such a goal by extracting or determining patterns or forecasting customer behavior from a large database with help of big data key factors for marketing decision (Farooqi & Iqbal, 2017). Big data analytics is also taken as a part of marketing and business intelligence because it constantly supports decision making for business with the help of reliable data, knowledge, and information (Farooqi & Iqbal, 2019). Big data analytics and business intelligence are common and basically focused upon data information and knowledge. Business and marketing intelligence include interactive visualization for data exploration land discovery. Tools such as view, spot fire, etc. also are considered the tools of big data analytics. This implies both business intelligence and big data in order to support marketing and business decision-making. Big data analytics and business intelligence share some common tools: mobile services technology cloud services and tree homology. Big data analytics social networking, technology eservices, and technologies have some common tools. Big data analytics in business and marketing intelligence in terms of technology and cloud servicing is given in Figure 5.2.

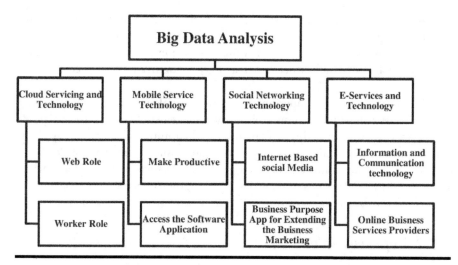

Figure 5.2 Big data analytics in business and marketing intelligence in terms of technology and cloud servicing.

Source: Sun & Yearwood, 2014

The diagram describes all four kinds of services that shape the most important markets for ecommerce and eservices. Furthermore, business marketing intelligence is a general concept for improving business and marketing decisions. On the other hand, big data analytics is a pivotal part of developing platforms (Sun & Yearwood, 2014).

5.5 Application of Big Data in Market Intelligences

Market and business intelligence is not only about sales, but it is also helpful for finding and using the information to create a business and marketing run flatter from top to bottom. However, big data is helpful for working internally to grow employee advocacy and firm regulation order. If they are using big data in order to grow their interchange with customers, big data is very helpful in this process. The use of big data and analytics is profitable in helping firms to understand their customers and target market, giving them a competitive advantage. There are more highlighted things that can be significant when market intelligence accepts big data in numerous actionable ways.

5.5.1 Enhance Supply Chain Management

As supply chain becomes complex and interlinked in the requirement to establish strong relationships with customers and the search for better efficiency in production, process have led business to adopt modern upgraded technology in order to retain the competitive status in the market place (Theyel et al., 2018). In support of the decision process, the role of big data is significant in various organizational activities from production and marketing to chain of supply management has been increasingly recognized (Waller & Fawcett, 2013).

Big data analytics is an important disruptive technology that helps in managing supplier relationships and improves inventory management for the delivery of product services based upon real-time demand. Big data initiates help in supply chain management in specifically safety or quality related issues (Shen et al., 2019). As an outcomes prediction abilities of big data permit the businesses to create a concrete and well informed decisions to increase and strengthen operations of supply chain (Tan & Zhan, 2017).

5.5.2 Improves Sales

Past data are used to improve sales forecast, allow to identify high value targets, and allocate potential opportunities, and new leads. The efficiency and effectiveness of sales efforts will increase at a rapid pace. The application of big data allows salespersons to influence customers on a personal basis in developing favorable loyal relationships and corporates to reach new client targets, boost sales, and increase conversion. Big data is an exciting new emerging field for marketers because the insights obtained through it are unmatched. In the area of sales management, it provides the vision such as which content is the most effective at each stage of a sales cycle. The customer relationship management can be improved besides that it is helpful for increasing conversion rate, prospects engagement revenue and customer. (Gupta et al., 2006).

5.5.3 Empowers Social Media

It is social media that provide knowledge and insight into purchasing behavior. Within a span of few years, the marketing industry has been actively involved in big data and how to apply it in order to decide what customers prefer. In fact big data has the potential to provide support to business and marketing industries to discover new consumption waves and market the demanded products more strategically (Boyd & Crawford, 2012). Social media plate forms played a significant role in producing and gathering used data related to customers as well as their purchasing behavior, which can be used for the analysis There are multiple social media platforms like Facebook, Instagram, YouTube, and Twitter created for the marketing industry to make better forecast. Social media analytics opens new avenues for new analytics to strengthen marketing strategies. Facebook and Twitter allowed people to follow, like, and comment freely about their favorite products and brands. Social media marketers are effectively using big data analytics to decide future buying trends. Big data increases the certainty regarding what the consumers wish and will. In fact, big data encourages personalization and provides complete knowledge and information about the world we live in and a better insight into consumers, not just a few people but billions (Tirunillai & Tellis, 2014).

5.5.4 Improving Competitiveness

The big data enables firms to generate and emphasize value for a technology-based competitiveness advantage. Big data provides businesses the potentiality to enhance decision making and improving products and process by extracting the value insights from data (Kitchens e al., 2018). The capabilities of big data include the growth of the models of innovative business in which the users can avail or excess the free services while offering revenue generated data stream (Trabucchi & Buganza, 2019). These approaches provide help and support to companies to establish reliable strong customer relationship management (CRM) and strengthen the value-added capabilities of marketing since the customers are supposed to be valuable sources of authentic and meaningful data. Big data enables business process to offer many opportunities for marketers. In addition, big data allows businesses to stay competitive by offering a quality price. Customer choices and preferences are based upon better campaign management. In response to this, the firm will gain a new market edge. As a result, firms can reach new market segments and a better knowledge and understanding of customers' needs and wants. The value-driven insight and big data decision allow companies to differentiate and deliver to superior customer needs. Big data gathered by firms and sometimes even generated by them can help market intelligence professionals to analyze their firms and where they fit within them relative to the competition. In short, big data helps companies to position their campaign and investment to outshine their competitors. In response to this, as results companies can obtain new segments of market (Chaudhary, 2012).

Big data results in the rise of well-focused companies that give due attention to the delivery of personalized products. In order to strengthen the performance of capital through spend a reasonable amount on customization.

5.5.5 Promoting Creativity and Innovation

In order to gear up innovation and creativity, firms use big data to create a new means of idea for the growth and development of products, services, pricing and channel of distribution (Erevelles et al., 2016). The analytics of big data and the creativity of marketing functions are closely associated (Johnson et al., 2019). The use of big data analytics makes a system (environment) where innovation can be easy to simulate, adopt, and implement. The higher the firm's capability to cultivate learning and experiment with big data, the higher the chances that the firm will maximize its value creation. Big data believes in promoting an environment that is based upon data-enabled insight that drives innovation in products, services, process and business models. Big data increases the speed of innovation and provides market information. In some contexts, big data is considered the solution to every problem in the areas of business, customized content creation, crisis management, and much more. Marketing is the area where creativity matters a lot, but that creativity is now in the most successful business firms being backed by powerful data analytics to give information about the needs and wants of customers (Khan et al., 2015). The combination of creativity and analytics proves to be far more powerful than individually, especially in driving content marketing (Zhan et al., 2017).The innovation of the product enabled by big data strengthens the ability of the firm, reduces the cost of the environment, and creates an efficient products or services framework that represents the potentialities of big data analytics in support of market intelligence through enhancing the comprehensive of the business environment, improving competitiveness, supporting customization, and stimulating innovation and creativity.

This diagram describes framework and potential business and eMarketing in big data worlds, which helps in understanding our achievable strategies in ecommerce business fields in the modern era. The traditional business and inbound business is given in Table 5.1.

Table 5.1 Traditional Business and Inbound Business

S. No	Aim	Traditional Business & Marketing	Inbound Business
1.	Basis	Interaction as a new customer	Interaction as request from new parties
2.	Method	Outbound push marketing	Inbound pull marketing
3.	Target	Mass business group	Individually or fans
4.	Time	Approval and planning procedures	Real-time competence is reinforced
5.	Location	At home	Using mobile and laptops at home
6.	Medium	Community and special events	Digital medium
7.	Billboards	By cash	Digital payments
8.	Sales	By person	Digital marketing sales

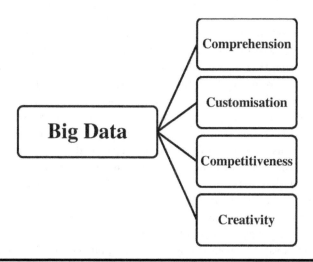

Figure 5.3 4C Framework of big data analytics potential in main market intelligence.

5.5.6 *Big Data and the Future of Business and Marketing*

Big data and market intelligence align with one and other and have shown their potential in the real world. The future of marketing and sales lies within big data analytics—marketing strategies have touched just the surface of big data, and a few firms have already shown to have found real above-market growth. Firms that use big data effectively show more profitability and productivity rates that are 5 to 6 percent higher than those of their peers.

Big data is not all about compressing a large amount of data and marketers using it to increase their profit. An analysis reveals firms that take a more data-centered of approach improve their marketing return on investment. By analyzing big data and transforming that knowledge into action with prospective strategies, it will lead to profit. Big data gives a foundation to predictive marketing. First predictive technology gives the marketer a better understanding of consumer behavior. It is slightly different from regular data analysis of marketing. Predictive marketing models suggest exactly what marketing strategy will likely work and which will not, therefore it will make it easier to make a decision. Predictive analysis is the backbone of data-driven marketing. It can provide help and support in six areas that include marketing mix modelling, cross selling, up selling, web optimization, customer acquisition, and method customer profiling. By using data analytics and big data, a marketer can track customers along the journey from initial interest to final buying with insight driven by cookies and click through rate (CTR). Marketers have a clear picture of what functions or what is not allowing them to invest their money in the right channels. Cookies blared on websites provide necessary information about online behavior of consumers. First-party data is personal information of a consume that includes interest, behavior, and action taken on a website. Third-party cookies travel across all sites. They can be generated on these visited sites and gather information from other websites. Big data provides a new dimension to market intelligence. It has been generated primarily from the ecommerce and web communities. Marking formation has been accomplished by ecommerce vendors such as Amazon through their innovative ecommerce platform. Most of the internet firms such as Amazon and Google and Facebook continue the development of web analytics closed computing etc. Various data meaning algorithms developed through artificial intelligence which is widely used in sales and marketing to cover, clustering affectation, regression, validation analysis land network analysis. These well-known popular algorithms are successfully incorporated in the commerce industry (Vogl et al., 2020). The big data analytics initiative in this domain, business and industries and from all the sectors, began to gain valuable insights through the structural data gathered through various enterprise systems and evaluated by commercial database management system. In recent times, web intelligence, web analytics, and Web 2.0 started a new era leading to unprocessed intelligence on consumer needs, consumer opinion, and new business opportunities (Farooqi & Iqbal, 2017).

5.5.7. Big Data in 2020: The Future Increase and Challenges of the Big Data Industry and Business

Enormous information is the misnomer. It can decrease the substances of the persistently expanding overwhelm of information to precisely in the following angle such as the downpour, the chaos and finally but not slightest, the magnitude perspective. In other words: something that alludes to this measurement of "big."

5.6 Advantages of Big Data in Business Intelligence Sectors

Enormous data's benefits for the marketers are various. The big data analytics benefits in business and market strategies are given in Table 5.2. They are utilized for the data available from a distant more prominent number of sources than ever some time recently, can you say as an advertiser:

- we can produce an extra-precise figure for your target consumer;
- we can predict consumer reaction to marketing messages and product benefaction;
- we can provide customization of the production marketing messages and product benefaction;
- we can enhance and add to our production and distribution strategy;
- we can produce and operate more accurate estimation measures;

Table 5.2 Big Data Analytics Benefits in Business and Market Strategies

S. No.	AIM	FUNDAMENTALS
1.	Precision	Target consumer in marketing
2.	Accuracy	Marketing message
3.	Personalize	Create market messages
4.	Optimization	Distribution strategies
5.	Digital marketing	Campaign-based strategies
6.	Innovation	Product-based innovation
7.	Identity	Vital-based audience targeting
8.	Analytics	Predictive scoring strategies

In spite of the fact that we realize the results, the incitement and great time of unstructured information and huge information analytics are all distant extra major than the greatness measurement such as speed, assortment, esteem, reason, matter more. Big information analytics: an expanding part within the quickly developing BDA market

A vast industry is that of huge information and trade analytics, in which huge information (analytics) is medium turn a huge portion.

5.7 Discussion and Conclusion

In this current era, the growing pace of data generation is full of challenges to gather data from various means of sources and find important, valuable information and insight related to business and marketing. The capabilities of big data are helpful for the firms to develop to enhance a deep understanding of the market and enhance the importance of decision making. Moreover, they try their level best to achieve a sharp competitive edge and believe in delivering highly customized products services and stimulate creativity and innovation in the field of business. Undoubtedly, big data analytics has created a new digital era and a variety of unique technologies allowing firms to track the behavior and purchasing habits of millions of consumers. The growth of big data analytics acts as a magnifying glass on the sequence or activities come from the internet in this digital age. Innovative products coming on the market now have better possibilities of finding ways to distinguish themselves, and the credit goes to big data; it will be much easier to pinpoint how to reach and find potential customers.

The availability of big data analytics and management of new information based effective technologies produced an unforgettable moment in the history of times, the age of big data. If this technology professionally continues to work together, it will deliver the promised. The practical application of big data analytics is evident in many fields of corporate and business management, especially in sales and marketing. Big data analytics revolves around more effective marketing. It generates innovations, creativity, new revenue opportunities, competitive advantage, customization, and other business benefits. Big data is a combination of both technical and strategic potential that gives a significant boost to the business firms of all sizes to generate value from data they gathered. The commercial impact of big data has the capacity to generate productivity and growth for a number of business firms. Data and analytics provide market intelligence, intensive and fruitful change, improving products, brand awareness, competition, etc. Big data have a significant step on marketing. It helps firms to them explore new opportunities that in turn lead to smart and profitable business moves, more efficient day-to-day operations, and happier customers, so finally understanding and using big data is a crucial competitive advantage for leading business and market firms. Data play a very important role of understanding a valuable insight data profile growing with a geometric pace. Firms can leverage analyze probabilities, then these valuable insights for enhancing business strategies and market campaign to full fill the target customer's needs. The innovative cost-effective technologies are emerging that make it easy for any business firm to implement big data solutions.

References

Ahmad, S., & Alam, M. (2014). Balanced-Ternary Logic for Improved and Advanced Computing. *International Journal of Computer Science and Information Technologies*, 5(4), 5157–5160, ISSN: 0975–9646.

Alam, B., Doja, M. N., Alam, M., & Malhotra, S. (2013). 5-Layered Architecture of Cloud Database Management System. *AASRI Procedia Journal*, 5, 194–199, ISSN: 2212–6716.

Alam, M., & Maurya, S. (2014). Database Development on Inborn Errors of Nucleotide Metabolism in Homo Sapiens and Tool Designing for Nucleotide Sequence Alignment. *Indian Journal of Applied Research*, 4(7), 12–15, ISSN: 2249–555x(Print), https://doi.org/10.15373/2249555X

Boyd, D., & Crawford, K. (2012). Critical Questions for Big Data: Provocations for a Cultural, Technological, and Scholarly Phenomenon. *Information, Communication & Society*, 15(5), 662–679.

Chaudhary, K. (2012). Emerging Trends of Investing and Financing Activities in Indian Companies. *International Journal of Research in Finance and Marketing (IJRFM)*, 2(4), 21–32, ISSN: 2231–5985.

Chaudhary, K., & Kumar, S. (2016). Customer Satisfaction Towards Flipkart and Amazon: A Comparative Study. *International Journal of Academic Research & Development JAR&D*, 35.

Chen, C. P., & Zhang, C. Y. (2014). Data-intensive Applications, Challenges, Techniques and Technologies: A Survey on Big Data. *Information Sciences, 275*, 314–347.

Delen, D., & Demirkan, H. (2013). Data, Information and Analytics as Services. *Decision Support Systems, 55*(1), 359–363.

Elgendy, N., & Elragal, A. (2014, July). Big Data Analytics: A Literature Review Paper. In *Industrial Conference on Data Mining* (pp. 214–227). Cham: Springer.

Erevelles, S., Fukawa, N., & Swayne, L. (2016). Big Data Consumer Analytics and the Transformation of Marketing. *Journal of Business Research, 69*(2), 897–904.

Farooqi, M. R., & Iqbal, N. (2017). Effectiveness of Data Mining in Banking Industry: An Empirical Study. *International Journal of Advanced Research in Computer Science, 8*(5), 827–830.

Farooqi, M. R., & Iqbal, N. (2019). Performance Evaluation for Competency of Bank Telemarketing Prediction Using Data Mining Techniques. *International Journal of Recent Technology and Engineering, 8*(2), 5666–5674.

Gandomi, A., & Haider, M. (2015). Beyond the Hype: Big Data Concepts, Methods, and Analytics. *International Journal of Information Management, 35*(2), 137–144.

Gupta, S., Hanssens, D., Hardie, B. G. S., Kahn, W., Kumar, V. L., Lin, N. N., & Ravishanker, N. (2006). Modeling Customer Lifetime Value. *Journal of Service Research, 9*(2), 139–155.

Iqbal, N., & Islam, M. (2016). From Big Data to Big Hope: An Outlook on Recent Trends and Challenges. *Journal of Applied Computing, 1*(1), 14–24.

Johnson, D. S., Muzellec, L., Sihi, D., & Zahay, D. (2019). The Marketing Organization's Journey to Become Data-driven. *Journal of Research in Interactive Marketing, 13*(2).

Kaur, G. (2017). The Importance of Digital Marketing in the Tourism Industry. *International Journal of Research- Granthaalayah, 5*(6), 72–77.

Khan, I., Naqvi, S. K., & Alam, M. (2015). Data Model for Big Data in Cloud Environment. *Computing for Sustainable Global Development (INDIACom), 2015 2nd International Conference* (pp. 582–585). New Delhi, India: IEEE, ISBN: 978-9-3805-4415-1.

Kitchens, B., Dobolyi, D., Li, J., & Abbasi, A. (2018). Advanced Customer Analytics: Strategic Value Through Integration of Relationship-oriented Big Data. *Journal of Management Information Systems, 35*(2), 540–574.

Mawed, M., & Aal-Hajj, A. (2017). Using Big Data to Improve the Performance Management: A Case Study from the UAE FM Industry. *Facilities, 35*(13–14, SI), 746–765. https://doi.org/10.1287/mksc.2015.0972

Shen, B., Choi, T. M., & Chan, H. L. (2019). Selling Green First or Not? A Bayesian Analysis with Service Levels and Environmental Impact Considerations in the Big Data Era. *Technological Forecasting and Social Change, 144*, 412–420.

Sun, Z., & Yearwood, J. (2014). A Theoretical Foundation of Demand Driven Web Services. In *Handbook of Research on Demand-Driven Web Services: Theory, Technologies, and Applications* (pp. 1–32). IGI Global.

Tan, K. H., & Zhan, Y. (2017). Improving New Product Development Using Big Data: A Case Study of an Electronics Company. *R & D Management, 47*(4), 570–582. https://doi.org/10.1111/radm.12242

Theyel, G., Hofmann, K., & Gregory, M. (2018). Understanding manufacturing location decision making: rationales for retaining, offshoring, reshoring, and hybrid approaches. *Economic Development Quarterly, 32*(4), 300–312.

Tirunillai, S., & Tellis, G. J. (2014). Mining Marketing Meaning from Online Chatter: Strategic Brand Analysis of Big Data Using Latent Dirichlet Allocation. *Journal of Marketing Research, 51*(4), 463–479.

Trabucchi, D., & Buganza, T. (2019). Data-driven Innovation: Switching the Perspective on Big Data. *European Journal of Innovation Management, 22*(1), 23–40. https://doi.org/10.1108/EJIM-01-2018-0017.

Turban, E., Volonino, L., Sipior, J. C., & Wood, G. R. (2011). *Information Technology for Management: Improving Strategic and Operational Performance.* New York: John Wiley.

Vogl, T. M., Seidelin, C., Ganesh, B., & Bright, J. (2020). Smart technology and the emergence of algorithmic bureaucracy: Artificial intelligence in UK local authorities. *Public Administration Review, 80*(6), 946–961.

Waller, M. A., & Fawcett, S. E. (2013). Data Science, Predictive Analytics, and Big Data: A Revolution that Will Transform Supply Chain Design and Management. *Journal of Business Logistics, 34*(2), 77–84.

Xu, Z., Frankwick, G. L., & Ramirez, E. (2016). Effects of Big Data Analytics and Traditional Marketing Analytics on New Product Success: A Knowledge Fusion Perspective. *Journal of Business Research, 69*(5), 1562–1566. https://doi.org/10.1016/j.jbusres.2015.10.017

Zhan, Y. Z., Tan, K. H., Ji, G., Chung, L., & Tseng, M. L. (2017). A Big Data Framework for Facilitating Product Innovation Processes. *Business Process Management Journal, 23*(3), 518–536.

Chapter 6

Advancements and Challenges in Business Applications of SAR Images

Prachi Kaushik and Suraiya Jabin

Contents

DOI: 10.1201/9781003175711-6

Biographical notes: Prachi is a research scholar in the Department of Computer Science at Jamia Millia Islamia (Central University), New Delhi, India. She received her bachelor's degree in 2013 and master's degree in 2015, both from the Department of Computer Science, YMCA University of Science and Technology, Faridabad, India. Her research interests include synthetic aperture satellite images, microwave remote sensing, and machine learning.

Suraiya Jabin is Professor in the Department of Computer Science, Jamia Millia Islamia (Central University), New Delhi, India. She received her PhD in 2009 from the Department of Computer Science, Jamia Hamdard University, New Delhi, India. Her research interests include artificial intelligence, pattern recognition, biometrics, soft computing, and remote sensing.

6.1 Introduction to SAR Imagery and Data Cubes

Remote sensing has the power to acquire information or monitor the physical characteristics of an area on earth without making any physical contact with it. Data collected from space have low spatial resolution and more global coverage as compared to the data collected from airlines. Imaging spectrometers are mounted on satellites to collect the energy reflected by the earth's surface in the form of bands. This forms the basis of spectral remote sensing.

The light energy reflected by the ground targets is collected by the imaging spectrometer. It can record the intensity of the red, green, blue (RGB) light for every band in the image pixel by pixel. A *band* here refers to a part of the electromagnetic spectrum consisting of a certain type of light. For example, an imaging spectrometer may capture a band consisting of wavelength values ranging between 500 nm and 900 nm.

6.1.1 *Multispectral Remote Sensing*

Multispectral remote sensing acquires the images in visible, near-infrared, and shortwave infrared bands. These remotely sensed images help to discriminate landforms based on the spectral signatures as every land surface pattern reflects and absorbs different wavelength. This data is composed of 5 to 10 spectral bands with large bandwidths (70–400 nm).

If the material has enough spectral resolution to differentiate it from other materials, then its "spectral reflectance signature" can be used to identify it. *Reflectance spectrum* is a graphical representation of the part of reflected radiation from a material that can be modeled as a function of the incident wavelength. This reflectance spectrum can be used as a unique signature for that material. Multispectral remote sensing widely uses this concept.

A multichannel detector is used as a sensor using some spectral bands. Every channel of this detector has sensitivity to the radiations of a certain range of wavelength bands.

The result of this is a multilayer image. This resulting image has the spectral (color) information of the target under observation along with its brightness. LANDSAT, SPOT, IKONOS, and SENTINEL-2 are some of the examples of optical satellites.

Synthetic aperture radar (SAR) uses the delay in time of the backscattered signals, thus utilizing the radar principle in the following steps:

■ An antenna transmits microwave pulses toward the surface of the Earth.
■ The scattering of microwave energy in return of this at the spacecraft end is thus measured.

A certain proportion of the energy is scattered back at the sensor's end in respect of the actual microwaves striking the surface. This proportion depends on a lot of factors such as:

■ The moisture content of any surface that acts as one of the deciding factors of the dielectric constant of that material.
■ The slope, orientation or roughness of the surface.
■ The land-cover type such as vegetation, soil or man-made objects.
■ Incident angle, polarization and microwave frequency.

SAR is especially very useful in the regions that are often covered under clouds for most of the year such as the tropical regions. This is because SAR captures cloud-free images irrespective of the weather conditions as the microwaves have the ability to penetrate the clouds. It can also be used in nighttime operations as it is an active remote-sensing device. For some applications, in order to gather data about the earth's surface, single-sensor data is not sufficient. For more sophisticated

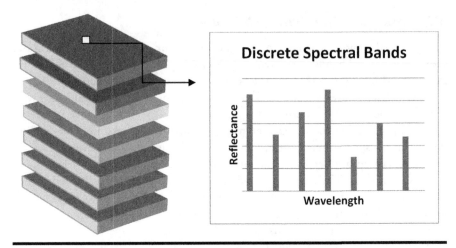

Figure 6.1 Multispectral Image with Discrete Spectral Bands.

information, we need to fuse satellite images with different spatial and spectral resolutions. To enhance the quality of the image interpretation, fusion of images with multiple bands improves the accuracy of classification. Multispectral images consisting of 3 to 10 bands are modeled as a high-dimensional data cube as shown in Figure 6.1. A hyperspectral image consists of hundreds of narrow bands having 10–20 nm wavelength recorded by the radiometer. In the coming subsections, we describe image fusion of SAR images with optical or different sensors.

6.1.2 Hyperspectral Remote Sensing

A multitemporal color composite image can be created by combining radar images captured at different time periods. This technique is used to detect the changes in land cover by assigning a red band to one image, a green band to the second image, and blue color to the next image to form an RGB color composite. The land cover that did not change over time appears grey in color, but the changed areas appear as colorful patches in the image.

The various types of spectral remote sensing is given in Table 6.1. Hyperspectral remote sensing captures images over hundreds of contiguous spectral bands to allow identification and quantification of molecular absorption in different surface materials. The advancement in sensor technology has led to the collection of images over several hundred bands over the spectrum. This technology groups imaging and spectroscopy in one system to study the absorption characteristics due to the chemical bonding in the material. A large number of bands gives an opportunity for more materials to be discriminated against based on the spectral responses. This technique is most widely used by geologists to detect the minerals from the earth's surface. This data is usually huge in size comprising 100 to 200 spectral bands of narrow bandwidths (5–10 nm), which

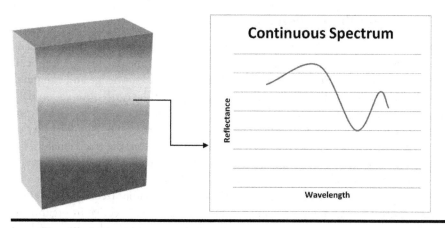

Figure 6.2 Continuous Spectrum of Hyperspectral Images.

Table 6.1   Types of Spectral Remote Sensing

Image Type	Bands	Bandwidth	Example	Applications
Multispectral Images	3–15 wider spectral bands	Large bandwidth (70–400 nm)	LANDSAT-8, SPOT, Sentinel2, IKONOS	Target tracking, agricultural studies, land use and land-cover classifications
Hyperspectral Images	100–1000 narrow spectral bands	Narrow bandwidth (10–20 nm)	AVIRIS (airborne visible/infrared imaging spectrometer) Proba-1 Prisma	Mining and oil industries, mineral mapping, differentiate soil types, atmospheric gases
Ultraspectral images	More than 1,000 narrow spectral bands	Narrow bandwidth	Tropospheric emission spectrometer (TES) with 9,000 bands	Gas spectral signature analysis, which requires high spectral resolutions

require new cloud-based processing methods shown in Figure 6.2. Precision agriculture and coastal management to monitor the phytoplankton, crop types, crop maturity and bathymetric changes are potential applications of hyperspectral remote sensing.

As the size of the datasets are huge, the hyperspectral imagery is modeled as a data cube with an X-Y axis representing the spatial data, and the z-axis in the data cube represents the spectral information.

6.1.3 Earth Observation Data Cube

The earth observation (EO) data potential is still underutilized as it requires scientific knowledge to understand the resolution and type of the satellite data (optical, RADAR) needed for processing. There is a lack of expert knowledge and computational resources in the field of storage and utilization of the earth observation data due to high cost and effort. As the demand for business-oriented decisions from this data continues to grow, there is a visual increase in the volume and velocity of image data. There is a requirement for a paradigm shift from the traditional methods and techniques of processing and data distribution at a local level to address the issues of handling and managing a high volume of data.

A new paradigm of EO data cubes (EODC) has revolutionized the interaction of users with the EO data. This solution has proven to be effective in organizing the data storage and management of spatio-temporal data to make quick analysis by using the analysis-ready format (ARD) of the earth data. It has bridged the gap between the expectation of the users and big data capabilities to address the issues of data volume and velocity Wani and Jabin (2018).

Several initiatives for the earth data cubes are operational like the Google Earth Engine and data cubes which focus on countries like Australia, Africa. The efficient implementation of the EO data cube has supported timely decision-making exploring the information power of the EO data. It converts the available information into significant geographical and physical variables. The below list gives a brief description of the current operational data cubes.

6.1.3.1 Open Data Cube (ODC)

This is an open-source technique to access, manage and analyze large amounts of EO data. It comprises a common analytical framework having data structures and tools for the analysis of a large, gridded collection of data to better manage the satellite data. It gives a foundation for several international, national as well as regional data cube architectures like Digital Earth Australia, African regional Data Cube, etc. The data cube efficiently works with preprocessed, ready-to-use analysis ready data (ARD) (Open Data Cube, 2020).

6.1.3.2 Digital Earth Australia (DEA)

This initiative has been developed as a part of the open data cube (ODC) use satellite data to detect the physical changes like soil erosion and water quality changes in Australia (Ticehurst et al., 2019). The data is prepared in advance as it reduces the cost and the time for processing the EO data to develop new applications.

The Commonwealth Scientific and Industrial Research Organization and Geoscience Australia agreed to develop a data cube collecting Sentinel-1 SAR images for Australia (Ticehurst et al., 2019). The SAR ARD included a series of preprocessing steps like calibration to (gamma naught, γ0) backscatter values, decomposition by eigenvectors and coherence calculation using Sentinel-1 data.

6.1.3.3 Africa Regional Data Cube

This data cube supports the countries of Central Africa like Kenya, Senegal, Sierra Leone, Ghana and Tanzania. It focuses on building the capacity of users to address the issues related to agriculture, food security, deforestation, urbanization and water shortage. It also aims to achieve the objectives laid down by the Group on Earth Observations (GEO) and to accomplish the goals set by the United Nations Sustainable Development (UN-SDG).

6.1.3.4 Swiss Data Cube

This data cube was the first data cube initiative to provide cloud-free mosaics of Landsat, Sentinel-1 or Sentinel 2 data. Initially it had 5 years of ARD in 2016, but now it covers Landsat data for the entire country for a period of 30 years. New data of interest like urbanization, snow cover etc. are updated in the data cube for analysis and future use. The different data cube initiative is given in Table 6.2.

Table 6.2   Different Data Cube Initiative

Data Cube Initiative	Applications	Area	Satellite data
Digital Earth Australia	Detect physical changes like soil erosion, water quality changes, intertidal extent, hotspots	Australia	Sentinel-1 SAR ARD
Africa Regional Data Cube	Agriculture, food security, deforestation, urbanization and water shortage	Central African countries: Kenya, Senegal, Sierra Leone, Ghana and Tanzania	Landsat: April 1984– December 2019 surface reflectance data Sentinel-2: 2017 onward Sentinel-1: 2017 onward (operational by mid 2021)
Swiss Data Cube	Urbanization, snow cover	Switzerland	Landsat: 33 years (1984–2017) Sentinel-2: 3 years (2015–2018) Sentinel-1: 2018

6.2 Business Applications of SAR Imagery

We have divided business applications of SAR images into the following broad categories of remote asset management, science and environment applications, security and defense etc. as shown in Figure 6.3.

6.2.1 Remote Management

Sensor technology has helped to remotely control the devices by sending commands, settings or configurations in real-time in isolated, hard-to-reach places. Some of the areas on the earth's surface, for example Antarctica and the Amazon basin, are hard-to-reach areas that are supported by satellite communications.

The RADARSAT-1 Antarctic mapping project (RAMP) comprises two missions: the first Arctic mapping mission (AMM-1) and the modified Antarctic mapping mission (MAMM) developed by the Canadian space agency. The goal of the RAMP mission was to create a mosaic map of Antarctica with a resolution of 25 m to study the relationship between the environmental factors between the southernmost continents. As the environmental conditions in Antarctica are inhospitible the imagery from the RADARSAT proved to be important for future missions. The geological features were displayed on the Antarctica map, taking into account the brightness and the texture features in the image. AMM-1 data measured the movement of ice sheets mathematically using the ice velocity vectors over the ice streams.

Liang et al. (2021) have highlighted a snowmelt detection method over large areas using Sentinel-1 SAR images for the period of 2015–2019 over Antarctica

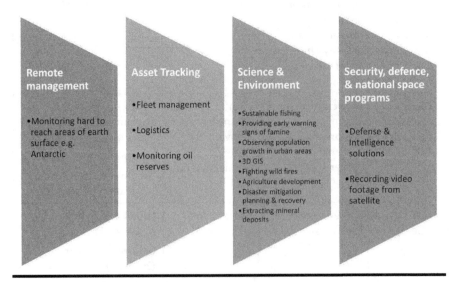

Figure 6.3 Business Applications of SAR Imagery.

using the Google Earth engine. The study aimed to observe spatiotemporal changes and anomalous events in Antarctica. Rosenqvist et al. (2020) in their paper studied the wetland inundation using the JERS-1 data and ALOS PALSAR data to generate annual maximum and minimum maps over the complete Amazon basin from 2014 to 2017. A decision tree-based classifier was trained resulting in an accuracy of 86%. Rosenqvist et al. (2020) in their paper have presented the flood inundation characteristics using the fusion of SAR C Sentinel-1 data, ALOS PALSAR L band data and ICESat-2 Lidar data to capture the water-level variations in the major rivers and water areas.

Çolak et al. (2019) used a combination of SAR and optical satellite images to study the land cover-changes due to the construction of the nuclear power plant in forest-dominated areas. The SAR image differencing support vector machine algorithm evaluated the annual changes between the period of 2016 and 2019 using these satellite images. Correlation between the two parameters like canopy structure and vegetation biomass from the Sentinel-2 dataset was analyzed along with the Sentinel-1 backscatter values to study the effect on the forest area as well as validate the changes in the vegetation.

6.2.2 Asset Tracking

SAR imagery has been widely used for a number of asset-tracking applications. In this section, we explain few asset-tracking applications of SAR imagery.

6.2.2.1 Fleet Management

The importance of fleet management is to maximize the efficiency and productivity of vehicles by vehicle tracking and maintenance. With the advancement of the satellite images, tracking of all types of vehicles has been possible even in isolated areas. One of the applications deals with the number of cars that can enter the parking lot. The information related to the count of the cars is augmented with different socioeconomic data files to predict the profit of the retailers. The satellite images give an accurate idea about the space requirement for the parking lots in a particular area.

Aprile et al. (2011) discuss a novel technique to find the velocity of ground moving targets using information regarding the road network from a single-channel SAR system.

The algorithm of doublet detection is divided into two steps; the first step focuses on detection tracking and moving target identification, and the second step deals with the estimation of the velocity of the moving target by extracting motion parameters and ground location. Henke et al. (2015) in their paper explore the data from the F-SAR system for evaluating methods for tracking the moving targets in single and multichannel SAR images. The methodology is used where the SAR images are temporally and spatially overlapped. An important filtering approach called *Kalman unscented filtering* is used to identify multitarget tracking in single-channel images showing promising results. The result validation is based on the ground measurements taken for the highway section. White et al. (2015) discussed the improvement of classical algorithms for vehicle tracking by fusion of multiple sources such as SAR and earth-observation data to model situations like vehicle tracking. The author implements a three-tier architecture of a vehicle tracker adding a hypothetical thinking layer with a goal to detect and resolve conflicts related to tracking.

Bethke et al. (2006) talk about traffic monitoring with radar (TRAMRAD). This project deals with wide-area monitoring of the road traffic to manage it with reliable information. The paper briefly describes the system and the complex conditions for the radar instrument to two processes the data for wide-area monitoring. Tanveer et al. (2020) used the synthetic-opportunity strip map imaging mode to monitor the traffic patterns using the Wuhan China case study. The study collected a long series of COSMO-SkyMed images to detect the increase in the number of vehicles across the bridges in Wuhan. This paper focuses on monitoring the traffic variation instead of detecting a single car. The validation of data was done using the TomTom traffic index to prove the effectiveness of detecting the traffic patterns. The algorithm was able to detect large vehicles such as trucks and buses, but it lagged in the detection of smaller vehicles.

6.2.2.2 Logistics

The movement of goods every day is an important characteristic of logistic companies. The GIS can solve many issues in the current world as it helps to know the location in real-time to estimate the time of arrival of a new product. Security control and traceability have been achieved with the help of the small satellite constellations in the logistics sectors. If the items or the goods are delicate there is also a requirement of the control transport conditions to maintain the quality of the product.

6.2.2.3 Monitoring Oil Reserves by Looking at Floating Oil Roof Tanks

The monitoring of the oil reserves from the satellite imagery has been made possible by interpreting the geometry. The circular geometry of the oil tanks with floating roof tanks prevents evaporation. The amount of oil can be measured from the sky based on the shadow of the floating roof without physically measuring the oil. If there is more shadow it means that there is less oil in the reserve. Del Frate et al. (2000) presented a semiautomatic neural-network approach to detect oil spills. The classifier inputs features that can characterize the oil spill for the classification process. Zeng et al. (2020) proposed an oil-spill convolution network OCSNet to perform the feature extraction and target classification for a dataset consisting of 20,000 images of dark spots. This system promised an accuracy of 94.01%, which is improved from the traditional machine-learning algorithms. Bianchi et al. (2020) have proposed a deep-learning model for classifying different kinds of oil spills based on the shape and textures based on the historical presence of oil spills worldwide. Chaturvedi et al. 2020 examined the oil spills in the Persian Gulf using the VV polarization of the Sentinel-1 SAR images. SAR images have played an important role in ocean and oil slick examination, propagation of oil spill and its documentation.

Another application is the estimation of oil inventory by detecting the shadows on it. Most of the fuel tanks have a floating top to calculate the volume and amount of oil in it utilizing simple trigonometry functions. These satellite images could be used to know the locations of oil with the oil tanks giving timely information to the agencies working with energy resources.

So, there is a lot of focus on fusing the earth-observation data with the machine-learning approach so that meaningful information could be extracted from the radar satellite images and transformed into actionable information.

6.2.3 Science and Environment

SAR imagery has been widely used for various science and environment-related applications. In this section, we explain a few such applications.

6.2.3.1 Sustainable Fishing

Sustainable fishing is an idea that ensures that the population and species of fishes in the ocean can be maintained for the livelihood of the people who depend on fishing. This shows that the fisheries could continue to exist in marine as well as freshwater habitats.

There are some specific satellites that have sensors to monitor the surface temperature and the ocean colors that depict a specific fish type. Remote sensing can be used to map the algal bloom, which is harmful to aquatic life.

Sasamal and Mallenahalli (2019) proposed a new approach of linearized moments in association with machine learning to detect fishing boats. This approach showed a better accuracy for identifying the fishing boats, which also improves the efficiency of machine-learning classifiers. Fitriani et al. 2020 explored the Sentinel-1 image for fishing-vessel detection in Indramayu sea waters. The overlay analysis is used to discriminate immovable and movable objects as well as validation of the ships. After experimental analysis, it can be concluded that SAR Sentinel-1 can detect more ships than the VMS software.

The SAR data has the capability of detecting the dark vessels in the water that do not transmit automatic identification signals location data. The monitoring of all the vessels in the sea has grown as satellites are being launched by private companies for illegal fishing. Capella Space has launched a constellation of 36 satellites into space in 2022 to detect the presence of any ship in the ocean or sea in the day as well as night. This is a huge revolution in real-time vessel detection as it has the capability to provide new images at an interval of 1 hour at the equator and poles.

6.2.3.2 Providing Early Warning Signs for Famine over Large Scales

There are several disasters that cause loss of life and damage to the economy. One of the most common types of disaster in the hilly areas is landslides, which could be detected using optical and SAR images along with the slope information. One of the techniques of IN-SAR can provide early warning for landslides as it gives ground-level displacements on the surface of the earth. Images capture the disasters irrespective of the weather conditions. During the floods, the SAR images were used to speed up the response time and evacuation plan to measure the floodwater. A very useful application of SAR data is to monitor the ice and glaciers on high altitudes based on the backscatter values deriving information on ice type and its concentration. On the ocean surface, illegal or accidental oil spills are easily visible and can be identified with radar imagery. Another useful application is to map the deformations and movement of few centimeters in the earth's surface due to earthquakes and landslides, which is made possible by the interferometry SAR (In-SAR) technique.

Some of the following recent studies show the effective techniques for famine and for monitoring famine and drought. Slinski et al. (2019) The European space agency Sentinel-1 satellite was used in monitoring the extent of water points in East African regions from 2014 to the present. The surface of the water is estimated using the famine early warning system and SAR-based water area extraction to derive the status of the water points. The fusion improved the ability to monitor the critical resource. In a paper, Keshavarz et al. (2014) presented a new index called the soil wetness deficit index (SWDI) derived from the soil wetness index to monitor the agricultural drought. The soil wetness index used a combination of land-surface temperature and vegetation index to estimate the soil moisture. The perfumes index showed a capability of spatial mapping of drought-affected areas by measuring the drought intensity. The presence of vegetation also showed the variation in the soil moisture both in wet and dry conditions. The effectiveness of this index was compared with the regional reports and other vegetation indices. Jeyaseelan (2003) in his lecture discusses the real-time monitoring of early warning systems and quick damage assessment with the help of the advancements in remote sensing and geographical information systems at the time of drought and flood disasters. The availability of high-resolution images at a low temporal frequency can be used for the long-term relief management and detailed monitoring of the damage assessment. One third of the area in South Africa is covered with natural vegetation called grasslands.

Abdel-Hamid et al. (2020) provide an impact assessment in the area of Eastern Cape Province with large grasslands with commercial importance with the help of the Sentinel-1 SAR data. Regression analysis was performed between the biophysical parameters derived from the Sentinel-1 data and the NDVI values derived from the Landsat 8 optical data. A significant correlation of 0.89 was observed between the backscattering coefficients of SAR data. The study also concluded that drought affects communal grasslands more than commercial grasslands. The paper by Li et al. (2020) focuses on the study of the rich texture features for landslide detection. A grayscale cooccurrence matrix was derived for Sentinel-1 and COSMO-SkyMed SAR images before and after the landslide event for the Jomda landslide in 2018. Landslide detection takes into account two parameters: the optimal window size and the optimal step size for the landslide detection. These parameters are obtained by rigorous analysis and comparison of the texture information for the mountain area. The temporal changes in the radar images are identified using the object-based image analysis as discussed in the paper by Lin et al. (2021). Polarimetric decomposition of the satellite images to extract the texture indices from the image data was useful for the object-based image analysis. Overall accuracy of 60% is achieved for the detection of landslides as compared to the in-situ landslide inventory data.

The paper by Noviello et al. (2020) addresses In-SAR methods for monitoring the buildings for natural hazards like landslides. It focuses on the systematic display displacements that affect the buildings during landslides and studies the vulnerability analysis and structural changes with improvements in 3D reconstruction. The SAR systems can provide critical and timely information over large areas to detect landslides. The study by Park and Lee (2019) focuses on the detection of landslides from single-, dual-, quad-polarization modes by a simple change detection technique based on the scattering properties. The areas affected by landslides were identified with a rate of 60% on the basis of the co-pol coherence and polarizing factors with quad polarization mode. Only half of the accuracy was achieved with single- or dual-pol parameters to produce a landslide map.

6.2.3.3 Observing Population Growth in Urban Areas

An important objective for urban planners is to observe the population growth as well as the distribution of the population within the cities. The modeling of the land-use change can be an important parameter to accurately measure the growth of the population, but it can also give a detailed analysis of the growth distribution for sustainable development and improved well-being. Koppel et al. (2017) discuss the dependence of sigma backscatter on physical building parameters like height, alignment, density, shape, and material. The strongest backscatter is due to the variable height of the buildings. Double-bounce scattering from wall-ground interactions is easily detected by Sentinel-1 SAR images. Dong et al. (1997) give a detailed understanding of the different types of radar backscattering from urban areas. They discuss single bounce from rooftops, double bounce from wall-ground structures and triple scattering from wall-wall-ground structures.

6.2.3.4 3D GIS

The 3D geographical information system (GIS) adds a third dimension to the satellite images mostly used for urban landscapes. The 3D technology gives a better visualization, making a significant impact on map creation.

The 3D GIS is used in the majority of applications such as city planning. Efficient city planning can help government agencies to evaluate the shortage of basic amenities like electricity, water requirements and space requirements that can meet the needs of future generations. It also helps the urban planners to find alternative solutions for smart cities.

Building information modeling (BIM) is a technique that, when used in combination with 3D GIS, can help to produce building management plans for more analysis of the data depicting the real-world settings in the environment.

Another application of 3D GIS is efficient and effective planning to understand the economic and environmental movement along with the coastal areas. It also helps us to recognize the factors that deal with the construction as well as maintenance of the ports, fisheries, and mining activities.

6.2.3.5 Fighting Wildfires

An unplanned fire that is difficult to control takes the shape of a wildfire, causing harm to life and property. There is a need to locate the fire with accuracy so that steps can be taken to lessen the impact of the fire and also control its spread in the neighboring areas. Satellites like AVHRR and MODIS also have the capability to detect and monitor wildfire by analyzing the thermal bands. These bands can capture the temperature information to detect the urban heat units.

6.2.3.6 Agriculture Development

As the population across the world is increasing, there is a need to increase the production of agricultural grains and crops to satisfy the need of the growing population. Proper management of agricultural resources needs information about the quality, quantity and location of the resources to be managed. GIS plays a significant role in generating agricultural maps to manage the crop data over a time series. SAR can capture images regardless of the weather conditions, so it proves to be an effective technique to monitor agricultural targets. Many words in the literature have focused on the fusion of optical and SAR images for detailed parameter extraction for the farmland crop identification classification model. Another application deals with crop yields and price prediction, focusing on the vegetation indices such as NDVI from the optical images from Landsat and Sentinel-2 images.

NDVI is used for agriculture-related models to extract the green content from the optical as well as radar images.

Abdikan et al. (2018) in their paper discussed the relationship between the maize height and sigma backscatter values (Sigma_VH, Sigma_VV). A high coherence was recorded in the early stages of plant growth, and the coherence reduced as the plant growth advanced. The backscattering coefficient discriminated against different kinds of crops with 80% accuracy. Vreugdenhil et al. (2018) have accessed the potential of SAR microwave indices (VV, VH) backscatter, VH/VV Ratio and cross-ratio (CR) to monitor the crop conditions. In-situ data such as vegetation water content, biomass, leaf area index (LAI) and height of the plant are collected for oilseed, corn and winter cereals in two growing seasons. The index CR is the best variable to estimate the water in the vegetation. The research demonstrates that microwave indices are highly sensitive to vegetation dynamics. Paloscia et al. (1998) in their paper investigated the influence of shape and dimensions (geometry) on the sigma backscattering coefficient for C and L band SAR images. The crops having the same biomass may have different sigma backscatter due to different geometry. Narrow-leaf crops show that with increasing biomass the backscatter decreases whereas for broadleaf crops the backscatter increases with the decrease in the biomass. Ulaby et al. (1990) discussed the radar backscattering from the forest canopies based on the Michigan microwave canopy-scattering model. Direct backscattering takes place from leaves and branches. Scattering from different regions such as trunk-ground or leaf-ground scattering is known as *multiple scattering*.

Dobson et al. (1992 examined the dependence of radar backscatter for P, L and C band SAR data on aboveground biomass for coniferous forests. The experiments show an increase in radar backscatter with increasing biomass until biomass saturation point, which varies with different bands. The C band is less sensitive to the total aboveground biomass. Ferrazzoli and Guerriero (1995) describe radiative transfer theory and the matrix doubling algorithm to compute backscatter coefficients for forests. The HV polarization is highly sensitive to woody volume and influenced by branch dimension and orientation.

6.2.3.7 Disaster Mitigation Planning and Recovery

Adverse events that occur due to the natural phenomena on the earth's surface are called *natural disasters*. It's difficult to assess the result of the natural disaster, which makes disaster risk assessment an important task for the rescue workers. The risk assessment needs to be quick and accurate so that a timely firsthand rescue plan can be prepared. Change-detection technique to classify the pre- and postdisaster event is a quick way to assess the damage. The shadows from the buildings and digital surface models can also be measured to assess the disaster changes in that particular area. SAR data has become an important source to provide actionable information to the first responders and rescue workers to provide relief solutions. Twele et al. (2016) have proposed a near real-time (NRT) processing chain for flood detection and monitoring, which provides the firsthand disaster information in less than 45 min. Some of the processing chain modules are automatic data ingestion of Sentinel-1 images, preprocessing Kaushik and Jabin's (2018) module comprising geometric correction, radiometric calibration and twofold classification first with automatic thresholding and refinement with fuzzy-logic classification. The results are encouraging with accuracy between 94% and 96.1%. Accuracy is higher for VV band than VH bands. To make the future flood-monitoring system robust and systematic acquisition of Sentinel-1 images, time-series analysis could be beneficial. The paper by Amitrano et al. (2018) proposes the use of ground range detected (GRD) Sentinel-1 images for rapid flood mapping. In the first level of processing, cooccurrence texture with amplitude information is fed into a fuzzy-classification system. The change detection of pre- and postdisaster event images is performed in the second level of processing. According to the experimental results based on five use cases from the Copernicus Emergency Management Service, the discussed methodology outperformed other methods like K means, neural network etc. Tsyganskaya et al. (2018) have exploited the time series of Sentinel-1 data to detect flooding of vegetation. The temporary flooded vegetation (TFV) is detected with the time series-analysis from September 2016 to July 2017 for SAR images due to short revisit time. Land cover information is combined with pixel- and object-based classification to generate time-series features. It reduces the classification of false water pixels and increases the accuracy by 27% due to the TFV feature.

DeVries (2020) et al. in their paper present an algorithm using a combination of Sentinel-1 SAR and historical Landsat and auxiliary data utilizing the computing power of the Google Earth engine. The proposed algorithm was able to produce flood maps for hundreds of images within minutes and provided the flexibility of rapid data processing. An automatic two-step processing chain was proposed by Alexandre et al. (2020) for change detection for flood mapping using Sentinel-1 images. The first step selects a reference image using the Jensen-Shannon index. The second step derives the probabilities of changed and unchanged classes to apply expectation maximization (EM) for saliency detection. This model effectively compares pixel-wise change information to prepare a final change map. It performs with the kappa coefficient of 0.9238. To provide a quick response and damage mapping, Uddin et al. (2019) developed an operational methodology to map flood inundation. The accuracy of this method comes out to be 96.44%. Mishra and Jabin (2020) have presented a case study of the 2013 Uttarakhand flash floods using the Landsat 7 and Landsat 8 images.

6.2.3.8 Extracting Mineral Deposits with Remote-Sensing-Based Spectral Analysis

The potential of the mineral exploration is essential during the prefeasibility and feasibility stages. Lithological mapping, geological mapping, and geomorphologic mapping enable the geoscientist to map the areas that can be considered potential zones for mineral exploration.

It also helps to recognize the hydrothermal alteration zones that indicate the presence of minerals using the spectral analysis of the bands in the satellite images. The geologist can confine their test drilling and physical and chemical activities in the high-potential zones after the mapping has been done by the image analysis.

6.2.4 Security, Defense, and National Space Programs

Recently, SAR imagery has been used in a number of security and defense applications, too.

6.2.4.1 Defense and Intelligence Solutions

SAR forms an indispensable system for defense applications due to its all-weather imaging capability. The SAR data has the capability to provide innovative geospatial intelligence solutions to support the critical and constantly evolving missions for the defense and intelligence community (Army, Air Force, Marine Corps, and intelligence agencies). The advancement of technology is integrated with geospatial solutions to extract timely, accurate, and actionable information to make informed, reliable decisions.

Identification of roads and vehicles, automatic target recognition, detection of camouflaged objects, location of the specific area of interest can be seen from the satellite images. Strip-map imaging mode with a resolution of 5 m by 5 m gives a great level of clarity to detect moving vehicles on the ground. These images have proved best to provide the crucial terrain information and topographic characteristics about the geographical area for the various missions. It helps to find suitable observation points for enemy tracking and identify areas suitable for forwarding operating bases (FOB) for the military force. The concept of command-control communication and coordination in a military operation is dependent on the availability of accurate spatial information to quickly identify and provide a means to access unknown targets that otherwise are difficult to detect.

Seasonal imaging is required for crop identification, forest insect infestation, and wetland monitoring. Only remote sensing from space can provide global repeatable and continuous observation of processors that can be used for defense purposes where the illegal activities can be tracked and appropriate action can be taken.

Maritime security includes reliable identification of ships entering and leaving the nation's terrestrial waters. Sea target detection from SAR data is important for application areas such as fishery management, vessel traffic service, naval warfare, and ship monitoring as well as detecting ships that are involved in illegal activities such as drug smuggling and identifying hidden tankers of enemies used for automatic harbor management and marine-rescue cargo shipping.

6.2.4.2 Recording Video Footage from Satellite

The approach of recording video footage using satellite video is a new practice that has been put in place. This practice can be used in fields of departure/landing of airplanes or monitoring the traffic during peak hours. So the future of remote sensing lies in the video rather than the still images.

6.3 Challenges in the SAR Image Applications

The previous review has exposed many challenges to exploring new methods and tools to organize large volumes of data to extract hidden patterns from the images. Significant geographical and physical features are collected from these images for change detection, time-series analysis, and disaster-risk events. Efficient data mining, machine learning, and knowledge-extraction techniques are developed to discover interesting and relevant patterns specific to the application of study. There is a need to evolve the most accurate and efficient model for designing a more robust framework for SAR image modeling and analysis. One-step satellite data applications are those in which the machine-learning techniques are applied directly onto the satellite images. Object detection deals with the actual information on buildings, urban areas that are important for municipalities, rescue teams, and other agencies. All the images in the data set must be normalized into ready-to-import data for the change-detection process and strong competence in machine learning and remote-sensing data.

Also, it is challenging to design templates in order to efficiently handle the following real-world problems involving SAR images: satellite images of border areas to identify hidden tankers of enemies, designing templates to identify terrorist activities on the border, identifying common patterns, cancer clusters to investigate environmental health hazards, etc. Very high-resolution imagery of 1 m resolution is mostly needed for some commercial satellite applications. This satellite imagery is critical in making decisions to predict the market analysis. Integrating remote-sensing data with the customer-data sources and existing workflows can provide some market-decision support answers. The increasing amount of data produced by satellites is due to the improvement in camera technology, data storage, and transfer capabilities to a wider audience. Around 163 remote-sensing satellites have been launched from 2006 to 2015.

The challenges in SAR image applications are identified as:

- The size and the amount of the SAR data is huge and complex, so handling such types of data with efficiency is still a concern.
- Characteristics of radar instruments such as angle of incidence, polarization, resolution, and sensitivity affect detection in SAR images.
- SAR image-processing errors and speckle noise in SAR images can interfere with the detection of the target object.

■ Speckle noise limits the minimum vessel size that can be detected as smaller vessels become difficult to detect.

■ Clouds, wind speed, the surface of the earth, and characteristics of the instruments used also affect the quality of the images and the identification of the objects.

■ The false-detection rate is increased in some algorithms because it becomes difficult to distinguish between target and nontarget objects due to the back-scatter produced by them.

■ The low-incidence angle can make the detection of the targets on the ground and water hard.

Excellent commercial packages are available that are used to model the high-dimensional spatial data, such as PCI Geomatica, ENVI-SARScape, and Gamma to provide processing of SAR data with accuracy. Some freeware and open-source alternatives are available that distribute their source codes freely to the developers. To some extent, all these packages limit themselves to one of the other real-life applications using SAR imagery. Table 6.3 lists the important features of some of the most useful open-source software.

Table 6.3 Useful Open Source Software

S.No	Software	Data products	Features	Support
1	SNAP Sentinel Toolbox Sentinel-1 Toolbox (SAR Applications) Sentinel-2 Toolbox (High-resolution optical applications) SNAP (Combination of S-1, S-2, and S-3 features)	Sentinel-1 ERS-1 & 2 ENVISAT ALOS PALSAR TerraSAR-X COSMO-SkyMed RADARSAT-2 RapidEye SPOT MODIS (Aqua and Terra) Landsat (TM)	Tools for calibration, speckle filtering, coregistration, ortho-rectification, mosaicking, data conversion, polarimetry and interferometry, Sen2cor plugin to correct atmospheric effects and classify images	Windows, MAC OS X, Unix

(Continued)

Table 6.3 (Continued)

S.No	Software	Data products	Features	Support
2	QGIS	Sentinel Data Landsat ASTER MODIS	Visualize, analyze, interpret, and understand spatial data Raster manipulation includes neighborhood analysis, map algebra, surface interpolation, hydrologic modeling, and terrain analysis like slope and aspect Semiautomatic classification plug-in provides tools for preprocessing and postprocessing of images	Windows, Linux, Mac OS X
3	SAGA GIS	Grid Data Vector data Field data Sentinel-2 LANDSAT TM	Rich library grid, imagery and terrain processing modules Vast library for raster-based tools, tools for photogrammetry and support vector machine (SVM), terrain tools like topographic position index, topographic wetness index, and soil classification	Windows, Linux, Free and open source
4	Opticks	Multispectral images Hyperspectral images	Eplugins for raster math, radar processing, and hyper-/ multispectral	Windows, Linux, solaris 10
5	GRASS	Aerial UAV Satellite data: MODIS, Landsat, Sentinel	Image classification PCA Edge-detection radiometric corrections 3D Geostatistics analysis LiDAR processing and analysis	Free and open source, OS X, Windows, Linux

S.No	Software	Data products	Features	Support
6	polsarpro PolSARPro	ENVISAT-ASAR ALOS-PALSAR RADARSAT-2 TerraSAR-X	Handle dual and full polarization SAR data, conversion, filtering, decompositions, inSAR processing and calibration, graph processing framework to automate workflow	Windows and Linux
7	Orfeo ToolBox ORFEO	Pleiades SPOT5 QuickBird Ikonos WorldView-1 WorldView-2	Radiometry, PCA, change detection, pan sharpening, image segmentation, classification and filtering Large-scale mean-shift segmentation	Linux, Mac OS X and Windows

6.4 Conclusions

Handling of the SAR data, which is spatial data, requires certain different tools and processing functions because the regular image-processing functions are often unsuitable to exploit the complexity of the spatial data. Regular processing functions are efficient to handle issues related to passive multispectral data in the visible thermal infrared wavelength range. Special solutions are required for the SAR images that are derived from active sensors. Hence, we need a different set of tools to work with SAR data.

There are various challenges in object detection as objects in the satellite imagery can be very small, approximately 20 pixels in size. The scarcity of the training data for the classification of high-resolution images leads to poor classification accuracy.

Another focus is usually on the change-detection applications that deal with crop land, urban infrastructure, disasters or deforestation, and crisis monitoring. Change detection focuses on the creation of maps for the areas that have changed over time. For the multiclass-classification supervised techniques there is a need for ground truth data and explicit labels to detect the transitions from one class to another. However, ground-data collection is a complex and time-consuming task, thereby making multiclass classification a complex application. A complex pipeline is designed for multilevel applications where the information is extracted from the satellite imagery and fused with data from nonsatellite sources to support the decisions useful for the government agencies.

In this chapter, we have focused on the various applications dealing with the business applications, keeping in view the SAR images. This contribution gives motivation to users for starting a new business, which requires them to overcome the hurdles in terms of technology, business model, and internal organization to be able to make use of satellite technology. And, through strategic collaboration, we can use this technology to further strengthen the foundation of a safer and more secure society that is more aware of the environment.

References

Abdel-Hamid, Ayman, Olena Dubovyk, Valerie Graw, and Klaus Greve. "Assessing the Impact of Drought Stress on Grasslands Using Multi-temporal SAR Data of Sentinel-1: A Case Study in Eastern Cape, South Africa." *European Journal of Remote Sensing* 53, no. sup2 (2020): 3–16.

Abdikan, S., A. Sekertekin, M. Ustunern, F. Balik Sanli, and R. Nasirzadehdizaji. "Backscatter Analysis Using Multi-temporal Sentinel-1 SAR Data for Crop Growth of Maize in Konya Basin, Turkey." *The International Archives of the Photogrammetry, Remote Sensing and Spatial Information Sciences* 42 (2018): 9–13.

Alexandre, Cyprien, Rosa Johary, Thibault Catry, Pascal Mouquet, Christophe Révillion, Solofo Rakotondraompiana, and Gwenaelle Pennober. "A Sentinel-1 Based Processing Chain for Detection of Cyclonic Flood Impacts." *Remote Sensing* 12, no. 2 (2020): 252.

Amitrano, Donato, Gerardo Di Martino, Antonio Iodice, Daniele Riccio, and Giuseppe Ruello. "Unsupervised Rapid Flood Mapping Using Sentinel-1 GRD SAR Images." *IEEE Transactions on Geoscience and Remote Sensing* 56, no. 6 (2018): 3290–3299.

Aprile, Angelo, Fabio Dell'Acqua, Tiziana Macrì Pellizzeri, and Niccolò Ricardi. *Fusion of Airborne MTI on SAR and Ancillary Information for Vehicle Tracking.* European Association of Remote Sensing Laboratories Symposium, EARSeL, Prague, Czech Republic, 2011.

Bethke, K.-H., Stefan Baumgartner, Martina Gabele, David Hounam, Erich Kemptner, Dieter Klement, Gerhard Krieger, and Robert Erxleben. "Air-and Spaceborne Monitoring of Road Traffic Using SAR Moving Target Indication—Project TRAMRAD." *ISPRS Journal of Photogrammetry and Remote Sensing* 61, no. 3–4 (2006): 243–259.

Bianchi, Filippo Maria, Martine M. Espeseth, and Njål Borch. "Large-scale Detection and Categorization of oil Spills from SAR Images with Deep Learning." *Remote Sensing* 12, no. 14 (2020): 2260.

Chaturvedi, Sudhir Kumar, Saikat Banerjee, and Shashank Lele. "An assessment of oil spill detection using Sentinel 1 SAR-C images." *Journal of Ocean Engineering and Science* 5, no. 2 (2020): 116–135.

Çolak, E., M. Chandra, and F. Sunar. "The Use of Multi-temporal Sentinel Satellites in the Analysis of Land Cover/land Use Changes Caused by the Nuclear Power Plant Construction." In *International Archives of the Photogrammetry, Remote Sensing & Spatial Information Sciences.* International Society of Photogrammetry and Remote Sensing (ISPRS), 2019.

Del Frate, Fabio, Andrea Petrocchi, Juerg Lichtenegger, and Gianna Calabresi. "Neural Networks for Oil Spill Detection Using ERS-SAR Data." *IEEE Transactions on Geoscience and Remote Sensing* 38, no. 5 (2000): 2282–2287.

DeVries, Ben, Chengquan Huang, John Armston, Wenli Huang, John W. Jones, and Megan W. Lang. "Rapid and Robust Monitoring of Flood Events Using Sentinel-1 and Landsat Data on the Google Earth Engine." *Remote Sensing of Environment* 240 (2020): 111664.

Dobson, Myron Craig, Fawwaz T. Ulaby, Thuy LeToan, Andre Beaudoin, Eric S. Kasischke, and Norm Christensen. "Dependence of Radar Backscatter on Coniferous Forest Biomass." *IEEE Transactions on Geoscience and Remote Sensing* 30, no. 2 (1992): 412–415.

Dong, Y., B. Forster, and C. Ticehurst. "Radar Backscatter Analysis for Urban Environments." *International Journal of Remote Sensing* 18, no. 6 (1997): 1351–1364.

Ferrazzoli, Paolo, and Leila Guerriero. "Radar Sensitivity to Tree Geometry and Woody Volume: A Model Analysis." *IEEE Transactions on Geoscience and Remote Sensing* 33, no. 2 (1995): 360–371.

Fitriani, Sarah Putri, Jonson Lumban Gaol, and Dony Kushardono. "Fishing-vessel Detection Using Synthetic Aperture Radar (sar) Sentinel-1 (Case Study: Java Sea)." *International Journal of Remote Sensing and Earth Sciences (IJReSES)* 16, no. 2 (2020): 131–142.

Henke, Daniel, Elias Mendez Dominguez, David Small, Michael E. Schaepman, and Erich Meier. "Moving Target Tracking in Single-and Multichannel SAR." *IEEE Transactions on Geoscience and Remote Sensing* 53, no. 6 (2015): 3146–3159.

Jeyaseelan, A. T. "Droughts & Floods Assessment and Monitoring Using Remote Sensing and GIS." *Satellite Remote Sensing and GIS Applications in Agricultural Meteorology* 291 (2003).

Kaushik, Prachi, and Suraiya Jabin. "A Comparative Study of Pre-processing Techniques of SAR Images." In *2018 4th International Conference on Computing Communication and Automation (ICCCA)*, pp. 1–4. IEEE, 2018.

Keshavarz, Mohammad Reza, Majid Vazifedoust, and Amin Alizadeh. "Drought Monitoring Using a Soil Wetness Deficit Index (SWDI) Derived from MODIS Satellite Data." *Agricultural Water Management* 132 (2014): 37–45.

Koppel, Kalev, Karlis Zalite, Kaupo Voormansik, and Thomas Jagdhuber. "Sensitivity of Sentinel-1 Backscatter to Characteristics of Buildings." *International Journal of Remote Sensing* 38, no. 22 (2017): 6298–6318.

Li, Baihui, Yan Chen, Yunping Chen, Youchun Lu, and Cunshi Ma. "Landslide Detection Based on GLCM Using SAR Images." In *IGARSS 2020–2020 IEEE International Geoscience and Remote Sensing Symposium*, pp. 1989–1992. IEEE, Hawaii, 2020.

Liang, Dong, Huadong Guo, Lu Zhang, Yun Cheng, Qi Zhu, and Xuting Liu. "Time-series Snowmelt Detection Over the Antarctic Using Sentinel-1 SAR Images on Google Earth Engine." *Remote Sensing of Environment* 256 (2021): 112318.

Lin, Shih-Yuan, Cheng-Wei Lin, and Stephan van Gasselt. "Processing Framework for Landslide Detection Based on Synthetic Aperture Radar (SAR) Intensity-Image Analysis." *Remote Sensing* 13, no. 4 (2021): 644.

Mishra, Sarthak, and Suraiya Jabin. "Land Use Land Cover Change Detection Using LANDSAT Images: A Case Study." In *2020 IEEE 5th International Conference on Computing Communication and Automation (ICCCA)*, pp. 730–735. Galgotias University Greater, IEEE, Noida, India, 2020.

Noviello, Carlo, Simona Verde, Virginia Zamparelli, Gianfranco Fornaro, Antonio Pauciullo, Diego Reale, Gianfranco Nicodemo, Settimio Ferlisi, Giovanni Gulla, and Dario Peduto. "Monitoring Buildings at Landslide Risk with SAR: A Methodology Based on the Use of Multipass Interferometric Data." *IEEE Geoscience and Remote Sensing Magazine* 8, no. 1 (2020): 91–119.

Open Data Cube, www.opendatacube.org/overview, Acessed on 27 February, 2020.

Paloscia, Simonetta, Giovanni Macelloni, and Paolo Pampaloni. "The Relations Between Backscattering Coefficient and Biomass of Narrow and Wide Leaf Crops." In *IGARSS'98. Sensing and Managing the Environment. 1998 IEEE International Geoscience and Remote Sensing. Symposium Proceedings. (Cat. No. 98CH36174)*, vol. 1, pp. 100–102. IEEE, Seattle, WA, 1998.

Park, Sang-Eun, and Sun-Gu Lee. "On the Use of Single-, Dual-, and Quad-polarimetric SAR Observation for Landslide Detection." *ISPRS International Journal of Geo-Information* 8, no. 9 (2019): 384.

Rosenqvist, Jessica, Ake Rosenqvist, Katherine Jensen, and Kyle McDonald. "Mapping of Maximum and Minimum Inundation Extents in the Amazon Basin 2014–2017 with ALOS-2 PALSAR-2 ScanSAR Time-Series Data." *Remote Sensing* 12, no. 8 (2020): 1326.

Sasamal, Sasanka Kumar, and Naresh K. Mallenahalli. "Detection of Fishing Boats in SAR Image Using Linear Moments and Machine Learning." In *2019 IEEE Recent Advances in Geoscience and Remote Sensing: Technologies, Standards and Applications (TENGARSS)*, pp. 21–25. IEEE, Kochi, India, 2019.

Slinski, Kimberly, Amy McNally, Christa D. Peters-Lidard, Gabriel B. Senay, Terri S. Hogue, and John E. McCray. "Synthetic Aperture Radar (SAR) Applications for Rangeland Famine Early Warning Systems." In *AGU Fall Meeting Abstracts*, vol. 2019, pp. H31F–04. AGU, San Francisco, CA, 2019.

Tanveer, Hashir, Timo Balz, Francesca Cigna, and Deodato Tapete. "Monitoring 2011–2020 Traffic Patterns in Wuhan (China) with COSMO-SkyMed SAR, Amidst the 7th CISM Military World Games and COVID-19 Outbreak." *Remote Sensing* 12, no. 10 (2020): 1636.

Ticehurst, Catherine, Zheng-Shu Zhou, Eric Lehmann, Fang Yuan, Medhavy Thankappan, Ake Rosenqvist, Ben Lewis, and Matt Paget. "Building a SAR-Enabled Data Cube Capability in Australia Using SAR Analysis Ready Data." *Data* 4, no. 3 (2019): 100.

Tsyganskaya, Viktoriya, Sandro Martinis, Philip Marzahn, and Ralf Ludwig. "Detection of Temporary Flooded Vegetation Using Sentinel-1 Time Series Data." *Remote Sensing* 10, no. 8 (2018): 1286.

Twele, André, Wenxi Cao, Simon Plank, and Sandro Martinis. "Sentinel-1-based Flood Mapping: A Fully Automated Processing Chain." *International Journal of Remote Sensing* 37, no. 13 (2016): 2990–3004.

Uddin, Kabir, Mir A. Matin, and Franz J. Meyer. "Operational Flood Mapping Using Multi-temporal Sentinel-1 SAR Images: A Case Study from Bangladesh." *Remote Sensing* 11, no. 13 (2019): 1581.

Ulaby, Fawwaz T., Kamal Sarabandi, K. Y. L. E. Mcdonald, Michael Whitt, and M. Craig Dobson. "Michigan Microwave Canopy Scattering Model." *International Journal of Remote Sensing* 11, no. 7 (1990): 1223–1253.

Fiscella, B., et al. "Oil Spill Detection Using Marine SAR Images." *International Journal of Remote Sensing* 21, no. 18 (2000): 3561–3566.

Vreugdenhil, Mariette, Wolfgang Wagner, Bernhard Bauer-Marschallinger, Isabella Pfeil, Irene Teubner, Christoph Rüdiger, and Peter Strauss. "Sensitivity of Sentinel-1 Backscatter to Vegetation Dynamics: An Austrian Case Study." *Remote Sensing* 10, no. 9 (2018): 1396.

Wani, Mudasir Ahmad, and Suraiya Jabin. "Big Data: Issues, Challenges, and Techniques in Business Intelligence." In *Big Data Analytics*, pp. 613–628. Springer, Singapore, 2018.

White, Jonathan, Anthony Helmstetter, Jared Culbertson, and Igor Ternovskiy. "Qualia Centric Hypothetical Thinking: Applications to Vehicle Tracking with the Fusion of EO and SAR Input Data Sources." In *Cyber Sensing 2015*, vol. 9458, p. 945806. International Society for Optics and Photonics, SPIE, Baltimore, MD, 2015.

Zeng, Kan, and Yixiao Wang. "A Deep Convolutional Neural Network for Oil Spill Detection from Spaceborne SAR Images." *Remote Sensing* 12, no. 6 (2020): 1015.

Chapter 7

Exploring Quantum Computing to Revolutionize Big Data Analytics for Various Industrial Sectors

Preeti Agarwal and Mansaf Alam

Contents

DOI: 10.1201/9781003175711-7

7.1 Introduction

We are living in the data era. Some of the major data sources are social media, company warehouses, transactional data, and, recently Internet of Things (IoT) sensors (Cloudmoyo 2020). These sources generate exabytes of data, which are increasing exponentially. Every day, a growing amount of audio and video is uploaded to social networking sites such as WhatsApp, Facebook, and Twitter. Each day an average of 300 hours of video is uploaded to YouTube. Business organizations are now investing a great deal in developing data warehouses containing historical records of their company related to customers, goods, sales, etc. (Chaudhary et al. 2021). The analysis of these historical records lets them gain insight into the patterns and trends that enable them to promote their business. This data can influence the business organization, as it can help understand the consumer's behavior and help predict what the customer is most likely to purchase. Big data analysis will help businesses develop smarter products and smarter services. It helps to improve operations, simplify their processes and improve the performance of their machines. IoT devices have also emerged as the next source of big data in recent years (Agarwal and Alam 2020c). Millions of IoT devices are deployed, which sense information that will make up the subsequent supply of big data (Agarwal and Alam 2020b). The number of IoT devices is projected to upsurge globally by 50 billion by 2025 (Bhatia and Sood 2020).

7.1.1 Need for Quantum Computing

The latest IoT buzzwords, artificial intelligence, machine learning, big data, generated data, and the classical computers will fail at a certain point in time. The data growth-rate graph shown in Figure 7.1 indicates an exponential trend in data growth, suggesting that classical computers will not handle it within a decade.

The storage and processing power needed to manage this enormous amount of data is beyond a classical computer's capability (Vamanan, Pandey, and Ramesh 2015). Many big data technologies, such as Hadoop and MapReduce, are available to store and process extensive unstructured data. Many analytical solutions are working at the top of these big data technologies. However, it is still expected that, beyond a certain point, the existing big data technologies cannot solve the current processing requirements, even if they are boosted by GPUs. The reason is that the processing power of current classical computers depends on the number of transistors. According to Moore's Law, computing power doubles every two years. The number of transistors needs to be increased for accommodating high computing power, resulting in transistors' size being miniatured. However, transistors' miniaturization is possible only to a limited extent, marking the end of Moore's law. Amdahl's law also restricts the degree of parallelization that can be achieved. Taking these two factors together, the processing of big data needs a paradigm

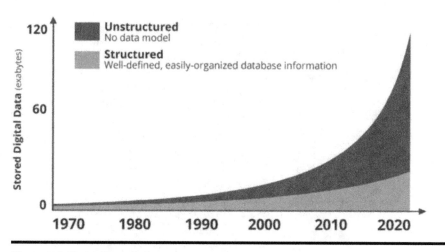

Figure 7.1 Data Growth Rate.

Source: Seekingalpha (2020)

shift. One of the potential solutions is in terms of quantum computing. Quantum computing is in its infancy at this stage but is expected to grow in the coming years. The processing power of quantum computers is several times faster than conventional computers as they operate in the order of 2^n in terms of qubits. Quantum computers, in a fraction of seconds, can answer the problem that can be answered by a traditional computer in hours.

In 2013, Google and NASA set up the first AI application lab using quantum computers. They worked on the theory to analyze exponentially increasing data. There is a need to minimize the number of operations to be performed on the data in a reverse manner, i.e., in a logarithmic manner. Researchers are attempting to integrate quantum computing into machine learning, deep learning, and AI to make computing faster and easier. Many companies, such as Facebook, Google, IBM, and Microsoft, which handle large volumes of data, are investing in quantum computers. According to current trends, quantum computing's global market is projected to reach 1.9 billion by 2023 and 8 billion by 2027 (Statista n.d.). Many computing giants are working on commercial quantum computers, including IBM, Facebook, Amazon, Microsoft, Google, and Alibaba (Mantra n.d.).

7.1.2 Industrial Applications of Quantum Computing

Some of the sectors that can benefit from quantum computers' computing capabilities are shown in Figure 7.2 (Chojecki n.d.).

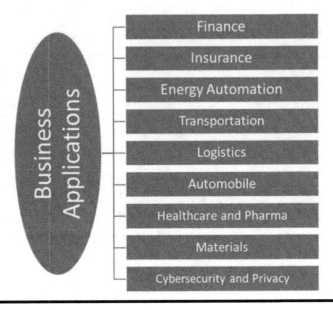

Figure 7.2 Various Business Applications.

- **Finance:** quantum computers can solve a range of problems in the banking industry, including portfolio optimization, asset pricing, risk analysis, fraud detection, and market forecasting. Many banking organizations have begun experimenting, e.g. Barclays, JP Morgan.
- **Insurance:** quantum computing's possible applications include valuing financial assets like bonds, valuing options and warranties on insured products, and reckoning operational risk. Allianz began its collaboration with 1QBit.
- **Energy sector:** improving current energy transmission network and forecasting usage are two large-scale problems that are well suited to quantum computer research. ExxonMobil is working as a quantum partner with IBM.
- **Transportation:** the greatest example of quantum computing in action is Volkswagen's traffic optimization project with D-Wave. With all its variations, the travelling salesman problem is an excellent problem to try on NISQ devices as it helps in route optimization.
- **Logistics:** supply-chain problems are often complicated and challenging to solve using traditional computers, implying that quantum computing has a bright future. Alibaba began experimenting with its hardware.
- **Automotive and aerospace:** Maintaining a large fleet of vehicles, whether autonomous or not, poses optimization problems that vary rapidly with the quantity of vehicles. That is the reason manufacturers such as Volkswagen, Daimler, and Ford have all entered the market. NASA, Airbus and Lockheed Martin are all very involved in the aerospace industry.

- **Healthcare, chemicals and pharmaceuticals:** drug development is an expensive procedure, and simulating molecules requires a lot of computing power. Quantum computers are a good fit for research and development in pharma, since they are ideal for simulating quantum phenomena due to their quantum existence. Biogen and Accenture worked on quantum-computing drug-discovery applications. The healthcare sector also benefited from quantum computing. Monitoring an individual's lifestyle is vital for chronic diseases (Agarwal and Alam 2020a).
- **Materials:** Industries that rely on improved batteries, processors or network architectures may use quantum computing to imitate new possibilities or improve current structures. Bosch and Honeywell were the first to try out this business model.
- **Cybersecurity and blockchain:** blockchain deals with encrypted transactions and contracts. It is heavily reliant on cryptographic methods and thus vulnerable to cyberattacks using cutting-edge technology. Exploring quantum blockchain is also an excellent way to prepare for the future. Only Accenture has listed blockchain and quantum so far. However, there is an increasing trend among cybersecurity firms to investigate post-quantum cryptography or algorithms that are safe to use in a world of powerful quantum computers, such as those developed by Microsoft or Google.

7.2 State-of-the-Art

Hey (Hey 1999) explored the basic principles of quantum computing. Qubits, architecture for quantum logic gates, quantum registers, the idea of reversible computation and quantum algorithms' complexity are among these concepts. Kumar et al. (Kumar et al. 2016) addressed the various core components, such as qubits, superposition and entanglement.

Quantum computation necessitates the use of special hardware and software. Buhrman et al. (Buhrman and Röhrig 2003) investigated the hardware in terms of distribution and topologies in different applications. S. Jain (Jain 2015) addressed various quantum architectures that could be effective. Menon looked at a variety of different transmission protocols. Due to the scarcity of real quantum systems, it is preferable to train on simulators. The research also looked at a variety of quantum simulators.

Gay et al. (Gay 2006) studied the idea of quantum programming languages. Various design principles for quantum programming languages, such as syntax, semantics, and compilers were explored as well as future directions. The numerous quantum algorithms were discussed by Rottler et al. (Roetteler and Svore 2018) and divided into three groups: "amplitude modification type algorithms," "hidden subgroup type algorithms," and the third category of algorithms that excludes the first two categories.

The execution of a quantum programming language necessitates the use of programming-language support tools. An analysis of existing quantum programming tools on the market was proposed by Sofge et al. (Sofge 2008). A comparative analysis was provided to assist in the selection of the best alternative. Han et al. (Han and Kim 2002) proposed a "Quantum Inspired Evolutionary Algorithm" to efficiently solve optimization problems. It is the product of combining evolutionary algorithms and quantum computing concepts.

In contrast to conventional systems, quantum computing can perform big data analytics more effectively. Shaikh et al. (Shaikh and On n.d.) backed up this idea by discussing a few big data analytics algorithms in a quantum environment. He demonstrated how quantum computers' processing capacity enhances quantum machine learning. Yan et al. (Yan, Iliyasu, and Venegas-Andraca 2016) addressed the various image-processing algorithms that have been enhanced in the context of quantum computers, as well as the principle of " quantum image processing."

7.3 Taxonomy of Quantum Computing

Quantum computing's taxonomy is characterized by basic elements, algorithms, softwares and tools used.

7.3.1 Basic Elements

Quantum computers use quantum mechanics to perform much faster computing than conventional computers. The basic components of quantum computing are data, operations and results (Nielsen, Chuang, and Grover 2002). The data in quantum computing is expressed in the form of 'quantum bits' called *qubits*. The operation on qubits is done using quantum gates. Quantum gates usually perform the unitary operation on qubits. The results are obtained by employing measurements. Each of these is explained in detail in the following subsections.

7.3.1.1 Qubits

Quantum computers have qubits, which are analogous to bits in classical computers.

$$0 \rightarrow |0>$$
$$1 \rightarrow |1>$$

The qubits are denoted by the letters $|0>$ and $|1>$, which stand for "zero ket" and "one ket," respectively. In quantum computing, they are the fundamental computational vectors. These qubits, unlike bits, are in Hilbert vector space. In vector space, a two-dimensional qubit is denoted as

$$|0>=[1\ 0]$$
$$|1>=[0\ 1]$$

Qubits states can be combined to form a product basis state as follows:

$$|00>=[1\ 1\ 0\ 0\ 0\ 10\ ]=[10\ 0\ 0\ ]$$
$$|01>=[1\ 0\ 1\ 1\ 0\ 0\ 0\ 1\ ]=[01\ 0\ 0\ ]$$
$$|10>=[0\ 1\ 0\ 0\ 1\ 1\ 10\ ]=[0\ 0\ 10\ ]$$
$$|11>=[0\ 0\ 0\ 1\ 1\ 1\ 0\ 1\ ]=[0\ 0\ 0\ 1]$$

In general, n qubits are represented by a superposition state vector in 2^n dimensional space.

Qubit state: a pure qubit exists as a superposition of its basis state known as *qubit state*. It is a linear combination of |0> and |1> as shown in equation 1

$$|\psi>=\alpha|0>+\beta|> \tag{1}$$

where ψ is a quantum vector and α and β can be real or complex numbers. α represents the probability of outcome |0> with value 0 and β represents the probability of outcome |1> with value 1. Therefore, it can be said that $|\alpha|^2+|\beta|^2=1$. Since α and β are complex numbers, each one has two degrees of freedom and can be visualized using bloch sphere. The bloch representation is shown in Figure 7.3.

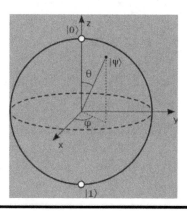

Figure 7.3 Bloch Sphere.

Source: "Qubit—Wikipedia" n.d.

7.3.1.2 Quantum Gates

Various operations on quantum computers can be carried out using logic gates. Quantum logic gates form the building blocks of quantum circuits for a quantum computer. Typically, they perform unit transformations on qubits.

The key gates are explained in the following, and Figure 7.4 shows the circuit for each quantum gate.

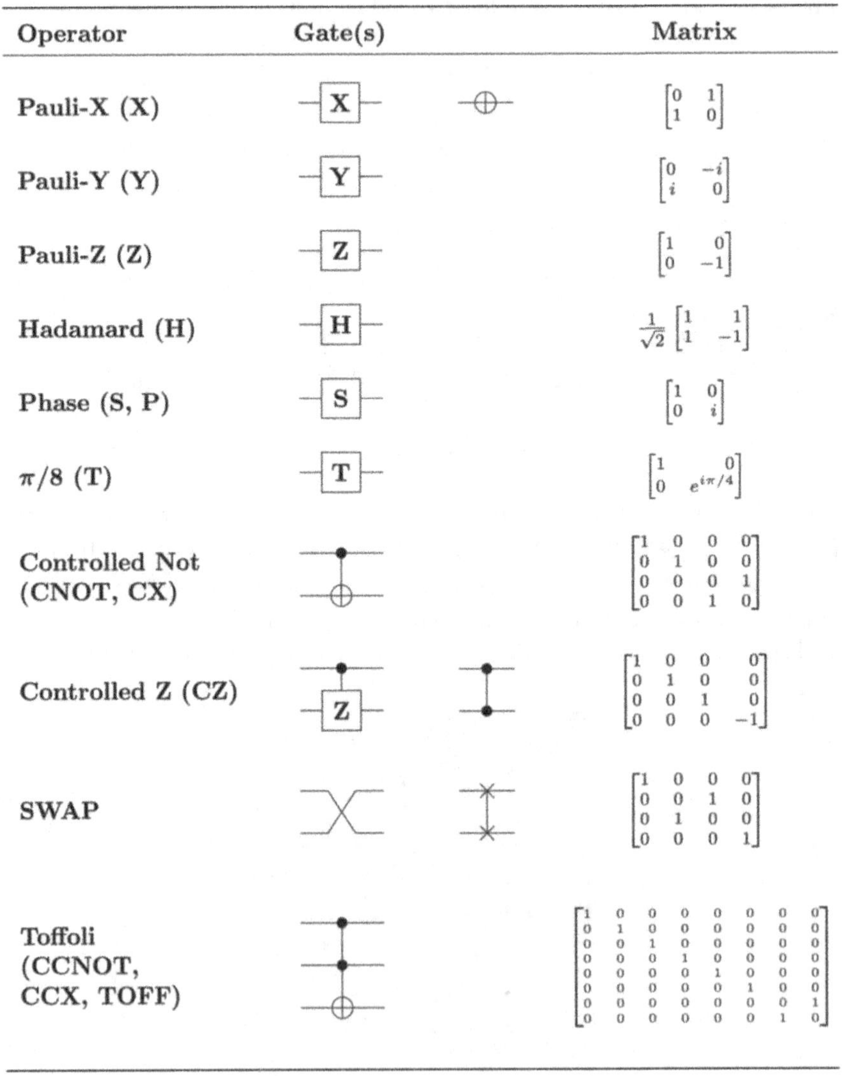

Operator	Gate(s)	Matrix
Pauli-X (X)		$\begin{bmatrix} 0 & 1 \\ 1 & 0 \end{bmatrix}$
Pauli-Y (Y)		$\begin{bmatrix} 0 & -i \\ i & 0 \end{bmatrix}$
Pauli-Z (Z)		$\begin{bmatrix} 1 & 0 \\ 0 & -1 \end{bmatrix}$
Hadamard (H)		$\frac{1}{\sqrt{2}} \begin{bmatrix} 1 & 1 \\ 1 & -1 \end{bmatrix}$
Phase (S, P)		$\begin{bmatrix} 1 & 0 \\ 0 & i \end{bmatrix}$
$\pi/8$ (T)		$\begin{bmatrix} 1 & 0 \\ 0 & e^{i\pi/4} \end{bmatrix}$
Controlled Not (CNOT, CX)		$\begin{bmatrix} 1 & 0 & 0 & 0 \\ 0 & 1 & 0 & 0 \\ 0 & 0 & 0 & 1 \\ 0 & 0 & 1 & 0 \end{bmatrix}$
Controlled Z (CZ)		$\begin{bmatrix} 1 & 0 & 0 & 0 \\ 0 & 1 & 0 & 0 \\ 0 & 0 & 1 & 0 \\ 0 & 0 & 0 & -1 \end{bmatrix}$
SWAP		$\begin{bmatrix} 1 & 0 & 0 & 0 \\ 0 & 0 & 1 & 0 \\ 0 & 1 & 0 & 0 \\ 0 & 0 & 0 & 1 \end{bmatrix}$
Toffoli (CCNOT, CCX, TOFF)		$\begin{bmatrix} 1 & 0 & 0 & 0 & 0 & 0 & 0 & 0 \\ 0 & 1 & 0 & 0 & 0 & 0 & 0 & 0 \\ 0 & 0 & 1 & 0 & 0 & 0 & 0 & 0 \\ 0 & 0 & 0 & 1 & 0 & 0 & 0 & 0 \\ 0 & 0 & 0 & 0 & 1 & 0 & 0 & 0 \\ 0 & 0 & 0 & 0 & 0 & 1 & 0 & 0 \\ 0 & 0 & 0 & 0 & 0 & 0 & 0 & 1 \\ 0 & 0 & 0 & 0 & 0 & 0 & 1 & 0 \end{bmatrix}$

Figure 7.4 Quantum Gates.

Source: "Quantum Logic Gate- Wikipedia" n.d.

- Pauli-X (X): similar to classical NOT gate. It maps |0> input to |1> and |1> to |0>. It maps the qubit rotation about x-axis through π radians in bloch sphere.
- Pauli-Y (Y): maps the qubit rotation about y-axis through π radians in bloch sphere.[ ] It converts |0 to i|1> and |1> to i|0>.
- Pauli-Z (Z): maps the qubit rotation about z-axis through π radians in bloch sphere. It keeps qubit |0> unchanged but changes |1> to -|1>.
- Hadamard (H): the Hadamard gate takes single a qubit as input and maps it to the output. It maps |0> to $\frac{|0>+|1>}{\sqrt{2}}$ and |1> to $\frac{|0>-|1>}{\sqrt{2}}$. The measurement has equal probability of outcome 0 or 1.
- Phase (S, P): this gate modifies the phase of the quantum state. It maps |0> to |0> and |1> to $e^{i\phi}$ |1>.
- Controlled Not (CNOT, CX): performs NOT operation on second qubit only when first qubit is |1>, otherwise leaves the output unchanged.
- Controlled Z (CZ): performs Pauli-Z operation about z-axis only when first qubit is |1>, otherwise leaves the output unchanged.
- SWAP: this gate swaps the qubits.
- Tofolli (CCNOT, CCX, TOFF): the Tofolli gate combined with the Hadamard gate acts as a universal gate. This gate takes 3 qubits as input. In case the first and second bit are state |1> then it applies Pauli-X on the third bit.

7.3.1.3 Measurement

The basic states of qubits are |0> and |1>. When a qubit is measured, it falls into one of two states: |0> or |1>. It's impossible to say with certainty which state a qubit would collapse in. The probability of a qubit collapsing to either |0> or |1> is calculated by measurement. This probability is equal to the square of the vector depth, known as Born's rule. Therefore, measuring a qubit that can be represented in the quantum state as $(a|0> + b|1>=\begin{bmatrix} a & b \end{bmatrix}$ will result in |0> with probability $|a|^2$ and |1> with probability $|b|^2$.

7.3.2 Quantum Algorithms

In this section, classical quantum algorithms, quantum machine learning algorithms, are described.

7.3.2.1 Classical Quantum Algorithms

Classic quantum-computing algorithms are used to speed up the application (Gyongyosi and Imre 2019). These are categorized as Fourier transform, amplitude implementation, and hybrid algorithm based on the operations.

7.3.2.1.1 Based on Fourier Transform

Algorithms in this category are useful in solving problems involving exponential queries, black-box problems, factoring, and logarithmic computing (Gill et al. n.d.). These algorithm categories are used to speed up and scale up the computation. The most popular algorithms in this group are the Bernstein-Vazirani algorithm and Shor's algorithm.

■ **Bernstein-Vazirani Algorithm (BSA)** (Bernstein and Vazirani 1997): given a function $f : \{0,1\}^n \mapsto \{0,1\}$, which can be represented as $f_s(x) = \oplus S_i x_i = <s, x>$, where s is an unknown string or hidden string. The BSA finds the hidden string by applying the oracle. The complexity of the algorithm depends on the number of times the oracle is applied. This is in contrast to classical computers, which on the application of $f(x)$ produce 1 bit with complexity $O(n)$. The oracle function is the black-box function denoted as $U_s = |x>|q \oplus <s, x>$ where x is data qubit and q is oracle qubit. The BSA procedure is as follows:
  - Perform the state initialization on n+1 qubit, $|00....0> \rightarrow |\varphi|>$.
  - Apply oracle U_s.
  - Apply $H \oplus n$ on first n qubits.
  - Measure all qubits.

■ **Shor's algorithm** (Shor 2002): Shor's algorithm is used to solve complex factorization problems in polynomial time, which classical computers cannot solve. Shor's algorithm is executed in two phases: First, the factorizing problem is reduced to an order-finding problem on the classical computer. Second, the order-finding problem is solved on the quantum computer.
  - First phase: the first phase is the classical computation phase and consists of the following steps:
    i. Choose a number randomly between $1 < a < n$.
    ii. Compute greatest common divisor (GCD) between a and n using Euclidean distance.
    iii. If GCD (a,n) = 1, then we go to the second phase of quantum computation to find the smallest positive integer r, such that for a given function $f(x) = a^x \bmod n$, $f(x+r) = f(x) = a^{x+r} \bmod n = a^x \bmod n$.
    iv. If r is odd or $a^{r/2} = -1 (\bmod n)$ then go to step 1.
    v. Otherwise GCD ($a^{r/2} + 1, n$) and GCD $(a^{r/2} - 1, n)$ are factors of n.
  - Second phase: this is the quantum-computing step. This step aims to find $Q = 2^q$, such that $n^2 \leq Q \leq 2n^2$, which implies $\frac{Q}{r} > n$. The various steps followed are as follows:
    i. Initialize the registers according to equation 2.

$$\frac{1}{\sqrt{Q}}\sum_{x=0}^{Q-1}|x>=\left(\frac{1}{\sqrt{2}}\sum_{x1}^{1}|x_1>\right)\otimes\dots\otimes\left(\frac{1}{\sqrt{2}}\sum_{xq}^{1}|x_q>\right) \tag{2}$$

ii. Construct $f(x)$ as a quantum function and apply it to the state created in step 1, $U_f|x,0^q>=|x,f(x)>$.

iii. Apply inverse quantum Fourier transform to the input register.

iv. Perform the measurement to obtain the output.

7.3.2.1.2 Based on Amplitude Modification

The algorithms in this category are generally used to perform generalized search and efficiently deal with large unstructured databases. The crucial algorithm in this category is Grover's algorithm.

■ **Grover's algorithm** (Grover 1996): Grover's algorithm is commonly used for searching for an item. In a randomly ordered n-item database, Grover's algorithm can search an item in $O\left(\sqrt{n}\right)$ operations, in contrast to the classical computers, which require $O(n)$ operations. Grover's algorithm can quadratically speed up the computations. Grover's algorithm's capability lies in the fact that, many a time, it can be used as the inverting function. For accomplishing this task, first we need to construct a "quantum oracle." If a given function is $y=f(x)$, Grover's algorithm calculates x given y, i.e., Grover's algorithm can find a function that produces y if the database entry matches x. Let n be the number of bit strings to perform the search. The Grover's operator is defined as $G=2|\psi>\psi|-I)O$, where $|\psi>=\frac{1}{\sqrt{n}}\sum_{i=0}^{n-1}|i>$ is the uniform superposition over all the basic states and O is the oracle. The inner working of the oracle is considered a black box. The oracle is a function f, as shown in equation 3, such that

$$f(x)=\{1, if \ |x> is \ a \ solution \ 0, otherwise \tag{3}$$

The oracle operator for a transformation is denoted as $|x>q>\rightarrow|x>|q\oplus f(x)$, where $|x>$ is the index qubit and $|q>$ is the oracle qubit. On the subsequent operations of Grover's algorithm, the amplitude is flipped about the mean amplitude.

The procedure for Grover's algorithm is as follows:

i. Initialize the basic state $|\psi>$

ii. Apply the Grover operator $\left\lceil\frac{\pi\sqrt{n}}{4}\right\rceil$ times.

iii. Perform the measurements on qubits.

7.3.2.1.3 Hybrid Computing Algorithm

The algorithms in this category are efficient in solving large graph problems. The algorithm belonging to this category is the quantum approximate optimization algorithm.

◼ **Quantum approximate optimization problem (QAOP)** (Farhi, Goldstone, and Gutmann 2014): This algorithm is used to solve combinatorial optimization problems, which can be formulated as

$$maximize : \sum_{\alpha=1}^{m} C_{\alpha}\left(z_i\right)$$

$$z_i \varepsilon \left\{0,1\right\} \forall i \varepsilon \left\{1,n\right\}$$

where n is the number of binary decision variables, z and m are binary functions, and C(z) are clauses.

In order to apply the quantum approximate optimization algorithm first, there is a need to convert clausal functions $C_{\alpha}\left(z\right)$ to the equivalent quantum clause C_{α}. After conversion, select the number of quantum rounds r, $r \geq 1$ and two angles per round.

$$\frac{0 \leq \beta[k] \leq \pi, and}{0 \leq \gamma[k] \leq 2\pi}$$

for the kth round.

The procedure is as follows:

i. Construct n qubit superstate.

ii. For r number of rounds

apply $\prod_{\alpha=1}^{m} e^{-i\gamma[k]C_{\alpha}}$ and $\prod_{j=1}^{n} e^{-i\beta[k]C_j}$

iii. The expected value of the final constructed state gives the approximate solution to the problem.

7.3.2.2 Quantum Machine Learning

The intersection of quantum computing and machine learning is known as *quantum machine learning*. Quantum machine learning looks at how quantum results can be used to solve machine-learning problems. The amount of data required to accurately train a classical computation model is increasing at a rate that exceeds the capabilities of current computing devices. In this case, quantum computation can help with ongoing training with large amounts of data. Quantum machine learning aims in building algorithms faster than traditional machine learning. Classically, there are three types of machine-learning algorithms: supervised machine learning, unsupervised machine learning and reinforcement learning (Mishra et al. 2021).

- Supervised machine learning: in this type of machine-learning algorithm, the machines are taught to work based on already labeled data based on specific characteristics.
- Unsupervised machine learning: in this type of machine learning, no labelled data is provided to the machines; they analyze data based on similarity and dissimilarity in the classes.
- Reinforcement learning: In this type of machine-learning, the machine analyzes feedback and learns.

Some widely used quantum machine-learning algorithms are discussed in the following paragraphs:

- **Quantum support vector machines (QSVM)** (Rebentrost, Mohseni, and Lloyd 2014): QSVM classifies a set of data points in a group and wants to find a line or hyperplane in the case of multidimensional data that separates the data into groups. This line or hyperplane is drawn with the help of kernels. In the case of quantum SVM, the data is first translated into quantum states, and then the kernel is built over the quantum state. After building the kernel matrix, the quantum SVM is trained in the same way as the classical SVM.

  The procedure for QSVM is as follows:

  i. Calculate kernel matrix using quantum inner product algorithm.

  $$k_{ij} = \vec{x_i} . \vec{x_j}$$

  where $\vec{x_i}$ and $\vec{x_j}$ is an n dimensional vector space.

  ii. Compute

  $$\left[0\,\vec{1}^T \ \vec{1}\,k + \gamma^{-1}1 \right] \left[b\,\vec{a} \right] = \left[0\,\vec{y} \right]$$

  where k is kernel matrix, γ is the tunning parameter and α is the normalizing vector, then find |b, $\vec{\alpha}$ for training data.

  iii. Perform classification on the data $\vec{x}$ against the training results |b, $\vec{\alpha}$ >.

- **Quantum principal component analysis (QPCA)** (Lloyd, Mohseni, and Rebentrost 2014): this algorithm is used to reduce the number of features in the dataset by eliminating redundant, nondominating features. QPCA is used to get the minimal set of the relevant features in the dataset. This algorithm is divided into four phases: classical preprocessing, state preparation, quantifying the purity and classical post preprocessing.

  The detailed procedure is as follows:

  i. This step consists of the following substeps.

      a. Convert raw data vectors to the covariance matrix.

      b. Normalize the covariance matrix.

      c. Convert to pure state $| \psi >$

  ii. Compute the unitary U_{pre} to pure state. U_{pre} acts on two qubits A and B and can be decomposed as $U_{prep} = (U_A \otimes U_B) CNOT_{AB} (U_A' \otimes 1_B)$.

iii. Perform purity calculations.
iv. Convert the output of step iii. to eigenvalues, select features with larger eigenvalues and discard others.

7.3.3 Quantum Software and Tools

Several quantum-software simulators supporting various programming languages are available in the market. Some of the most popular software development kits (SDKs) are Ocean by D-Wave and Qiskit by IBM. Some open-source SDKs are ProjectQ and Forest. Various popular simulators available for quantum computation are QDK by Microsoft, Cirql by Google, Strawberry Fields by Xanadu and QX Simulator. Some of the popular quantum programming languages are QCL, Q#, and Q language. Popular quantum processors are Google Bristlecone, IBM Q5 Tenerife, Rigetti 8Q Agave, and D-wave 2000Q. The comparison between different popular quantum softwares and their tolls are given in Table 7.1.

Table 7.1 Comparison of Popular Quantum Software and Tools

Tool/ Library	Open-Source	Cloud-Based	GUI Support	Support for Quantum Circuits	Language Support	SDK Support
Qiskit	Yes	Public cloud	Yes	Yes	Python	IBM SDK
pyQuil (Rigetti forest)	Yes	Private cloud	Yes	Yes	Python	Forest SDK
Q#	Yes	Private cloud	No	No	Q# visual studio, python for NET framework	Microsoft SDK
ProjectQ	Yes	No	No	Yes	Python	IBM SDK
Cirq	Yes	No	No	Yes	Python	Google Quantum AI
Strawberry Fields	Yes	Private cloud	Yes	Yes	Python combined with many other simulator SDKs	Supports various cross platform SDKs

7.4 Conclusions and Future Directions

Quantum computing is expected to be mature within a decade. It finds significant applications in finance, operations, cybersecurity, robotics, healthcare, drug discovery etc. The significant challenges that future research needs to address are:

■ The unreliability and design issues in quantum computers, as quantum technology has a very short coherence time of qubits, lead to large error rates. Developing efficient error correction methods is still challenging in quantum research because qubits forget their information in a fraction of seconds (Paler and Devitt 2015).

■ Many physical qubits are required to execute a problem involving big data; thus, continuous communication is required between the computation platform and quantum chip, leading to increased overhead and complexity. The design of fault-tolerant quantum systems is still open to research, as quantum states are fragile and operate at a very low temperature. The present quantum architecture is not efficient enough to handle fabrication errors (Devitt, Munro, and Nemoto 2013).

■ Efficiency and scalability of quantum machine-learning algorithms for larger datasets requiring 100 to 1000 qubits (Perdomo-Ortiz et al. 2018) must be improved. Efficient data preparation and training models need to be designed (Usman et al. 2019).

■ It is necessary to speed the quantum-computation algorithms to meet the demand for high-performance computing. The significant factors that need to be addressed for this are improving qubit connectivity and lowering noise in the device (Perdomo-Ortiz et al. 2018).

■ Quantum computing is a significant step toward green computing, as quantum computers consume less energy than classical computers (Gill and Buyya 2018). Therefore, quantum computers are considered energy-efficient computers. Since quantum computing is still in its infancy, hybrid frameworks for tasks can be developed where high-energy tasks are performed on quantum computers and low-energy tasks are performed on the classical system on clouds (Toosi, Calheiros, and Buyya 2014). Implementing the hybrid computing model to solve business problems is still a challenging task.

■ The development of quantum internet enables distributed quantum computing and designing communication protocols, though efficient error detection and correction mechanism are still flourishing research areas (Cacciapuoti et al. 2020).

■ Quantum computing finds its primary application in cryptography. The cryptographic algorithms enable secure online communication. The number of critical algorithms is designed to protect data from attackers. Still, there is a need to develop future quantum systems that can prevent and predict security attacks (Bernstein and Lange 2017).

References

Agarwal, Preeti, and Mansaf Alam. 2020a. "A Lightweight Deep Learning Model for Human Activity Recognition on Edge Devices." *Procedia Computer Science*, 167: 2364–2373. https://doi.org/10.1016/j.procs.2020.03.289.

———. 2020b. "Investigating IoT Middleware Platforms for Smart Application Development." *Lecture Notes in Civil Engineering*, 58: 231–244. Springer. https://doi.org/10.1007/978-981-15-2545-2_21.

———. 2020c. "Open Service Platforms for IoT." In *Internet of Things (IoT): Concepts and Applications*: 43–59. Springer International Publishing. https://doi.org/10.1007/978-3-030-37468-6_3.

Bernstein, Daniel J., and Tanja Lange. 2017. "Post-Quantum Cryptography." *Nature*. Nature Publishing Group. https://doi.org/10.1038/nature23461.

Bernstein, Ethan, and Umesh Vazirani. 1997. "Quantum Complexity Theory." *SIAM Journal on Computing*, 26(5): 1411–1473. https://doi.org/10.1137/S0097539796300921.

Bhatia, Munish, and Sandeep K. Sood. 2020. "Quantum Computing-Inspired Network Optimization for IoT Applications." *IEEE Internet of Things Journal*, 7(6): 5590–5598. https://doi.org/10.1109/JIOT.2020.2979887.

Buhrman, Harry, and Hein Röhrig. 2003. "Distributed Quantum Computing." *Lecture Notes in Computer Science (Including Subseries Lecture Notes in Artificial Intelligence and Lecture Notes in Bioinformatics)*, 2747: 1–20. https://doi.org/10.1007/978-3-540-45138-9_1.

Cacciapuoti, Angela Sara, Marcello Caleffi, Francesco Tafuri, Francesco Saverio Cataliotti, Stefano Gherardini, and Giuseppe Bianchi. 2020. "Quantum Internet: Networking Challenges in Distributed Quantum Computing." *IEEE Network*, 34(1): 137–143. https://doi.org/10.1109/MNET.001.1900092.

Chaudhary, K., M. Alam, M. S. Al-Rakhami, and A. Gumaei. 2021. "Machine Learning Based Mathematical Modelling for Prediction of Social Media Consumer Behaviour Using Big Data Analytics." *Journal of Big Data*, 8. https://europepmc.org/article/ppr/ppr287687.

Chojecki, Przemek. n.d. "Quantum Computing for Business." Accessed March 16, 2021. https://towardsdatascience.com/quantum-computing-for-business-347b95d400f9.

Cloudmoyo. 2020. "Sources of Big Data: Where Does It Come from? | CloudMoyo." *Cloudmoyo.com*. 2020. www.cloudmoyo.com/blog/data-architecture/what-is-big data-and-where-it-comes-from/.

Devitt, Simon J., William J. Munro, and Kae Nemoto. 2013. "Quantum Error Correction for Beginners." *Reports on Progress in Physics*, 76(7): 076001. https://doi.org/10.1088/0034-4885/76/7/076001.

Farhi, Edward, Jeffrey Goldstone, and Sam Gutmann. 2014. "A Quantum Approximate Optimization Algorithm." *arXiv:1411.4028*, November. http://arxiv.org/abs/1411.4028.

Gay, Simon J. 2006. "Quantum Programming Languages: Survey and Bibliography." *Mathematical Structures in Computer Science*, 16: 581–600. https://doi.org/10.1017/S0960129506005378.

Gill, S. Singh, and Rajkumar Buyya. 2018. "A Taxonomy and Future Directions for Sustainable Cloud Computing: 360 Degree View." *ACM Computing Surveys*, 51(5). https://doi.org/10.1145/3241038.

Gill, S. Singh, A. Kumar, H. Singh, M. Singh, K. Kaur, M. Usman, and R. Buyya. n.d. "Quantum Computing: A Taxonomy, Systematic Review and Future Directions." *Ui.Adsabs.Harvard.Edu.* Accessed March 16, 2021. https://ui.adsabs.harvard.edu/abs/2020arXiv201015559S/abstract.

Grover, Lov K. 1996. "A Fast Quantum Mechanical Algorithm for Database Search." In *Proceedings of the Annual ACM Symposium on Theory of Computing*, Part F1294:212–19. New York: Association for Computing Machinery. https://doi.org/10.1145/237814.237866.

Gyongyosi, Laszlo, and Sandor Imre. 2019. "A Survey on Quantum Computing Technology." *Computer Science Review.* Elsevier Ireland Ltd. https://doi.org/10.1016/j.cosrev.2018.11.002.

Han, Kuk Hyun, and Jong Hwan Kim. 2002. "Quantum-Inspired Evolutionary Algorithm for a Class of Combinatorial Optimization." *IEEE Transactions on Evolutionary Computation*, 6(6): 580–593. https://doi.org/10.1109/TEVC.2002.804320.

Hey, T. 1999. "Quantum Computing: An Introduction." *Computing & Control Engineering Journal*, 10(3): 105–112. https://doi.org/10.1049/cce:19990303.

Jain, Saumya. 2015. "Quantum Computer Architectures: A Survey." In *2015 International Conference on Computing for Sustainable Global Development, INDIACom 2015*, 2165–2169. https://ieeexplore.ieee.org/abstract/document/7100621/.

Kumar, Kunal, Neeraj Anand Sharma, Ramendra Prasad, Aman Deo, Md Tanzim Khorshed, Mishal Prasad, Aaron Dutt, and A. B. M. Shawkat Ali. 2016. "A Survey on Quantum Computing with Main Focus on the Methods of Implementation and Commercialization Gaps." In *2015 2nd Asia-Pacific World Congress on Computer Science and Engineering, APWC on CSE 2015*. IEEEXplore. https://doi.org/10.1109/APWCCSE.2015.7476130.

Lloyd, Seth, Masoud Mohseni, and Patrick Rebentrost. 2014. "Quantum Principal Component Analysis." *Nature Physics*, 10(9): 631–633. https://doi.org/10.1038/NPHYS3029.

Mantra. n.d. "Business Applications of Quantum Computing—Mantra AI." Accessed March 16, 2021. www.mantra.ai/blogs/business-applications-of-quantum-computing/.

Mishra, Nimish, Manik Kapil, Hemant Rakesh, Amit Anand, Nilima Mishra, Aakash Warke, Soumya Sarkar, et al. 2021. "Quantum Machine Learning: A Review and Current Status." *Advances in Intelligent Systems and Computing*, 1175: 101–145. Springer Science and Business Media Deutschland GmbH. https://doi.org/10.1007/978-981-15-5619-7_8.

Nielsen, Michael A., Isaac Chuang, and Lov K. Grover. 2002. "Quantum Computation and Quantum Information." *American Journal of Physics*, 70(5): 558–559. https://doi.org/10.1119/1.1463744.

Paler, Alexandru, and Simon J. Devitt. 2015. "An Introduction into Fault-Tolerant Quantum Computing." In *Proceedings—Design Automation Conference*. Vol. 2015–July. Institute of Electrical and Electronics Engineers Inc. arXiv. https://doi.org/10.1145/2744769.2747911.

Perdomo-Ortiz, Alejandro, Marcello Benedetti, John Realpe-Gómez, and Rupak Biswas. 2018. "Opportunities and Challenges for Quantum-Assisted Machine Learning in near-Term Quantum Computers." In *Quantum Science and Technology*. Institute of Physics Publishing. arXiv. https://doi.org/10.1088/2058-9565/aab859.

"Quantum Logic Gate- Wikipedia." n.d. Accessed March 16, 2021. https://en.wikipedia.org/wiki/Quantum_logic_gate.

"Qubit—Wikipedia." n.d. Accessed March 16, 2021. https://en.wikipedia.org/wiki/Qubit.

Rebentrost, Patrick, Masoud Mohseni, and Seth Lloyd. 2014. "Quantum Support Vector Machine for Big Data Classification." *Physical Review Letters*, 113(3): 130503. https://doi.org/10.1103/PhysRevLett.113.130503.

Roetteler, Martin, and Krysta M. Svore. 2018. "Quantum Computing: Codebreaking and Beyond." *IEEE Security and Privacy*, 16(5): 22–36. https://doi.org/10.1109/MSP.2018.3761710.

Seekingalpha. 2020. "Splunk: Strong Prospects for the Foreseeable Future (NASDAQ:SPLK) | Seeking Alpha." *Seekingalpha.* https://seekingalpha.com/article/4350544-splunk-strong-prospects-for-foreseeable-future.

Shaikh, T.A., and R. Ali On. n.d. "Quantum Computing in Big Data Analytics: A Survey." In *IEEE International Conference on Computer and Information Technology (CIT).* IEEEXplore.

Shor, P.W. 2002. "Algorithms for Quantum Computation: Discrete Logarithms and Factoring." In *Proceedings 35th Annual Symposium on Foundations of Computer Science*, 124–134. Institute of Electrical and Electronics Engineers (IEEE). IEEEXplore. https://doi.org/10.1109/sfcs.1994.365700.

Sofge, Donald A. 2008. "A Survey of Quantum Programming Languages: History, Methods, and Tools." In *Proceedings—The 2nd International Conference on Quantum-, Nano- and Micro-Technologies, ICQNM 2008*, 66–71. IEEEXplore. https://doi.org/10.1109/ICQNM.2008.15.

Statista. n.d. "Quantum Computing Market Global Scenario Market Size." Accessed March 16, 2021. www.statista.com/statistics/936010/quantum-computing-future-market-outlook-forecast/.

Toosi, Adel Nadjaran, Rodrigo N. Calheiros, and Rajkumar Buyya. 2014. "Interconnected Cloud Computing Environments: Challenges, Taxonomy, and Survey." *ACM Computing Surveys*. New York: Association for Computing Machinery. https://doi.org/10.1145/2593512.

Usman, Muhammad, Yi Zheng Wong, Charles D. Hill, and Lloyd C.L. Hollenberg. 2019. "Atomic-Level Characterisation of Quantum Computer Arrays by Machine Learning." *ArXiv*. www.nature.com/articles/s41524-020-0282-0.

Vamanan, Ramesh, Abhishek Pandey, and V. Ramesh. 2015. "Quantum Computing for Big Data Analysis." *Indian Journal of Science*, 14(43): 98–104. www.researchgate.net/publication/274195911.

Yan, Fei, Abdullah M. Iliyasu, and Salvador E. Venegas-Andraca. 2016. "A Survey of Quantum Image Representations." *Quantum Information Processing*, 15(1): 1–35. Springer. https://doi.org/10.1007/s11128-015-1195-6.

Chapter 8

Evaluation of Green Degree of Reverse Logistic of Waste Electrical Appliances

Li Qin Hu, Amit Yadav, Hong Liu, and
Rumesh Ranjan

Contents

DOI: 10.1201/9781003175711-8

8.1 Introduction

This chapter refers to the existing literature on greenness evaluation, combined with the characteristics and connotations of reverse logistics and green logistics It comprises the following index system and briefly introduces each secondary index, which is shown in Table 8.1 (Spicer and Johnson 2004;

Table 8.1 Reverse Logistics Green Degree Evaluation Index System

Target layer	First-level indicator layer	Second-level indicator
Evaluation of green degree of reverse logistics	Green level X_1	Environmental goal achievement rate X_{11}
		Energy consumption rate X_{12}
		Investment rate of environmental protection X_{13}
	Green remanufacturing X_2	Waste disposal X_{21}
		Process design X_{22}
		Resource recycling X_{23}
	Green recycling X_3	Environmental awareness X_{31}
		Waste recycling rate X_{32}
		Waste treatment technology X_{33}
	Green storage X_4	Environmental protection technology X_{41}
		Storage environment X_{42}
		Space utilization X_{43}
	Green transportation X_5	Gas pollution X_{51}
		Solid and liquid pollution X_{52}
		Noise pollution X_{53}

Source: Logistics Management Association

Tian and Chen 2014; Shokouhyar and Aalirezaei 2017; Islam and Huda 2018; Goodship et al. 2019).

8.2 Related Works

The multilevel fuzzy-comprehensive evaluation method is a method combining Analytical Hierarchy Process (AHP) and fuzzy comprehensive evaluation. This method generally determines the weight of the index weight through the AHP first and then performs comprehensive analysis through the fuzzy evaluation. This method has the characteristic of combining the qualitative and quantitative, which can avoid the deficiency of a single method to a certain extent (Tian and Chen 2014).

8.2.1 AHP Is Used to Obtain the Weight of Each Indicator

8.2.1.1 Establish a Hierarchical Structure Model

The hierarchical structure model is given in Figure 8.1.

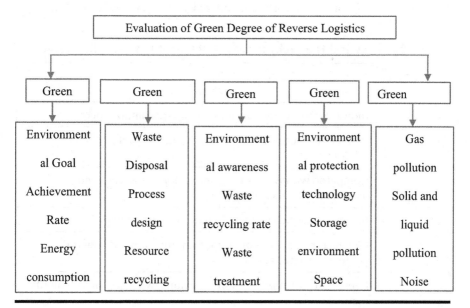

Figure 8.1   Hierarchical Structure Model.

8.2.1.2 Construct a Pair of Judgment Matrices

Starting from the second layer of the hierarchy model, for the factors of the same layer subordinate to each factor of the upper layer, the pairwise comparison matrix is constructed by using the pairwise comparison method and the 1–9 comparison scale until the lowest layer. AIJ (Architectural Institute of Japan) model is used to scale the general judgment matrix. Table 8.2 shows the specific scale of the judgment matrix in AHP (Yadav et al. 2015a, 2015b; Saaty and Vargas 2012).

8.2.1.3 Hierarchical Order and Consistency Check

The average random consistency index of the judgment matrices follow from the previous study (Saaty and Vargas 2012; Goodship et al. 2019).

8.3 Fuzzy-Comprehensive Evaluation of Reverse Logistic Green Degree

8.3.1 Determine the Set of Evaluation Indicators

This chapter uses a collection $X = \{X_1, X_2, ...X_n\}$ to represent the set of first-level indicators of evaluation objects and uses $X_i (i = 1,2,3 \ldots n)$ to represent a collection of secondary indicators where n is the number of second-level indicators where the

Table 8.2   Analytical Hierarchy Process 1–9 Quantity Description Table

Evaluation scale	Description
1	Indicates that the two factors are of equal importance
3	Two factors—one factor is slightly more important than the other factor
5	Compared with two factors, one factor is obviously more important than the other factor
7	Indicates that two factors are more important than the other
9	One factor is much more important than the other factor compared to two factors
2、4、6、8	Represents the median of the previous two adjacent judgment matrices
Reciprocal	If the comparison between factors i and j is aij, then the comparison between factors j and i is aji = 1 / aij

first-level indicators are located (Georgiadis and Athanasiou 2013; Islam and Huda 2018; Liu et al. 2014; Kalita et al. 2020). Based on the previous green evaluation system of reverse logistics operation mode, the first-level index set in this chapter is $X = \{X_1, X_2, \ldots\ldots X_n\}$. The set of secondary indicators is: X1 = $\{X_{11}, X_{12}, X_{13}\}$; X2 = $\{X_{21}, X_{22}, X_{23}\}$; X3 = $\{X_{31}, X_{32}, X_{33}\}$; X4 = $\{X_{41}, X_{42}, X_{43}\}$; X5 = $\{X_{51}, X_{52}, X_{53}\}$

X1 = green-level indicators

X11 = environmental-goal achievement rate (achievement rate of environmental goals = environmental goals completed at the end of the year/environmental goals set at the beginning of the year)

X12 = energy-consumption rate (The energy consumption rate mainly refers to the energy consumed per 10,000 Yuan of output value.)

X13 = Investment rate of environmental protection (Funds invested in environmental protection in the implementation of reverse logistics, that is, the environmental protection investment rate = one year of environmental protection investment/one year of the company's total investment.)

X2 = green remanufacturing indicators

X21 = waste disposal (that is to say, whether the treatment situation and treatment methods of waste water, waste gas and other pollutants are discharged in the remanufacturing process of waste household appliance parts by household appliance manufacturers meet the requirements of being green and pollution-free)

X22 = process design (in the remanufacturing of waste household appliances, whether the production technology and process of the enterprise have been improved to achieve the effect of green production)

X23 = resource recycling (refers to the recovery and utilization of valuable resources (parts/raw materials) in the implementation of reverse logistics by home-appliance companies. That is, resource recycling utilization rate = resources recycled/recycled/total resources recycled.)

X3 = green recycling index

X31 = waste recovery rate (That is, the recycling ratio of used home appliances in the consumption area, waste recovery rate = used home appliances recovered/total amount of home appliances theoretically scrapped in the consumption area.)

X32 = waste treatment technology (refers to the level of dismantling of waste household appliances that have no reuse value after recycling. Generally speaking, the more advanced the technology, the higher the degree of recycling.)

X33 = environmental awareness (refers to the environmental-protection awareness of consumers and home-appliance companies during the recycling process. Generally speaking, the stronger the environmental protection awareness, the more waste household electricity that enters the formal recycling channels.)

X4 = green warehousing indicators

X41 = environmental protection technology (Green and environmentally friendly warehousing technology can be stored separately according to the different chemical characteristics of the storage, and the whole parts, parts and raw materials can be stored separately to avoid mutual pollution.)

X42 = storage environment (Waste household appliances have the dual characteristics of high value and heavy pollution. These two characteristics determine the special storage environment of waste household appliances. Targeted establishment of green storage can ensure the value of waste household appliances while avoiding secondary pollution to the environment or human body.)

X43 = space utilization (warehouse space utilization = used storage space/total storage space)

X5 = green transportation index

X51 = gas pollution (refers to various types of atmospheric pollutants emitted during transportation such as carbon monoxide (CO), hydrocarbons (HC), nitrogen oxides (NOX), sulphur dioxide (SO2), inhalable particulate matter (PM10) and fine particulate matter (PM5.2). When the emitted air pollutants reach a certain concentration, they will endanger human health.)

X52 = solid and liquid pollution (Solid and liquid pollutants are also produced in the process of reverse recycling of used household appliances, mainly referring to the aging of internal components due to the severe damage of used household appliances, which produces unpleasant and harmful solid and liquid substances to pollute the environment.)

X53 = noise pollution (The noise pollution generated during transportation is mainly: the noise generated by the engine and the refrigerator; the noise generated by the friction between the wheel and the ground; the noise such as the driver whistle.)

8.3.2 Determine the Level of Evaluation

In this chapter, there are 5 evaluation levels for each indicator set $Q = \{Q_1, Q_2, Q_3, Q_4, Q_5\}$ to describe the level for each indicator and whether the degree corresponding to each indicator is very poor, poor, fair, good, or excellent as shown in Appendix A. For each indicator, a fuzzy subset of its review grade must be constructed.

8.3.3 Establish Fuzzy Relation Matrix R

This chapter uses a questionnaire with each index as the survey content to conduct a survey and obtains the membership of each index by recovering the data. Suppose there are M experts participating in the assessment of green reverse logistics and their scores correspond to the above 5 levels: very poor, poor, average, good, and excellent. Refer to Table 8.2 for details on the green degree evaluation questionnaire of reverse logistics (Suyabatmaz et al. 2014; Tian and Chen 2014; Xiong and Li 2010).

Based on this result, the fuzzy relation matrix R can be established as follows:

$$
R = \begin{bmatrix}
r_{i11} & r_{i12} & \cdots & r_{i1k} \\
r_{i21} & r_{i22} & \cdots & r_{i2k} \\
\cdots & \cdots & \cdots & \cdots \\
r_{ij1} & r_{ij2} & \cdots & r_{ijk}
\end{bmatrix}
\tag{2.4}
$$

In the matrix R, i represents the number of first-level indicators of the evaluation object, i = 1,2,3,4,5; j represents the number of second-level indicators corresponding to the first-level indicators; k represents the number of comment levels of each indicator = 1,2,3,4,5.

8.3.4 Determine the Weight of Evaluation Indicators

This chapter uses a collection $w = \{w_1, w_2, w_3 \ldots w_n\}$ to represent the set of weights of the first-level indicators of the evaluation object and uses $w_i \, (i = 1,2,3 \ldots n)$ to represent the set of weights of the secondary indicators, where n is the number of secondary indicators where the primary indicators are located (Yadav et al. 2015a; Saaty and Vargas 2012).

8.3.5 Synthetic Fuzzy-Comprehensive Evaluation Result Vector

Synthesize w and R of each evaluated object to obtain a fuzzy-comprehensive evaluation result vector B of various objects (Xiong and Li 2010).

a. Index Comprehensive Evaluation Vector

For the fuzzy-comprehensive evaluation vector of first-level indicators, the calculation model should be followed. For the fuzzy-comprehensive evaluation vector of the overall goal, the calculation model is used for calculation (Xiong and Li 2010; Ayvaz et al. 2015).

b. Greenness Evaluation Score of Each Indicator

The first-level indicator performance and performance evaluation score of the overall target have been calculated. Through the previous fuzzy-comprehensive evaluation results and scores, the green degree of reverse logistics under a certain operation mode can be comprehensively evaluated to determine whether the mode meets the development needs of green logistics (Xiong and Li 2010). Various studies have been conducted in decision-making; however, waste of electrical appliances was missing, which is one of the major causes of environmental pollution. This study will help in decision-making and managing waste of electrical appliances and to create a sustainable environment (Sharif et al. 2018; Zarbakhshnia et al. 2019).

8.4 Greenness Evaluation

8.4.1 Determination of Weight by AHP

The home-appliance manufacturer selected in this chapter is a home-appliance manufacturer in Sichuan Province. With the help of multiple teachers, 30 experts (including 15 reverse-logistics experts and 15 green-assessment experts) were interviewed and selected. The relevant indicators are scored with weights (Islam and Huda 2018).

8.4.1.1 Determination of the Weight of First-Level Indicators

There are 5 first-level indicators under the target layer, and the judgment matrix is constructed according to their relatively important relationship as shown in Table 8.3.

According to the calculation: $\lambda \approx 5.150$, $C.I. = 0.037$, $R.I. = 1.12$, $C.R. = 0.033 < 0.1$. Meet the consistency check, single layer weight vector, w= {0.4962, 0.2301,0.1585,0.0792,0.0360}.

Table 8.3 Judgment Matrix of the First-Level Indicator Layer to the Target Layer

	Green level	Green remanufacturing	Green recycling	Green storage	Green transportation
Green level	1	3	4	6	9
Green remanufacturing	1/3	1	2	3	7
Green recycling	1/4	1/2	1	4	5
Green storage	1/6	1/3	1/3	1	3
Green transportation	1/9	1/7	1/5	1/3	1

8.4.1.2 Determination of the Weight of the Second-Level Indicators

There are three secondary indicators under the green level, and the judgment matrix is constructed according to their relatively important relationship as shown in Table 8.4.

According to the calculation: $\lambda \approx 3.066$, $C.I. = 0.033$, $R.I. = 0.52$, $C.R. = 0.063 < 0.1$. Meet the consistency check, single-layer weight vector (w), w = {0.7235, 0.1932, 0.0833}. There are three secondary indicators under green remanufacturing, and the judgment matrix is constructed according to their relatively important relationship as shown in Table 8.5.

According to the calculation: $\lambda \approx 3.054$, $C.I. = 0.027$, $R.I. = 0.52$, $C.R. = 0.052 < 0.1$, Meet the consistency check, single-layer weight vector, w = {0.5247, 0.3338, 0.1416}. There are three secondary indicators under green recycling, and the judgment matrix is constructed according to their relatively important relationship as shown in Table 8.6.

According to the calculation: $\lambda \approx 3.003$, $C.I. = 0.002$, $R.I. = 0.52$, $C.R. = 0.004 < 0.1$.

Meet the consistency check, single-layer weight vector $w = \{0.5813, 0.3092, 0.1096\}$.

Table 8.4   Judgment Matrix of Green-Level Secondary Indicators

	Environmental goal-achievement rate	Energy-consumption rate	Investment rate of environmental protection
Environmental goal-achievement rate	1	5	7
Energy-consumption rate	1/5	1	3
Investment rate of environmental protection	1/7	1/3	1

Table 8.5   Judgment Matrix for the Secondary Indicators of Green Remanufacturing

	Waste disposal	Process design	Resource recycling
Waste disposal	1	2	3
Process design	1/2	1	3
Resource recycling	1/3	1/3	1

Table 8.6 Judgment Matrix of Green Recycling Secondary Indicators

	Environmental awareness	Waste recycling rate	Waste-treatment technology
Environmental awareness	1	2	5
Waste recycling rate	1/2	1	3
Waste-treatment technology	1/5	1/3	1

Table 8.7 Judgment Matrix of Green Storage Secondary Indicators

	Environmental-protection technology	Storage environment	Space utilization
Environmental-protection technology	1	2	5
Storage environment	1/2	1	3
Space utilization	1/5	1/3	1

Table 8.8 Judgment Matrix of Green Transportation Secondary Indicators

	Gas pollution	Solid and liquid pollution	Noise pollution
Gas pollution	1	7	7
Solid and liquid pollution	1/7	1	3
Noise pollution	1/7	1/3	1

There are three secondary indicators under green storage, and the judgment matrix is constructed according to their relatively important relationship as shown in Table 8.7. According to the calculation: $\lambda \approx 3.025$, $C.I. = 0.012$, $R.I. = 0.52$, $C.R. = 0.024 < 0.1$. Meet the consistency check, single-layer weight vector, w={0.5679, 0.3340, 0.0982}. There are three secondary indicators under green transportation, and the judgment matrix is constructed according to the relatively important relationship as shown in Table 8.8.

According to the calculation: $\lambda \approx 3.054$, $C.I. = 0.027$, $R.I. = 0.52$, $C.R. = 0.052 < 0.1$. Meet the consistency check, single-layer weight vector, w={0.5247, 0.3338, 0.1416}. In summary, the weights of the primary and secondary indicators are shown in Table 8.9.

Table 8.9 Weights of Green Evaluation Indicators of Reverse Logistics Operation Mode

Target layer	First-level indicator layer	Index weight	Second- level indicator	Second-level index weight
Evaluation of green degree of reverse logistics	Green level X_1	0.4962	Environmental goal-achievement rate X_{11}	0.7235
			Energy-consumption rate X_{12}	0.1932
			Investment rate of environmental protection X_{13}	0.0833
	Green remanufacturing X_2	0.2301	Waste Disposal X_{21}	0.5247
			Process design X_{22}	0.3338
			Resource recycling X_{23}	0.1416
	Green recycling X_3	0.1585	Environmental awareness X_{31}	0.5813
			Waste-recycling rate X_{32}	0.3092
			Waste-treatment technology X_{33}	0.1096
	Green storage X_4	0.0792	Environmental-protection technology X_{41}	0.5679
			Storage environment X_{42}	0.3340
			Space utilization X_{43}	0.0982
	Green transportation X_5	0.0360	Gas pollution X_{51}	0.5247
			Solid and liquid pollution X_{52}	0.3338
			Noise pollution X_{53}	0.1416

8.4.2 Analysis of Fuzzy-Comprehensive Evaluation Method

8.4.2.1 Data Collection

The review grade of this chapter is designed in Likert5 scale format. The evaluation criteria of the indicator are divided into 5 grades: excellent, good, fair, poor and very poor. In order to facilitate the calculation, this chapter quantifies the comments and assigns the 5 levels 100, 80, 60, 40 and 20 in sequence (Islam and Huda 2018; Liu et al. 2014). The standard for comprehensive evaluation and ranking is shown in Table 8.10.

Data statistics are collected for the valid questionnaires recovered. The questionnaire statistics and membership results are shown in Table 8.11 and 8.12.

Table 8.10 Evaluation and Rating Standards

Evaluation value	Grade
$X_i > 80$	Excellent
$60 < X_i \leq 80$	Good
$40 < X_i \leq 60$	General
$20 < X_i \leq 40$	Poor
$X_i \leq 20$	Very Poor

Table 8.11 Questionnaire Statistics

Evaluation index	Excellent	Good	General	Poor	Very Poor
Environmental goal-achievement rate X_{11}	15	10	2	2	1
Energy-consumption rate X_{12}	10	10	8	1	1
Investment rate of environmental protection X_{13}	12	7	5	5	1
Waste disposal X_{21}	16	8	5	1	0
Process design X_{22}	14	8	7	0	1
Resource recycling X_{23}	10	9	6	2	3
Environmental awareness X_{31}	10	13	6	1	0
Waste-recycling rate X_{32}	12	9	3	4	2

Evaluation index	Excellent	Good	General	Poor	Very Poor
Waste-treatment technology X_{33}	10	9	6	5	0
Environmental-protection technology X_{41}	14	6	3	3	4
Storage environment X_{42}	9	12	6	1	2
Space utilization X_{43}	10	12	3	2	3
Gas pollution X_{51}	15	7	2	3	3
Solid and liquid pollution X_{52}	15	9	4	0	2
Noise pollution X_{53}	10	7	10	0	3

Table 8.12 Results Of the Membership Of the Questionnaire

Evaluation index	Excellent	Good	General	Poor	Very Poor
Environmental goal-achievement Rate X_{11}	0.5000	0.3333	0.0667	0.0667	0.0333
Energy-consumption rate X_{12}	0.3333	0.3333	0.2667	0.0333	0.0333
Investment rate of environmental protection X_{13}	0.4000	0.2333	0.1667	0.1667	0.0333
Waste disposal X_{21}	0.5333	0.2667	0.1667	0.0333	0.0000
Process design X_{22}	0.4667	0.2667	0.2333	0.0000	0.0333
Resource recycling X_{23}	0.3333	0.3000	0.2000	0.0667	0.1000
Environmental awareness X_{31}	0.3333	0.4333	0.2000	0.0333	0.0000
Waste-recycling rate X_{32}	0.4000	0.3000	0.1000	0.1333	0.0667
Waste-treatment technology X_{33}	0.3333	0.3000	0.2000	0.1667	0.0000
Environmental-protection technology X_{41}	0.4667	0.2000	0.1000	0.1000	0.1333
Storage environment X_{42}	0.3000	0.4000	0.2000	0.0333	0.0667
Space utilization X_{43}	0.3333	0.4000	0.1000	0.0667	0.1000
Gas pollution X_{51}	0.5000	0.2333	0.0667	0.1000	0.1000
Solid and liquid pollution X_{52}	0.5000	0.3000	0.1333	0.0000	0.0667
Noise pollution X_{53}	0.3333	0.2333	0.3333	0.0000	0.1000

8.4.2.2 Establish Fuzzy-Relation Matrix

$$R_1 = \begin{Bmatrix} 0.5000 & 0.3333 & 0.0667 & 0.0667 & 0.0333 \\ 0.3333 & 0.3333 & 0.2667 & 0.0333 & 0.0333 \\ 0.4000 & 0.2333 & 0.1667 & 0.1667 & 0.0333 \end{Bmatrix}$$

$$R_2 = \begin{Bmatrix} 0.5333 & 0.2667 & 0.1667 & 0.0333 & 0.0000 \\ 0.4667 & 0.2667 & 0.2333 & 0.0000 & 0.0333 \\ 0.3333 & 0.3000 & 0.2000 & 0.0667 & 0.1000 \end{Bmatrix}$$

$$R_3 = \begin{Bmatrix} 0.3333 & 0.4333 & 0.2000 & 0.0333 & 0.0000 \\ 0.4000 & 0.3000 & 0.1000 & 0.1333 & 0.0667 \\ 0.3333 & 0.3000 & 0.2000 & 0.1667 & 0.0000 \end{Bmatrix}$$

$$R_4 = \begin{Bmatrix} 0.4667 & 0.2000 & 0.1000 & 0.1000 & 0.1333 \\ 0.3000 & 0.4000 & 0.2000 & 0.0333 & 0.0667 \\ 0.3333 & 0.4000 & 0.1000 & 0.0667 & 0.1000 \end{Bmatrix}$$

$$R_5 = \begin{Bmatrix} 0.5000 & 0.2333 & 0.0667 & 0.1000 & 0.1000 \\ 0.5000 & 0.3000 & 0.1333 & 0.0000 & 0.0667 \\ 0.3333 & 0.2333 & 0.3333 & 0.0000 & 0.1000 \end{Bmatrix}$$

8.4.3.3 Fuzzy-Comprehensive Evaluation

$$B_1 = w_1 \bullet R_1 \begin{Bmatrix} 0.7235 \\ 0.1932 \\ 0.0833 \end{Bmatrix}^{-1} \bullet \begin{Bmatrix} 0.5000 & 0.3333 & 0.0667 & 0.0667 & 0.0333 \\ 0.3333 & 0.3333 & 0.2667 & 0.0333 & 0.0333 \\ 0.4000 & 0.2333 & 0.1667 & 0.1667 & 0.0333 \end{Bmatrix}$$

$$= \{0.4600 \bullet 0.3250 \bullet 0.0686 \bullet 0.1404 \bullet 0.0333\}$$

$$B_2 = w_2 \bullet R_2 = \begin{Bmatrix} 0.5247 \\ 0.3338 \\ 0.1416 \end{Bmatrix}^{-1} \bullet \begin{Bmatrix} 0.5333 & 0.2667 & 0.1667 & 0.0333 & 0.0000 \\ 0.4667 & 0.2667 & 0.2333 & 0.0000 & 0.0333 \\ 0.3333 & 0.3000 & 0.2000 & 0.0667 & 0.1000 \end{Bmatrix}$$

$$= \{0.4828 \bullet 0.2714 \bullet 0.1937 \bullet 0.0269 \bullet 0.0253\}$$

$$B_3 = w_3 \bullet R_3 = \begin{Bmatrix} 0.5813 \\ 0.3092 \\ 0.1096 \end{Bmatrix}^{-1} \bullet \begin{Bmatrix} 0.3333 & 0.4333 & 0.2000 & 0.0333 & 0.0000 \\ 0.4000 & 0.3000 & 0.1000 & 0.1333 & 0.0667 \\ 0.3333 & 0.3000 & 0.2000 & 0.1667 & 0.0000 \end{Bmatrix}$$

$$B_4 = w_4 \bullet R_4 = \begin{Bmatrix} 0.5679 \\ 0.3340 \\ 0.0982 \end{Bmatrix}^{-1} \bullet \begin{Bmatrix} 0.4667 & 0.2000 & 0.1000 & 0.1000 & 0.1333 \\ 0.3000 & 0.4000 & 0.2000 & 0.0333 & 0.0667 \\ 0.3333 & 0.4000 & 0.1000 & 0.0667 & 0.1000 \end{Bmatrix}$$

$$= \{0.3980 \bullet 0.2865 \bullet 0.1334 \bullet 0.0745 \bullet 0.1078\}$$

$$B_5 = w_5 \bullet R_5 = \begin{Bmatrix} 0.5247 \\ 0.3338 \\ 0.1416 \end{Bmatrix}^{-1} \bullet \begin{Bmatrix} 0.5000 & 0.2333 & 0.0667 & 0.1000 & 0.1000 \\ 0.5000 & 0.3000 & 0.1333 & 0.0000 & 0.0667 \\ 0.3333 & 0.2333 & 0.3333 & 0.0000 & 0.1000 \end{Bmatrix}$$

$$= \{0.4764 \bullet 0.2556 \bullet 0.1267 \bullet 0.0525 \bullet 0.0889\}$$

Overall evaluation vector of greenness:

$$B_0 = w_0 \bullet R_0 \begin{Bmatrix} 0.4962 \\ 0.2301 \\ 0.1585 \\ 0.0792 \\ 0.0360 \end{Bmatrix}^{-1} \bullet \begin{Bmatrix} 0.4600 & 0.3250 & 0.0686 & 0.1404 & 0.0333 \\ 0.4828 & 0.2714 & 0.1937 & 0.0269 & 0.0253 \\ 0.3540 & 0.3780 & 0.1691 & 0.0788 & 0.0206 \\ 0.3980 & 0.2865 & 0.1334 & 0.0745 & 0.1078 \\ 0.4764 & 0.2556 & 0.1267 & 0.0525 & 0.0889 \end{Bmatrix}$$

$$= \{0.4441 \bullet 0.3155 \bullet 0.1203 \bullet 0.0961 \bullet 0.0373\}$$

The evaluation results of the greenness of each first-level indicator layer are as follows:

$$V_1 = B_1 \bullet Q^T = 82.4, V_2 = B_2 \bullet Q^T = 83.2, V_3 = B_3 \bullet Q^T = 79.3, V_4 = B_4 \bullet Q^T$$
$$= 75.9, V_5 = B_5 \bullet Q^T = 79.5, V_0 = B_0 \bullet Q^T = 81.5$$

Overall final score of greenness is calculated in the same way; the greenness evaluation results of each secondary index can also be obtained. Due to the limited space, this chapter will not calculate the final score of the secondary index one by one. The evaluation results of each primary index and the total target are shown in Table 8.13.

It can be drawn Table 8.13 that the comprehensive score of the reverse logistics of the example enterprise is 81.5, the corresponding grade is "excellent", and its first-level indicator green level and green remanufacturing evaluation result are "excellent"; Green transportation is "good". Through calculation examples, if home-appliance manufacturers want to improve the greenness of reverse logistics, they must strengthen the environmental awareness and environmental protection technologies in the three aspects of recycling, storage and transportation.

Table 8.13 Evaluation Results of Various First-Level Indicators and General Targets

Target layer	Green score	Green degree	First-level indicator layer	Greenness-evaluation results	Green degree
Reverse-logistics green degree	81.5	Excellent	Green level X1	82.4	Excellent
			Green remanufacturing X2	83.2	Excellent
			Green recycling X3	79.3	Good
			Green storage X4	75.9	Good
			Green transportation X5	79.5	Good

8.5 Conclusion

This chapter builds a green evaluation index system for reverse logistics of used home appliances. It is best to combine the data of case companies to evaluate the greenness of the reverse logistics of used home appliances. It is concluded that the green level, green remanufacturing and green recycling of the current home appliances in China reverse logistics has a greater impact on the greenness. Therefore, it is recommended that enterprises implement environmental protection awareness and environmental protection technologies in the areas of recycling, warehousing and transportation in the process of implementing reverse logistics of waste household appliances so that the development of reverse logistics is more in line with green logistics.

References

Ayvaz, B., B. Bolat, and N. Aydın. "Stochastic reverse logistics network design for waste of electrical and electronic equipment." *Resources, Conservation and Recycling* 104 (2015): 391–404.

Georgiadis, P., and E. Athanasiou. "Flexible long-term capacity planning in closed-loop supply chains with remanufacturing." *European Journal of Operational Research* 225, no. 1 (2013): 44–58.

Goodship, Vannessa, Ab Stevels, and Jaco Huisman, eds. *Waste Electrical and Electronic Equipment (WEEE) Handbook*. Sawston, Cambridge: Woodhead Publishing, 2019.

Islam, Md Tasbirul, and Nazmul Huda. "Reverse logistics and closed-loop supply chain of Waste Electrical and Electronic Equipment (WEEE)/E-waste: A comprehensive literature review." *Resources, Conservation and Recycling* 137 (2018): 48–75.

Kalita, H., K. Kumar, and J. P. Davim. "Classification of factors associated with a closed-loop supply chain system, their modelling methods and strategies." In *Supply Chain Intelligence* (pp. 19–35). Cham: Springer, 2020.

Liu, Yang, Yun Feng Zhang, and Yu Xin Jin. "Reverse logistics network design of waste electrical appliances." In *Applied Mechanics and Materials*, vol. 513, pp. 474–477. Stafa-Zurich, Switzerland: Trans Tech Publications Ltd, 2014.

Saaty, Thomas L., and Luis G. Vargas. *Models, Methods, Concepts & Applications of the Analytic Hierarchy Process*. Vol. 175. Berlin, Germany: Springer Science & Business Media, 2012.

Sharif, N. S., M. S. Pishvaee, A. Aliahmadi, and A. Jabbarzadeh. "A bi-level programming approach to joint network design and pricing problem in the municipal solid waste management system: A case study." *Resources, Conservation and Recycling* 131 (2018): 17–40.

Shokouhyar, Sajjad, and Armin Aalirezaei. "Designing a sustainable recovery network for waste from electrical and electronic equipment using a genetic algorithm." *International Journal of Environment and Sustainable Development* 16, no. 1 (2017): 60–79.

Spicer, A. J., and M. R. Johnson. "Third-party demanufacturing as a solution for extended producer responsibility." *Journal of Cleaner Production* 12, no. 1 (2004): 37–45.

Suyabatmaz, Ali Çetin, F. Tevhide Altekin, and Güvenç Şahin. "Hybrid simulation-analytical modeling approaches for the reverse logistics network design of a third-party logistics provider." *Computers & Industrial Engineering* 70 (2014): 74–89.

Tian, Ting, and Ya Ping Chen. "The decision-making model of the Electrical appliances enterprise Reverse logistics with Government monitoring." In *Applied Mechanics and Materials*, vol. 448, pp. 4465–4470. Stafa-Zurich, Switzerland: Trans Tech Publications Ltd, 2014.

Xiong, Guojing, and Xian Li. "Empirical studies on the fuzzy comprehensive evaluation to the Performance of reverse logistics system based on the fuzzy AHP model." In International Conference of Logistics Engineering and Management (*ICLEM) 2010*, pp. 3444–3450. Chengdu, China: Logistics for Sustained Economic Development: Infrastructure, Information, Integration, 2010.

Yadav, Amit, Maira Anis, Mohsin Ali, and Sadhana Tuladhar. "Analytical hierarchy process (ahp) for analysis: Selection of passenger airlines for gulf country." *International Journal of Scientific and Engineering Research* (2015a): 379–383.

Yadav, Amit, Gokul Bhandari, Daji Ergu, Mohsin Ali, and Maira Anis. "Supplier selection by AHP in KMC pharmaceutical: Use of GMIBM method for inconsistency adjustment." *Journal of Management Research* 7, no. 5 (2015b): 19–46.

Zarbakhshnia, N., H. Soleimani, M. Goh, and S. S. Razavi. "A novel multi-objective model for green forward and reverse logistics network design." *Journal of Cleaner Production* 208 (2019): 1304–1316.

Chapter 9

Nonparametric Approach of Comparing Company Performance: A Grey Relational Analysis

Tihana Škrinjarić

Contents

9.1 Introduction

Measurement of business performance is not a new topic in the literature and business practices. However, the concept of performance measurement, definitions, methods, and other relevant issues are still under debate (see Neely et al., 1995, 2001; Choong, 2013). Nevertheless, it is a crucial part of the company management when making decisions about current and future plans, as well as decisions on how to improve the results (Narkunienė and Ulbinaitė, 2018). To obtain better results

DOI: 10.1201/9781003175711-9

of an issue, it needs to be able to be measured. That is why a part of the literature focuses on the measures that are mostly concentrated on the financial ratios of a company (e.g. Prieto and Revila, 2006; Fernandes et al., 2006; Wier et al., 2007; Chen et al., 2009; Cardinaels and van Veen-Dirks, 2010; etc.). Although data from financial statements are not the only thing important in the whole process of the performance measurement, they are widely accepted in evaluation methods. If one assumes that no data manipulation was made within the financial statements, objective information could be extracted and compared within an industry. The information can be used either to compare the company with its peers from the company's management point of view or the side from potential investors on stock markets (Škrinjarić and Šego, 2021). The growing dynamics in business and especially in financial markets is forcing managers and investors to continuously evaluate business performance (Škrinjarić, 2021).

If we focus on the quantitative aspect of the business-performance evaluation, there exist many approaches that have been developed over the decades. These range from econometric models and methods, over a wide range of operational research ones, to other ones that combine either existing approaches or machine-learning ones. The complexity of the performance evaluation of a business has been recognized for a long time now, as Venkatraman and Ramanujam (1986) have already observed. Due to greater data availability today, the issue of big data emerges. Although big data is useful when making important decisions within business conduction (see Matthias et al., 2017 or Li et al., 2016), much research has indicated the complexities of using big data within the analysis of the financial ratios. Some of them are Beaver (2010); Myšková and Hájek (2017); and Laitinen (2018). These issues do not solely include problems referring to computational issues. Parker (2000) stated that business-performance measurement should address if the business can cover the needs of the customer and reveal potential issues with the activities and that decisions should not be made based on emotions or assumptions. The author emphasizes that decisions should be made on real data. Big data problems in general can be observed in Samiya et al. (2017, 2019), Malhotra et al. (2015, 2017), Khan et al. (2015, 2018a, 2018b, 2017a, 2017b), Alam and Shakil (2016), Shakil and Alam (2014, 2018), Alam et al. (2013a, 2013b, 2013c), Shakil et al. (2015), Chaudhary et al. (2021), Alam (2012), and Kaur and Alam (2013).

However, dealing with real data imposes the big data problem. The manager or the investor has to make fast and timely decisions, based on much available information. That is why the purpose of this chapter is to examine how to utilize specific quantitative tools in the assessment part of the business performance. The most quantifiable approach today is to observe the financial ratios from the financial statements. The sheer volume of literature focusing on these ratios is huge. Despite this, there are still some literature gaps. First of all, there exist problems in utilizing variables in the analysis that are not grounded in the financial theory or the business practice (Škrinjarić and Šego, 2021). Next, the comparability issue arises in the research as well. This refers to comparing different types of industries, which are usually not comparable at all, just to show how a quantitative model or method works. Sometimes, there is not a connection between the "quant" and the decision-maker who does not possess quantitative knowledge, to combine the best of both aspects. That is why this chapter will deal not only with big data but also with comparisons between the industries that are comparable from the economic, i.e. financial, aspect. Furthermore, the methodological approach used in this chapter is a relatively newer one. It refers to the grey relational analysis (GRA), part of the grey systems theory (GST), which has been developing since the 1980s. GST could either be used by itself or in combination with existing approaches that deal with big data. The development and history of GST is given in Liu et al. (2016) and Liu and Lin (2010, 2006). Here, we utilize the GRA methodology, as it is used to rank alternatives based on specified criteria.

The motivation for this chapter is found in the lack of research that combines the big data and methodological aspects of analysis from one side and theoretical grounding in finance on the other side. Some previous research is focused on the methodological standpoint. Although this is useful, the decision-maker cannot understand the methodology fully if he is not a quantitative analyst. Other research has focused on the economic and financial interpretations but without utilizing the methodology to the fullest. Thus, the motivation here is to combine the best from both aspects. Namely, the purpose of the chapter is to use big data, in terms of including the available information on data from financial statements for S&P 500 companies, to assess their business performance. Thus, the GRA methodology can be applied so that a robust ranking system can be made based on many different criteria Of course, we will take into consideration the company comparability by differentiating their type of industry or sector. The contribution of this research is as follows: this research gives an overview of several steps within the GRA methodology that need to be taken so that a robust ranking system can be obtained. In that way, the decision-maker without much quantitative knowledge can obtain similar results on a day-to-day basis. Furthermore, we incorporate the result from finance theory into the construction of the ranking system so that the decision-making is based on a rational basis. This is seen from the criteria definition; as the financial ratios are the criteria used to compare the companies, the rationale on which ratio should be the highest or smallest possible is determined based on financial theory. Finally, the majority of previous work does not observe the ratio increase or decrease amounts needed to improve the efficiency of a business. Here, we introduce such analysis as well. Although the DEA approaches of modeling incorporate such analysis, the GRA approach usually does not. Thus, the company can obtain insights into its ranking compared to others, but what is needed is input reduction and output increase in order to increase the business efficiency.

The GRA methodology can handle many data at once, but as it is still not so much known today (Škrinjarić, 2019, 2020). One other purpose of this chapter is to popularize this approach in the decision-making process. That is why the rest of this chapter is structured as follows: the second section deals with a related literature review, which will focus on research closely linked to this one. The third section describes the methodology used in the study and how the manager or the potential investor could obtain useful insights. The fourth section is the empirical one, in which the empirical analysis is done, and the fifth, final section concludes the chapter with implications and recommendations.

9.2 Related Literature Review

Since we are focusing on the financial ratios as the main variables in the analysis and the GRA methodology, the majority of this section gives an overview of the literature that is closest to this research. There are several conclusions based on the literature overview. First, a lot of papers exist that incorporate some typical variables that contrast one company with another, such as the book to market ratio (BMR), popular for a long time now (see DeBondt and Thaler, 1987; Keim, 1988; or Fama and French, 1992, 1993; Asness et al., 2015 for a newer analysis); dividend yields (since Litzenberger and Ramaswamy, 1979; or Brennan, 1970; to newer research in Leary and Michaely, 2011); Basu (1977, 1983); the price to earnings ratio (P/E) (Modigliani and Miller, 1958); and the total debt ratio. Earnings per share (EPS) is also popular due to Beaver (1989) and McDonald (1999). The mentioned papers are within other methodological approaches that show that the mentioned ratios differentiate companies and the values of their stocks based on the value of a ratio. The analysis was usually made via regression, panel regression, and similar approaches. Second, it is not a surprise that a great part of the empirical research focuses on the more developed markets due to the liquidity of such markets and more publicly available data about the companies listed on the stock markets. Big data is, thus, more relatable to such markets and businesses in more-developed countries, as the problems of other smaller markets and developing countries today are still a thing. Finally, the research employing the GRA and other GST approaches has slowly grown in the last decade. As the rest of the section will focus on financial ratios and the GRA methodology, here we briefly mention the rest of the research employing GRA in the construction of a ranking system within economics and finance. Bankruptcy prediction is often observed in the literature, as this is always a relevant issue, especially during the financial crisis (Delcea et al., 2013; Delcea et al., 2012; Lin et al., 2009); bank performance in general (Wu et al., 2010; Doğan, 2013; Pashaki et al., 2018); and economic applications in general (Yildirim et al., 2015; Pan and Leu, 2016), Camelia (2015a, 2015b) provide a bibliometric analysis.

When talking about business performance, one cannot mention the great bulk of literature that deals with financial ratios in general. The research deals with sometimes ordinary regression or probit/logit approaches due to failure prediction; earlier research includes McDonald and Morris (1984); Beaver (1966); Altman (1968, 2005); Ohlson (1980); and Bhargava et al. (1998), and newer approaches are found in Achim et al. (2016); du Jardin and Séverin (2011); Campbell et al. (2011); Altman et al. (2017); and Morris (2018). Authors try to describe the return series of stock returns by using financial ratios or try to predict business failure based on previous success and failure characteristics. Other econometric approaches include some form of an asset pricing model in a panel regression or vector autoregression (VAR), such as Lau et al. (2002); Penman et al. (2007); Deaves et al. (2008); or Gregoriou et al. (2015). Furthermore, the majority of these papers focus on the stock-return prediction based on financial ratios "health" and mentioned probability for business failure and do not focus so much on the business performance from the management point of view. This literature is more focused on the investor's point of view, when making decisions about portfolio (re)structuring or the point of view of a bank (granting a loan or not). It is not said that such analysis is not useful for decision-making within a business; it provides useful information, but not some specific details when compared to the studies focusing on shortfalls or surpluses of some aspects of the business itself. Such approaches are mentioned in the next passage.

However, we are interested in the performance measurement, in terms of constructing a ranking system. Thus, a greater focus will be on such papers. Some of the prominent approaches are data envelopment analysis (DEA) and multiple-criteria decision-making (MCDM) methodologies. These approaches enable the decision-maker to obtain a ranking system of observed companies and can provide information on the sources of the inefficiencies of a company. The GRA approach is somewhat relatable to the two aforementioned ones, but it has been getting more attention only in the last decade (details on the methodology are provided in the next section). Earlier work includes Powers and McMullen (2002), where 185 companies were included as well as several market-performance measures (such as the CAPM beta) within a DEA approach, and Edirisinghe and Zhang (2007), where 230 companies were evaluated via a generalized DEA approach but this time with financial ratios included. These papers focused more on the investor's point of view in terms of portfolio (re)structuring analysis over time. Other examples include Škrinjarić (2014)—where a dynamic DEA approach was made with investment guidance given over time—and Zamani et al. (2014), where a superefficiency DEA approach was utilized. Some of the research solely uses stock-market variables in the analysis, which is beneficial for speculators that aim to exploit market inefficiencies. Others include the financial ratios in the analysis as well, as there exist investors who observe long-term investment horizons. Combinations of ranking approaches are given in Huang et al. (2015) where a two-level DEA and GRA are used, Rosini and Gunawan (2018) where technique for ordered preference by similarity to ideal solution (TOPSIS) and DEA are combined, or Ding and Sickles (2018) where panel regression is combined with the DEA approach.

Different countries were included in all of the analyses. As already mentioned, the majority of data comes from more developed markets. But there are still papers that use data within the country in which the author(s) originate. This is due to simplicity of collecting "local" data, as the main purpose of the paper was to show how a model or methodology works. Some of the papers that are within the GST are as follows: Fang-Ming and Wang-Ching (2010) focused on electronics-sector companies and contrasted the DEA to the GSD. The latter approach had discriminated bad from good performance with an accuracy of 79%. As previously mentioned, failure prediction, i.e. probability of business failure, is popular in the literature. This is also true within the GST (see Huang et al., 2015 for an overview). The GST models and methods are applied in the following papers as well, but the problem here is that very small samples are used in the research. This is seen in Zhao et al. (2014), where only 9 companies, i.e. tourist hotels, were ranked, or Salardini (2103), where 16 companies were compared via stock-market measures, etc. Škrinjarić (2021) has utilized the DEA approach and MCDM for robustness-checking of the ranking system, based on financial ratios for 292 companies constituting the NASDAQ stock-market index. Due to some restrictions of the data and the number of input and output variables within the DEA approach, from more than 40 different financial ratios a total of 9 were left in the analysis. Thus, the shortfall of this study is the shortfall of DEA itself; when the correlation between inputs or outputs exists, the decision-maker needs to identify those variables that should stay in the analysis and those that should not. This includes some subjectivity in the analysis. Finally, as can be seen from this overview, although the research regarding the topic of business performance is huge, it could be improved, from the methodological point of view, when there are shortcomings within the data or the method or when the approach lacks an economic interpretation, often ignored in the data-science literature.

9.3 Methodology Description

The focus of the methodology is the GRA, with the description following Kuo et al. (2008) and Liu and Lin (2010, 2006). Some terminology will be changed so that it is in line with the performance measurement of a company within the industry. Suppose that the decision-maker has to compare M companies, with respect to their business performance in terms of financial ratios. The decision-maker has to compare K different financial ratios. Thus, every company within an industry is denoted with k, and each ratio with m, where $m \in \{1, 2, \ldots, M\}$ and $k \in \{1, 2, \ldots, K\}$. The original data is collected and put into a matrix form as follows:

$$
Z = \begin{bmatrix}
z_1(1) & z_1(2) & \cdots & z_1(K) \\
z_2(1) & z_2(2) & & z_2(K) \\
\vdots & \vdots & \ddots & \vdots \\
z_M(1) & z_M(2) & \cdots & z_M(K)
\end{bmatrix}, \tag{1}
$$

where each row is the individual financial ratio for every company k, and each column is one company k and values of each of the m ratios. As different values of every ratio cannot be compared one to another directly due to different measurements, the data has to be normalized in the first step. The process of normalization depends on the criteria, i.e. the financial ratio that is observed. Some ratios should be aimed to be the highest possible, others have to be lower to be better, and some should be around specific values in order to say that the business is "healthy". Thus, the normalization of the ratios that should be the highest possible is performed via the formula:

$$x_m(k) = \frac{-\min_m z_m(k) + z_m(k)}{-\min_m z_m(k) + \max_m z_m(k)}. \tag{2}$$

Ratios that need to be the lowest possible are normalized via the following formula:

$$x_m(k) = \frac{\max_m z_m(k) - z_m(k)}{\max_m z_m(k) - \min_m z_m(k)}, \tag{3}$$

and the ratios that should be around a specific value $z^*(k)$ are normalized as follows:

$$x_m(k) = \frac{|z_m(k) - z^*(k)|}{\max_m z_m(k) - z^*(k)}. \tag{4}$$

Thus, all of the obtained normalized values are easier to work with and are comparable across different criteria, i.e. financial ratios. Now, data in (1), (2), and (3) will be within the range [0,1], with 1 being the best value. Since companies have different performances across financial ratios, the idea is not that the new data should be contrasted to a referent sequence $x^*(k)$. This value is the best performing one in terms of what a company should be aiming for regarding a financial ratio, what experts advise to obtain, what is the usual practice, etc. Thus, some subjectivity can be included in this approach, as in the MCDM (multiple criteria decision making) and similar approaches. To be as objective as possible, due to the nature of the normalization of the data, the referent sequence is set to be a sequence of unit values, as this value represents the best value when the original dataset is normalized. This is usually done in literature (see Kuo et al., 2008) when the researcher does not explain why other values should be used. Thus, within every industry, we normalize the data via formulas (1)–(3) and compare the data to the referent sequence $x^*(k)$ via the Grey Relational Coefficient (GRC) as follows:

$$GRC_m(k) = \frac{\Delta_{\min} + p\Delta_{\max}}{\Delta x_m(k) + p\Delta_{\min}}, \tag{5}$$

where $\Delta x_m(k)$ is the absolute difference between each normalized value and the referent sequence within a criterion, i.e. $\Delta x_m(k) = |x_m(k) - x^*(k)|$, and p is called the distinguishing coefficient and takes value from the range [0,1]. Liu and Lin (2010, 2006) state that empirical applications usually set $p = 0.5$. The only difference in changing the value of p is that it will change the values in (5) to be increased or decreased. However, this will not change the rankings.

Finally, the grey relational grade (or degree, GRG or GRD) is a weighted average of (5) GRC values as follows:

$$GRD_m = \sum_{K=1}^{K} w_k G_m(k), \forall m. \tag{6}$$

The weights w_k could be set from the manager's point of view of which financial ratios are more important or less based on previous practice etc. It should hold that $\sum_{K=1}^{K} w_k = 1$. In order to be objective, in this study we assign equal weights to every financial ratio. Now, value in (6) for every company m within an industry can be interpreted as the degree of similarity between this company and the best possible sequence, i.e. a company that would perform in the best possible way when observing all of the ratios. It could be said that the value in (6) could be observed as a coefficient of correlation between a company performance and an ideal company. The greater the value in (6) is, the better performing the company is. Values in (6) will be contrasted one to another within an industry in order to obtain a ranking system.

9.4 Empirical Analysis

9.4.1 Data Description

The empirical part of the analysis includes the performance of S&P 500 companies. All of the available data on financial ratios was downloaded from Investing (2021) and refers to the most recent quarter, i.e. the last quarter of 2020. The initial dataset included 495 companies, which were divided into the sectors, i.e. different industries. Then, if a sector had only one company, it was excluded from the analysis, as we need at least two of them for comparison purposes. In the end, a total of 403 companies was left in the analysis. The publicly available data on Investing (2021) is for the following ratios, given in Table 9.1, with explanations as to what they represent (full descriptions with explanations on higher/lower values are given in Škrinjarić and Šego, 2021). In total, we use 47 ratios, and contrasting them one to another within each industry across 403 companies makes this a problem of big data.

Table 9.1 Used Financial Ratios for Company Performance Evaluation

Full name	Abbreviation	Explanation	H/L
5-year capital-spending growth, average	CSG	Capital investment to maintain and grow business-growth rate	High
5-year EPS growth, average	EPS_G	Earnings-per-share growth rate, 5 year average	High
5-year sales growth, average	S_G	Company-sales growth rate, 5 year average	High
Asset turnover TTM	AT	Net-sales revenue/average total assets value.	High
Basic EPS ANN	BEPS	Net income minus preferred dividends/no. of outstanding shares.	High
Book value/share MRQ	BV/S	Total equity value minus preferred equity/no. of outstanding shares	High
Cash flow/share TTM	CF/S	After-tax earnings plus depreciation/number of outstanding shares	High
Cash/share MRQ	C/S	Total cash/no. of outstanding shares.	Low
Current ratio MRQ	CR	Current assets/current liabilities.	1
Diluted EPS	DEPS	Net income minus preferred dividends/no. of shares outstanding increased plus conversion of dilutive securities	High
Dividend growth rate	DGR	Dividend yield growth rate	High
Dividend yield 5 year, average	DY5 year	Dividend payment/market capitalization	High
Dividend yield	DY	Dividend payment/market capitalization	High
EPS(MRQ) vs. qtr. 1 year. ago MRQ	EPS_Q	Net profit/no. of common shares	High
EPS(TTM) vs. TTM 1 year ago TTM	EPS_TTM		High

(Continued)

Table 9.1 (Continued)

Full name	Abbreviation	Explanation	H/L
Gross margin 5 year average	GM5 year	Company's revenue minus cost of sold goods/revenues	High
Gross margin TTM	GM		High
Inventory turnover TTM	IT	Net sales/average inventory	High
LT debt to equity MRQ	LTD/E	Long-term debts/total shareholders' equity	Low
Net income/employee TTM	NI/E	Net income/no. of employees	High
Net profit margin 5 year average	NPM5 year	Net profit/revenues	High
Net profit margin TTM	NPM		High
Operating margin 5 year average	OM5 year	Operating earnings/ operating revenues	High
Operating margin TTM	OM		High
P/E ratio TTM	P/E	Share price/earnings per share	High
Payout ratio TTM	PR	Paid dividends/net income	High
Pretax margin 5 year average	PM5 year	Profit/sales before tax reduction.	High
Pretax margin TTM	PM		High
Price to book MRQ	P/B	Market capitalization/total book value	Low
Price to cash flow MRQ	PCF	Market capitalization/ operating cash flow	Low
Price to free cash flow TTM	PFCF	Market capitalization/free cash flow	Low
Price to sales TTM	P/S	Market capitalization/ revenues	Low
Price to tangible book MRQ	P/TB	Share price/tangible book value per share	Low

Full name	Abbreviation	Explanation	H/L
Quick ratio MRQ	QR	Liquid assets/quick liabilities	1
Receivable turnover TTM	RT	Net credit sales/average receivable accounts	High
Return on assets 5 year average	ROA5 year	Net income/total assets	High
Return on assets TTM	ROA		High
Return on equity 5 year average	ROE5 year	Net income/equity	High
Return on equity TTM	ROE		High
Return on investment 5 year average	ROI5 year	Net income/cost of investment	High
Return on investment TTM	ROI		High
Revenue/employee TTM	R/E	Total revenue/no. of employees	High
Revenue/share TTM	R/S	Total revenues/no. of shares outstanding	High
Sales (MRQ) vs. qtr. 1 year. ago MRQ	S_Q	Sales growth rate, quarter of this year compared to same quarter of last year	High
Sales (TTM) vs. TTM 1 year ago TTM	S_TTM	Company sales growth rate, this year compared to last year	High
Tangible book value/ share MRQ	TBV/S	Total tangible assets/no. of shares outstanding	High
Total debt to equity MRQ	D/E	Total liabilities/the total shareholders' equity	Low

Note: H/L denotes highest or lowest possible or unit value for specific ratios. *MQR* denotes most recent quarter and *TTM* is trailing twelve months. *No.* is number. Best values of current and current ratios is around 1 (Tracy, 2004).

Source: Investing (2021)

After cleaning the dataset, all of the financial ratios were transformed based on formulas (2)–(4) within each industry, and the final values in (6) were calculated. The next subsection deals with the results.

9.4.2 Main Results

First of all, the GRD values within every industry have been calculated as in (6), and the descriptive statistics for every industry are given in Table 9.2. It can be seen that the number of companies within the industry ranges from 2 to 26. Furthermore, the results provide some information about the dispersion of the results when observing the standard-deviation column. In that way, the greatest discrepancies can be observed, and the interested decision-maker can focus on a specific group (industry). This focus can be made so that he can see what are sources of greater dispersion of financial ratios within this group, which has as a consequence contribution to the greater variability of GRD values. Next, if some industries are found to be similar (e.g. IT one sector and IT another sector) and could be compared one to another, here the decision-maker can compare the results in greater detail if needed: why is the mean GRD value of one sector better- or worse-performing when compared to the other? An individual company can contrast its results with the results in Table 9.2 to see its relative position within an industry and overall efficiency (although less comparable). Finally, to add another comment on Table 9.2, if the investor's point of view is observed, he can utilize the results from this table in terms of observing the maximal value of the GRD coefficient within each industry. In that way, he chooses the best-performing company when all financial ratios are taken into consideration, for portfolio diversification purposes.

Next, the decision-maker can visualize the GRD values within every industry, so that the individual performance is contrasted better with others within the industry. This is done in Figure 9.2 for all industries, and Figure 9.3 is an example of focusing on one industry. Although the company may not be the best performer, it can see how much it is lagging behind the best-performing one. In particular, company 6 within industry 64 is the best-performing one (Figure 9.2, greatest GRD value), but it is very closely followed by companies 1 and 2. Such visualizations of the results provide the management with a simple approach, yet they give so much information. Since the management is interested in how much the company needs to improve particular segments, the next analysis is done as an example in which we focus on industry 64. For every company, percentages of how much each one needs to increase or decrease a financial ratio have been calculated based on the ideal company (the referent sequence in the methodology description part) and based on company 6, which performs the best overall within this group. The results are provided in Table 9.3.

Table 9.2   GRD Values, Descriptive Statistics for Every Industry

Industry	Mean	Max	Min	Std. Dev.	Obs.
1	0.525259	0.810461	0.285120	0.227176	5
2	0.515440	0.609514	0.452458	0.083016	3
4	0.506192	0.648260	0.317561	0.138017	4
5	0.503006	0.634146	0.371866	0.185460	2
6	0.477466	0.771443	0.270168	0.139107	17
9	0.500146	0.632928	0.366081	0.103866	7
11	0.481754	0.584135	0.265518	0.145759	4
15	0.414229	0.621835	0.264222	0.097835	17
16	0.480877	0.503545	0.429310	0.035059	4
17	0.497563	0.655347	0.373402	0.126795	6
20	0.483151	0.566313	0.350224	0.116323	3
21	0.442230	0.546787	0.232295	0.068561	26
23	0.415024	0.593527	0.079406	0.149897	10
24	0.460112	0.633308	0.263009	0.124993	9
25	0.534814	0.692465	0.352698	0.111335	12
26	0.385056	0.551150	0.261912	0.094705	10
27	0.451469	0.614238	0.390018	0.108854	4
29	0.515132	0.714590	0.384759	0.130535	6
30	0.472263	0.609908	0.373317	0.087517	6
31	0.453174	0.543133	0.325142	0.113873	3
33	0.466057	0.680167	0.348152	0.123778	6
34	0.487556	0.617080	0.214286	0.188946	4
39	0.507565	0.659574	0.355556	0.214974	2
42	0.509306	0.590041	0.428571	0.114176	2
43	0.425514	0.712559	0.287106	0.173590	5
44	0.478983	0.650943	0.279777	0.096927	10
45	0.461743	0.552883	0.352001	0.099924	5

(Continued)

Table 9.2 (Continued)

Industry	Mean	Max	Min	Std. Dev.	Obs.
46	0.474055	0.593741	0.332681	0.084260	11
47	0.501501	0.744186	0.258816	0.343208	2
48	0.384466	0.402230	0.366702	0.025122	2
50	0.558040	0.655980	0.368612	0.084371	9
52	0.484486	0.613636	0.082609	0.987294	2
53	0.539229	0.701751	0.263895	0.239738	3
55	0.433546	0.737092	0.345896	0.114542	11
56	0.598485	0.772727	0.250000	0.301797	3
57	0.498647	0.611227	0.383698	0.066401	12
59	0.455023	0.605859	0.244717	0.099260	12
60	0.407966	0.658318	0.280311	0.137853	7
63	0.448768	0.651583	0.313984	0.097846	19
64	0.448337	0.662839	0.274457	0.131025	12
66	0.507685	0.731022	0.354089	0.179735	5
67	0.437167	0.577901	0.314978	0.063495	23
68	0.478327	0.622582	0.315807	0.073418	21
69	0.495532	0.712683	0.337927	0.146009	9
70	0.390668	0.581107	0.236351	0.101778	18
72	0.450943	0.508697	0.393630	0.051411	5
73	0.542008	0.629259	0.275346	0.152882	5
75	0.485879	0.695561	0.235974	0.182557	6
76	0.495401	0.674932	0.242121	0.182033	4
77	0.470392	0.615505	0.359803	0.114300	5
78	0.421420	0.476987	0.365854	0.078583	2
81	0.462392	0.639156	0.228790	0.211005	3
All	0.461798	0.810461	0.082609	0.133063	403

Note: Obs denotes number of companies within an industry, *Std. Dev.* denotes standard deviation of the values within an industry

Source: Author's calculation

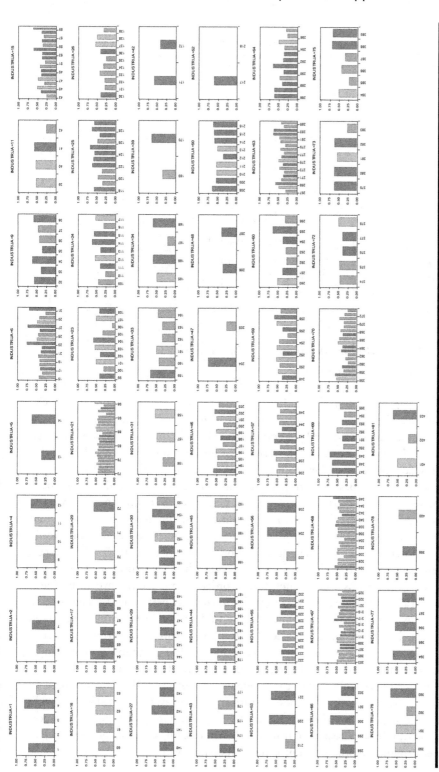

Figure 9.1 GRDs of Every Company within an Industry.

Source: Author's calculation

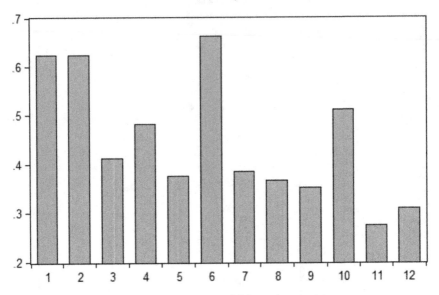

Figure 9.2   GRD of Every Company within Industry 64.
Source: Author's calculation

Since the calculation of required increase or decrease of individual financial ratios within the industry is similar across all ratios, Table 9.3 and 9.4 depict examples of some ratios across all 12 companies. Detailed results are available upon request; here we show a part of the results, for interpretation purposes. First, Table 9.3 provides the results when companies are contrasted with the ideal company. This means that the best-performing financial ratio is examined and used as a basis for the results. As company 6 was the best performer overall, it does not need to increase revenue per employee and net profit margins. However, it needs to increase return on assets (ROA) by 6.5%. Thus, the management of a company would see from such results that they need to work on ROA more than other aspects of the business. Some of the worst performers, such as companies 11 or 12, need to increase their ratios a far greater deal in order to improve the overall business. Second, Table 9.4 compares the companies to the best performer, i.e. company 6. That is why this company is not included in Table 9.4, as its performance is taken as a basis. Negative values indicate that some companies are performing better than company 6 when a specific ratio is considered. Thus, a double analysis can be made: one, in which companies are compared to the ideal one, as in Table 9.3, so that the worst-performing ratios can be identified. Then the other one, in which all companies are compared to the best-performing one on average, based on the GRD results. As the ideal company characteristics are very hard to achieve, it is important to maintain some aspect of realism in terms of comparing the performance to real performance of others, not just the ideal company.

Table 9.3   Needed Increases or Decreases of Selected Financial Ratios across Companies, Industry 64, All 12 Companies, Ideal Company, in %

Company	Revenue/employee TTM	Net profit margin 5YA	Return on assets 5YA
1	8.2	38.2	38.6
2	8.2	38.2	38.6
3	73.4	71.5	44.6
4	79.9	22.3	1.1
5	52.5	83.8	92.8
6	0.0	0.0	6.5
7	76.7	60.6	75.5
8	100.0	64.0	65.3
9	81.8	64.7	84.7
10	77.9	7.4	0.0
11	52.3	59.5	77.7
12	100.0	86.8	88.2

Source: Author's calculation

Table 9.4   Needed Increases or Decreases of Selected Financial Ratios across Companies, Industry 64, 11 Companies, Compared to Company 6, In %

Company	Operating margin TTM	Return on Assets TTM	EPS(MRQ) vs. qtr. 1 year ago MRQ
1	40.6	32.1	53.7
2	40.6	32.1	53.7
3	61.6	43.6	−507.7
4	-0.8	−3.8	111.6
5	55.8	91.0	163.2
7	68.3	94.1	77.3
8	83.4	81.7	188.4
9	29.4	72.9	132.2
10	−25.9	−21.3	133.1
11	106.2	150.4	130.8
12	88.8	93.7	190.5

Source: Author's calculation

There are several implications from such an analysis. First, the methodology utilized in this chapter is not a highly complicated one when compared to other ranking approaches. However, it deals with uncertainty in data very well (for details, see Škrinjarić, 2020). The focus was made on the interpretation of the results, from the management point of view. Quantitative research often lacks this part of the study as the rankings are obtained as shown in Figure 9.1, but there is lacking a greater in-depth analysis of why such results were obtained. Although maybe not immediately apparent, the calculations done in this chapter fall within big data research, as many companies within different sectors are evaluated via more than 40 financial ratios at once. The calculations shown in Tables 9.3 and 9.4 are just one part of the calculation and results process. If the management of a company deals with these issues, the analysis is a bit smaller, as they will focus on a specific industry or several interesting industries. However, if we take the point of view of an investor, he would need to observe simultaneously all companies at once. Nevertheless, it was shown how to implement a quantitative tool in estimating concrete numbers, which at least tells the decision-maker what needs to be improved and by how much—and what is relatively fine.

9.5 Conclusion

The approach provided in this chapter provides simple interpretations regarding measuring business performance to the interested parties involved. This is important for many people in the position of making important decisions about future business conduct and planning. Due to problems of big data today, much available information, fake news, etc., the idea of the chapter was to provide several insights into how to simplify the quantitative approach and use it when a company is compared to another. Direct results obtained show that the management of a company can focus on crucial problems when they are detected in one aspect of the business. Although we start with a lot of data at the beginning, the rankings obtained provide simple information. The analysis can be done every time new data arrives. Then, when problems are detected, the interested parties can focus solely on the problems so that they are resolved as quickly as possible. Of course, the analysis can be made in greater detail, based on the needs of the decision-maker.

The contributions of the chapter lie in the critical overview of the literature and focusing on sectoral analysis of the business performance, often lacking in existing research. Next, we have observed what is needed, increase or decrease of certain financial ratios in order to achieve better results within an industry. Previous literature focuses solely on constructing the ranking system, without further analysis on what needs to be done in order to enhance future business performance. Thus both quantitative and economic aspects have been made. Another advantage of such analysis is its simplicity in terms of being relatively easy and quick to calculate when compared to other approaches. The results are easy to interpret and understand, even if the analysis is performed by someone whose job is not primarily quantitative. The practitioners, e.g. managers, within business can make decisions more easily, as the results are not complicated sheets of numbers. Quite the opposite, the results can be formatted in a way that is based on fewer numbers to deal with; one can make good decisions about future business.

Although a more holistic approach is needed in business-performance measurement, this chapter focused on the part that refers to the quantification of the business results. The performance measurement in general needs both quantitative analysts and the managers who bring other aspects to the final decision-making process. We focused on the quantitative tools that are just one part of the whole process. Thus, there are some shortfalls in the study. Previous research has indicated that nonfinancial variables should also be included in the evaluation of the business performance (see Abdel-Maksoud et al., 2005; Modi, 2016; Milost, 2013; Kotane, 2015; Kotane and Kuzmina-Merlino, 2011). Thus, future research and applications should include incorporating the nonfinancial variables in the whole process of performance measurement. Next, our analysis was a static one. This was due to data unavailability. We have collected the latest publicly available data, but future research, both academic and empirical, which can retrieve data over time, could do a dynamic analysis. Moreover, we have assigned all financial ratios equal weights in the ranking system. Changing the weights will change the obtained results. However, the idea was to show how to obtain a robust and reliable ranking system that provides easy interpretations. The weighting schemes should be left for practitioners to decide within each industry and time period what is relevant and why. It is hoped that this chapter provided answers to some of the open questions in the literature and that future work and practice will implement such ideas more.

References

Abdel-Maksoud, A., Dugdale, D., and Luther, R. 2005. Non-financial Performance Measurement in Manufacturing Companies. *The British Accounting Review* 37(3):261–297.

Achim, M. V., Borlea, S. N., and Gaban, L. V. 2016. Failure Prediction from the Investors' View by Using Financial Ratios. *Lesson from Romania* 19(4):117–133.

Alam, B., Doja, M. N., Alam, M., and Malhotra, S. 2013a. Security Issues Analysis for Cloud Computing. *International Journal of Computer Science and Information Security* 11(9):117–125.

Alam, M. 2012. Cloud Algebra for Cloud Database Management System. In *Second International Conference on Computational Science, Engineering and Information Technology*, 26–29. New York, NY: Association for Computing Machinery.

Alam, M., and Shakil, K. A. 2013b. Cloud Database Management System Architecture. *International Journal of Advances in Computer Science and its Applications* 3(1):27–31.

Alam, M., and Shakil, K. A. 2013c. A Decision Matrix and Monitoring Based Framework for Infrastructure Performance Enhancement in a Cloud Based Environment. *Advances in Engineering and Technology Series* 7:147–153.

Alam, M., and Shakil, K. A. 2016. Big Data Analytics in Cloud Environment Using Hadoop. *arXiv*, preprint arXiv:1610.04572.

Altman, E. I. 1968. Financial Ratios, Discriminant Analysis and the Prediction of Corporate Bankruptcy. *The Journal of Finance* 23(4):589–609.

Altman, E. I. 2005. An Emerging Market Credit Scoring System for Corporate Bonds. *Emerging Markets Review* 6(4):311–323.

Asness, C. S., Ilmanen, A., Israel, R., and Moskowitz, T. J. 2015. Investing with Style. *Journal of Investment Management* 13(1):27–63.

Altman, E. I., Iwanicz-Drozdowska, M., Laitinen, E. K., and Suvas, A. 2017. Financial Distress Prediction in an International Context: A Review and Empirical Analysis of Altman's Z-Score Model. *Journal of International Financial Management & Accounting* 28(2):131–171.

Basu, S. 1977. The Investment Performance of Common Stocks in Relation to Their Price to Earnings Ratio: A Test of the Efficient Markets Hypothesis. *The Journal of Finance* 32(3):663–682.

Basu, S. 1983. The Relationship Between Earnings Yield, Market Value, and Return for NYSE Common Stocks: Further Evidence. *Journal of Financial Economics* 12(1):129–156.

Beaver, W. H. 1966. Financial Ratios as Predictors of Failure. *Journal of Accounting Research* 4(7):71–111.

Beaver, W. H. 1989. *Financial Accounting: An Accounting Revolution*. Engle-wood Cliffs, NJ: Prentice-Hall.

Beaver, W. H. 2010. Financial Statement Analysis and the Prediction of Financial Distress. *Foundations and Trends in Accounting* 5(2):99–173.

Bhargava, M., Dubelaar, C., and Scott, T. 1998. Predicting Bankruptcy in the Retail Sector: An Examination of the Validity of Key Measures of Performance. *Journal of Retailing and Consumer Services* 5(2):105–117.

Brennan, M. J. 1970. Taxes, Market Valuation, and Corporate Financial Policy. *National Tax Journal* 23(4):417–427.

Camelia, D. 2015a. Grey Systems Theory in Economics—A Historical Applications Review. *Grey Systems Theory and Application* 5(2):263–276.

Camelia, D. 2015b. Grey Systems Theory in Economics—Bibliometric Analysis and Applications' Overview. *Grey Systems Theory and Application* 5(2):244–262.

Campbell, J. Y., Hilscher, J. D., and Szilagyi, J. 2011. Predicting Financial Distress and the Performance of Distressed Stocks. *Journal of Investment Management* 9(2):14–34.

Cardinaels, E., and van Veen-Dirks, P. M. G. 2010. Financial Versus Non-financial Information: The Impact of Information Organization and Presentation in a Balanced Scorecard. *Accounting, Organizations and Society* 35(6):565–578.

Chaudhary, K., Alam, M., Al-Rakhami, M. S., and Gumaei, A. 2021. Machine Learning Based Mathematical Modelling for Prediction of Social Media Consumer Behaviour Using Big Data Analytics. *Research Square*. Preprint.

Chen, J.-S., Hung Tai, T., and Huang, Y.-H. 2009. Service Delivery Innovation: Antecedents and Impact on Firm Performance. *Journal of Service Research* 12(1):36–55.

Choong, K. K. 2013. Understanding the Features of Performance Measurement System: A Literature Review. *Measuring Business Excellence* 17(4):102–121.

Deaves, R., Miu, P., and White, C. B. 2008. Canadian Stock Market Multiples and Their Predictive Content. *International Review of Economics and Finance* 17(3):457–466.

DeBondt, W., and Thaler, R. 1987. Further Evidence on Investor Overreactions and Stock Market Seasonality. *The Journal of Finance* 42(3):557–581.

Delcea, C., Bradea, I., Maracine, V., Scarlat, E., and Cotfas, L. A. 2013. GM(1,1) in Bankruptcy Forecasting. *Grey Systems: Theory and Application* 3(3):250–265.

Delcea, C., Scarlat, E., and Maracine, V. 2012. Grey Relational Analysis Between Firm's Current Situation and Its Possible Causes: A Bankruptcy Syndrome Approach. *Grey Systems: Theory and Application* 2(2):229–239.

Ding, D., and Sickles, R. C. 2018. Frontier Efficiency, Capital Structure, and Portfolio Risk: An Empirical Analysis of U.S. Banks. *BRQ Business Research Quarterly* 21(4):262–277.

Doğan, M. 2013. Measuring Bank Performance with Grey Relational Analysis: The Case of Turkey. *Ege akademik bakiş/Ege Academic Review* 13(2):215–225.

du Jardin, P., and Séverin, E. 2011. Predicting Corporate Bankruptcy Using a Self-organizing Map: An Empirical Study to Improve the Forecasting Horizon of a Financial Failure Model. *Decision Support Systems* 51(3):701–711.

Edirisinghe, N. C. P., and Zhang, X. 2007. Generalized DEA Model of Fundamental Analysis and Its Application to Portfolio Optimization. *Journal of Banking & Finance* 31(11):3311–3335.

Fama, E. F., and French, K. 1992. The Cross-section of Expected Stock Returns. *The Journal of Finance* 47(2):427–465.

Fama, E. F., and French, K. 1993. Common Risk Factors in the Returns on Stocks and Bonds. *Journal of Financial Economics* 33(1):3–56.

Fang-Ming, L., and Wang-Ching, C. 2010. A Precaution Diagnosis of Financial Distress via Grey Situation Decision. *Journal of Grey System* 22(4):395–403.

Fernandes, K. J., Raja, V., and Whalley, A. 2006. Lessons from Implementing the Balanced Scorecard in a Small and Medium Size Manufacturing Organization. *Technovation* 26(5–6):623–634.

Gregoriou, A., Healy, J., and Gupta, J. 2015. Determinants of Telecommunication Stock Prices. *Journal of Economic Studies* 42(4):534–548.

Huang, C., Dai, C., and Guo, M. 2015. A Hybrid Approach Using Two-level DEA for Financial Failure Prediction and Integrated SE-DEA and GCA for Indicators Selection. *Applied Mathematics and Computation* 251:431–441.

Investing. 2021. www.investing.com (acessed January 20, 2021).

Kaur, A., and Alam, M. 2013. Role of Knowledge Engineering in the Development of a Hybrid Knowledge Based Medical Information System for Atrial Fibrillation. *American Journal of Industrial and Business Management* 3(1):36–41.

Keim, D. B. 1988. Stock Market Regularities: A Synthesis of the Evidence and Explanations. In *Stock Market Anomalies*, ed. Dimson, E., 16–39. Cambridge: Cambridge University Press.

Khan, I., Naqvi, S. K., and Ala, M. M. 2015. Data Model for Big Data in Cloud Environment. *Computing for Sustainable Global Development (INDIACom) 2nd International Conference*, 582–585. New Delhi, India: IEEE.

Khan, I., Naqvi, S. K., Alam, M. M., and Rizvi, S. N. A. 2018b. A Framework for Twitter Data Analysis. In *Big Data Analytics: Advances in Intelligent Systems and Computing*, ed. Aggarwal, V., Bhatnagar, V., and Mishra, D., 297–303. Singapore: Springer.

Khan, S., Kashish, A., and Shakil, M. A. 2017a. Big Data Computing Using Cloud-Based Technologies: Challenges and Future Perspectives. In *Networks of the Future: Architectures, Technologies and Implementations*, ed. Elkhodr, M., Hassan, Q. F., and Shahrestani, S., 803–849. Boca Raton, FL: Chapman and Hall/CRC Press.

Khan, S., Liu, X., Shakil, K. A., and Alam, M. 2017b. A Survey on Scholarly Data: From Big Data Perspective. *Information Processing & Management* 53(4):923–944.

Khan, S., Liu, X., Shakil, K. A., and Alam, M. 2019. Big Data Technology—Enabled Analytical Solution for Quality Assessment of Higher Education Systems. *International Journal of Advanced Computer Science and Applications* 10(6):292–304.

Khan, S., Shakil, K. A., and Alam, M. 2018a. Cloud-Based Big Data Analytics—A Survey of Current Research and Future Directions. In *Big Data Analytics. Advances in Intelligent Systems and Computing*, ed. Aggarwal, V., Bhatnagar, V., and Mishra, D., 595–604. Singapore: Springer.

Kotane, I. 2015. Evaluating the Importance of Financial and Non-financial Indicators for the Evaluation of Company's Performance. *Management Theory and Studies for Rural Business and Infrastructure Development* 37(1):80–94.

Kotane, I., and Kuzmina-Merlino, I. 2011. Non-financial Indicators for Evaluation of Business Activity. European Integration Studies. *Research and Topicalities* 5:213–219.

Kuo, Y., Yang, T., and Huang, G.-W. 2008. The Use of a Grey-based Taguchi Method for Optimizing Multi-response Simulation Problems. *Engineering Optimization* 40(6):517–528.

Laitinen, E. K. 2018. Financial Reporting: Long-Term Change of Financial Ratios. *American Journal of Industrial and Business Management* 8(9):1893–1927.

Lau, S. T., Lee, T. C., and McInish, T. H. 2002. Stock Returns and Beta, Firms Size, E/P, CF/P, Book-to-market, and Sales Growth: Evidence from Singapore and Malaysia. *Journal of Multinational Financial Management* 12(3):207–222.

Leary, M. T., and Michaely, R. 2011. Determinants of Dividend Smoothing: Empirical Evidence. *The Review of Financial Studies* 24(10):3197–3249.

Li, X., Song, J., and Huang, B. 2016. A Scientific Workflow Management System Architecture and Its Scheduling Based on Cloud Service Platform for Manufacturing Big Data Analytics. *The International Journal of Advanced Manufacturing Technology* 84(1–4):119–131.

Lin, R. S., Wang, Y. T., Wu, C. H., and Chuang, C. L. 2009. Developing a Business Failure Prediction Model via RST, GRA and CBR. *Expert Systems with Applications* 36(2):1593–1600.

Litzenberger, R., and Ramaswamy, K. 1979. The Effects of Personal Taxes and Dividends on Capital Asset Prices: Theory and Empirical Evidence. *Journal of Financial Economics* 7(2):163–195.

Liu, S., and Lin, Y. 2006. Grey *Information Theory and Practical Applications*. New York: Springer.

Liu, S., and Lin, Y. 2010. *Grey Systems, Theory and Applications*. Berlin/Heidelberg: Springer.

Liu, S., Yang, Y., and Forrest, J. 2016. *Grey Data Analysis: Methods, Models and Applications*. Singapore: Springer Science + Business Media.

Malhotra, S., Doja, M. N., Alam, B., and Alam, M. 2015. Data Integration of Cloud-based and Relational Databases. In *International Conference on Soft Computing Techniques and Implementations*, 83–86. IEEEXplore: Faridabad, India.

Malhotra, S., Doja, M. N., Alam, B., and Alam, M. 2017. Big Data Analysis and Comparison of Big Data Analytic Approaches. *Computing, Communication and Automation (ICCCA) 2017 International Conference*, 309–314. India: IEEE.

Matthias, O., Fouweather, I., Gregory, I., and Vernon, A. 2017. Making Sense of Big Data—Can It Transform Operations Management? *International Journal of Operations & Production Management* 37(1):37–55.

McDonald, B., and Morris, M. H. 1984. The Statistical Validity of the Ratio Method in Financial Analysis: An Empirical Examination. *Journal of Business Finance and Accounting* 11(1):89–97.

McDonald, J. T. 1999. The Determinants of Firm Profitability in Australian Manufacturing. *Economic Record* 75(229):115–126.

Milost, F. 2013. Information Power of Non-financial Performance Measures. *International Journal of Business Management and Economic Research* 4(6):823–828.

Modi, S. 2016. A Review on the Literature of Value Relevance of Nonfinancial Variables or Information. *International Journal of Advance Research in Computer Science and Management Studies* 4(2):81–85.

Modigliani, F., and Miller, M. 1958. The Cost of Capital, Corporation Finance and the Theory of Investment. *American Economic Review* 48(3):261–297.

Morris, R. 2018. *Early Warning Indicators of Corporate Failure: A Critical Review of Previous Research and Further Empirical Evidence*. London: Rutledge Revivals.

Myšková, R., and Hájek, P. 2017. Comprehensive Assessment of Firm Financial Performance Using Financial Ratios and Linguistic Analysis of Annual Reports. *Journal of International Studies* 10(4):96–108.

Narkunienė, J., and Ulbinaitė, A. 2018. Comparative Analysis of Company Performance Evaluation Methods. *Entrepreneurship and Sustainability Issues* 6(1):125–138.

Neely, A. D., and Adams, C. 2001. Perspectives on Performance: The Performance Prism. *Journal of Cost Management* 15(1):7–15.

Neely, A. D., Gregory, M. J., and Platts, K. W. 1995. Performance Measurement System Design: A Literature Review and Research Agenda. *International Journal of Operations and Production Management* 15(4):80–116.

Ohlson, J. A. 1980. Financial Ratios and the Probabilistic Prediction of Bankruptcy. *Journal of Accounting Research* 18(1):109–131.

Pan, W.-T., and Leu, Y. 2016. An Analysis of Bank Service Satisfaction Based on Quantile Regression and Grey Relational Analysis. *Mathematical Problems in Engineering*:1–9.

Parker, C. 2000. Performance Measurement. *Work Study* 49(2):63–66.

Pashaki, M. K., Ahadzadeh, M., and Shahverdiani, S. 2018. Ranking Active Companies in Cement Industry with the Combined Approach of Grey Relational Analysis and Data Envelopment Analysis. *The Third International Conference on Intelligent Decision Science (IDS-2018)*. Iran: Iranian Data Envelopment Analysis (DEA) Association.

Penman, S. H., Richardson, S. A., and Tuna, I. 2007. The Book-to-price Effect in Stock Returns: Accounting for Leverage. *Journal of Accounting Research* 45(2):427–467.

Powers, J., and McMullen, P. 2002. Using Data Envelopment Analysis to Select Efficient Large Cap Securities. *Journal of Business and Management* 7(7):31–42.

Prieto, I. M., and Revilla, E. 2006. Learning Capability and Business Performance: A Non-financial and Financial Assessment. *Learning Organization* 13(2):166–185.

Rosini, I., and Gunawan, J. 2018. Financial Ratio and Performance Airlines Industry with DEA and TOPSIS Model. *International Journal of Pure and Applied Mathematics* 119(10):367–374.

Salardini, F. 2013. An AHP-GRA Method for Asset Allocation: A Case Study of Investment Firms on Tehran Stock Exchange. *Decision Science Letters* 2(4):275–280.

Samiya, K., Ali, S.A., Hasan, N., Shakil, K.A., and Alam, M. 2019. Big Data Scientific Workflows in the Cloud: Challenges and Future Prospects. *Cloud Computing for Geospatial Big Data Analytics* 49: 1–28.

Samiya, K., Liu, X., Ara Shakil, K., and Alam, M. 2017. A Survey on Scholarly Data: From Big Data Perspective. *Information Processing & Management* 53(4):923–944. DOI: 10.1016/j.ipm.2017.03.006.

Shakil, K. A., and Alam, M. 2014. Data Management in Cloud Based Environment Using k-Median Clustering Technique. *International Journal of Computer Applications* 3:8–13.

Shakil, K. A., and Alam, M. 2018. Cloud Computing in Bioinformatics and Big Data Analytics: Current Status and Future Research. In *Big Data Analytics*, ed. Aggarwal, V. B., Bhatnagar, V., and Mishra, D. K., 629–640. Singapore: Springer.

Shakil, K. A., Sethi, S., and Alam, M. 2015. An Effective Framework for Managing University Data Using a Cloud Based Environment. In *2nd International Conference on Computing for Sustainable Global Development*, 1262–1266. New Delhi, India.

Škrinjarić, T. 2014. Investment Strategy on the Zagreb Stock Exchange Based on Dynamic DEA. *Croatian Economic Survey* 16(1):129–160.

Škrinjarić, T. 2019. Using Grey Relational Analysis with Fuzzy Logic in Portfolio Selection. *CEA Journal of Economics* 14(2):39–56.

Škrinjarić, T. 2020. Dynamic Portfolio Optimization Based on Grey Relational Analysis Approach. *Expert Systems with Applications* 147:1–15.

Škrinjarić, T. 2021. Comparing Company's Performance to Its Peers A Data Envelopment Approach. In *Big Data Analytics in Supply Chain Management Theory and Application*, ed. Rahimi, I., Gandomi, A. H., Fong, S. J., and Ülkü, M. A., 79–108. Boca Raton, FL: Taylor & Francis Group.

Škrinjarić, T., and Šego, B. 2021. Evaluating Business Performance Using Data Envelopment Analysis and Grey Relational Analysis. In *Handbook of Research on Engineering, Business, and Healthcare Applications of Data Science and Analytics*, ed. Patil, B., and Vohra, M., 115–148. Hershey, PA: IGI Global.

Tracy, J. A. 2004. *How to Read a Financial Report: Wringing Vital Signs Out of the Numbers*. New York: John Wiley and Sons.

Venkatraman, N., and Ramanujam, V. 1986. Measurement of Business Performance in Strategy Research: A Comparison of Approaches. *The Academy of Management Review* 11(4):801–814.

Wier, B., Hunton, J., and Hassab Elnaby, H. R. 2007. Enterprise Resource Planning Systems and Non-financial Performance Incentives: The Joint Impact on Corporate Performance. *International Journal of Accounting Information Systems* 8(3):165–190.

Wu, C.-R., Lin, C.-T., and Tsai, P.-H. 2010. Evaluating Business Performance of Wealth Management Banks. *European Journal of Operational Research* 207(2):971–979.

Yildirim, B. F., Hepsen, A., and Onder, E. 2015. Grey Relational Analysis Based Ranking of Latin American and Caribbean Economies. *Journal of Economics, Finance and Accounting* 2(3):301–312.

Zamani, L., Beegam, R., and Borzoian, S. 2014. Portfolio Selection Using Data Envelopment Analysis (DEA): A Case of Select Indian Investment Companies. *International Journal of Current Research and Academic Review* 2(4):50–55.

Zhao, D., Kuo, S.-H., and Wang, T. C. 2014. The Evaluation of the Business Operation Performance by Applying Grey Relational Analysis. In *Intelligent Data Analysis and Its Applications, Volume I. Advances in Intelligent Systems and Computing*, ed. Pan, J. S., Snasel, V., Corchado, E., Abraham, A., and Wang, S. L., 441–450. Cham: Springer.

Chapter 10

Applications of Big Data Analytics in Supply-Chain Management

Nabeela Hasan and Mansaf Alam

Contents

DOI: 10.1201/9781003175711-10

10.1 Introduction

Big data is described as complex and massive data sets, typically extending beyond exabytes. It surpasses conventional systems with limited storage, handling, monitoring, decoding and visualization capability (Kaisle, Armour, Espinosa, Money 2013). Currently, data are growing significantly and are expected to stretch to zettabytes each coming year (Tiwari, Wee, Daryanto 2018). The community of professionals and researchers agree that such a rise in the flow of data provides advance opportunities; many organizations have consequently tried to generate and improve their big data analytics (BDA) potential to explain or to gain a greater and better knowledge from BDA. The research in the field of big data is consistently extended and progressive, and the majority of big data's properties are currently expanded to include the 5 V's model of velocity, volume, value, veracity and variety (Addo-Tenkorang, Helo 2016; White 2012). Akter, Wamba, Gunasekaran, Dubey 2016 suggested that BDA is one of the major aspects affecting corporate execution.

By developing BDA, businesses can better understand the needs of their customers, provide adequate services to meet their needs, boost incomes and sales and enter the neoteric marketplace. Numerous investigations have indicated applications of BDA in different areas, for instance, insurance, banking, marketing, logistics, financial services and production (Zhong, Newman, Huang 2016). However, this chapter shows the advances of big data in acquiring new perspectives and building various new types of constructs that have influenced relationships in the logistic network. For this objective, we defined the significant concepts of BDA and its function in forecasting the future. Second, we discussed the role of optimization, simulation and statistical analysis in supply-chain analytics (SCA). Third, we reviewed the role of BDA in the field of supply-chain network. Consequently, we gave concise information on the application of BDA in various supply-chain categories in fourth section. Fifth, we provided some insight into how BDA will be used in the supply chain and, finally, conclude with a number of decision-making recommendation and implications for further research.

10.2 Big Data Analytics Competencies

In order to truly comprehend the consequence and implementation of BDA, it is mandatory to understand clearly what it really is. Generally, *big data* indicates large quantities of data. It refers in particular to huge sets of data whose volume is so great that it becomes impossible to get it equipped with available storage. These data can be collected, saved, transmitted, accumulated and evaluated. As the amount of data has grown exponentially, the tools used to analyze it must be restructured. Such data should not be placed in ordered rows and columns as conventional data sets, which cannot be analyzed by modern technology, were in earlier times. Big data occurs in various data types. They include all kinds of data across all potential sources. Data consisting of big data can be completely unstructured, semistructured or completely structured. It can consist of text, images, speech, numeric data and communication as a further categorization. It can also exist in the form of point-of-sale (POS), radio-frequency identification (RFID), global positioning system (GPS) or from Twitter feeds, Facebook, Instagram, customer blogs or call centers. The analytical advancements of today enable us to gather relevant information from all types of data. Analytics is a mixture of statistical and mathematical data in huge quantity. BDA means the use of mathematics and statistics to evaluate large data. Big data are only a lot of data without analytics. For years, the authors have analyzed a lot of data. Big data analytics is simply an advanced statistical and mathematical technologies. Companies can extract information from these enormous data volumes. This is possible due to today's huge computational capabilities at a lower cost than they have ever been. Integrating big data and analytics therefore does provide various tools for evaluation to gain insight and transform extracted knowledge into business intelligence.

10.3 Supply-Chain Analytics

The *supply chain* is the series of companies ranging from suppliers of raw materials to manufacturing organizations, retailers, consumers and wholesalers. This chain involves not just substantial movement including transmission of products and materials but also financial flows and information. Supply-chain analytics (SCA) is used to retrieve relevant meaningful information from the supply chain with BDA techniques (Wang, Gunasekaran, Ngai, Papadopoulos 2016). Such analysis can also be divided into prescriptive, predictive and descriptive analytical analysis (Wang, Gunasekaran, Ngai, Papadopoulos 2016; Souza 2014). Implemented and well-formulated decisions translate directly to potential outcome by reducing the costs of sourcing, transport, storage, inventory and disposal. The use of BDA techniques to resolve the issues that arise in supply-chain management therefore has a significant and positive impact on the implementation of these strategies. For years, researchers and managers have used operational and statistical research methods to resolve problems of balance between demand and supply (Souza 2014; Trkman, McCormack, De Oliveira, Ladeira 2010). However, current advancements in analytics usage have given researchers and managers new horizons. Table 10.1 shows the summary of the features and challenges of different types of analytics. Figure 10.1 shows the correlation among prescriptive, predictive and descriptive analytics in making decisions and taking action.

Table 10.1 Types of Analytics

Category	Features
Descriptive Analytics • What happened	• Foundational • Filters big data into useful nuggets and interpretable information • Provides a historical summary of what happened in the past • Focus on minimizing bias • Example: providing historical insights regarding the company's production, financials, operations, sales, finance, inventory, and customers.
Predictive Analytics • What might happen	• Insightful • What-if-analysis • Focus on minimizing the combined bias and variance • Forecasting supply chain requirements • Example: Analyzing past trends to estimate future needs, supply and demand, set accurate delivery time and etc.
Prescriptive Anaytics • What should we do	• Strategic • Scenario and knowledge based • Optimization and automation of decisions • Example: optimizing production, scheduling and inventory.

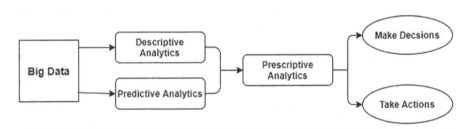

Figure 10.1 Using Various Analytics to Make and Take Decisions.

Integrating data can transform methods that are used at present because of the possible benefits that are generated. This has prompted an increase in academic work on this subject in recent years. BDA strategies play a crucial role in effective management of SCM. Since 2011, several journals have published papers about the new research into SCM and its benefits. In 2011 to 2015, Mishra et al. recognized the famous and popular articles and researchers with the highest citations. The findings showed that the number of publications in the area of Broad-based Black Economic Empowerment Act (BBE) has been increased. Barbosa et al. looked at the introduction of BDA in the investment and trade divisions. The findings showed that statistical and prescriptive techniques are commonly used in BDA methodology. Researchers wanted to explore the impacts of big data and statistical learning on environmental and social factors. In this analysis, data were obtained from manufacturing firms, and a structural equation model was used to evaluate the variables. Big data appear to have optimistic and important impacts on environmental and social maintenance. Gupta, Altay and Luo 2017 observed that using

BDA strategies contributes to an efficient form of relaxation in daily life. Gupta et al., based on 28 journal articles, were able to summarize the application of big data to humanitarian service management. They offered ideas for future studies using resource dependency theory, social network theory, transaction cost economics, complexity theory, stakeholder theory, resource-based perspective, structural theory and ecological modernization theory. Zhao et al. implemented a multiobjective and goal-driven approach for green supply-chain management employing the BDA paradigm. In order to optimize the possible benefits extracted from hazardous materials transportation through the United States, three scenarios were developed. They used big data methodology to control device efficiency. Song et al. researched "environmental performance evaluation along with latest developments in environmental management using big data" (Song, Fisher, Wang, Cui 2018).

- **Descriptive analytics**—answers questions like *why* and *what*. In this process, reporting tools (e.g., GPS, RFID and transaction bar codes) and online analytical processing tools (OLAP) and real-time information are used and supported to identify new challenges and opportunities. For the purpose of collection, description and analysis of raw data for historical events, descriptive statistics are used. They evaluate and represent events of the past and make them interpretable and comprehensible. Descriptive analytics allow an organization to gain knowledge from its past events and learn how variables are related and about their impact on future results. It can be used, for example, to elucidate average wealth, yearly sale changes and inventory stock. Descriptive analytics are also useful for the accounting, sales, transaction and production reports of an entire organization.
- **Predictive analysis**—this technology is used to give an explanation of what is occurring or is probable to occur by analyzing historic data patterns using programming, simulation and mathematical techniques. These approaches attempt to determine the causes of a phenomenon and event as well as to predict precisely what will happen and to fill in the nonexistent information and data. Statistical tools cannot be used for 100-percent-accurate predictions of the future. Predictive analytics are used to forecast consumer preferences and buying patterns in order to predict and identify the inclination in future sales. This technique is also used to forecast consumer requirements, operations and stock documents.
- **Prescriptive analysis**—discusses what needs to be done and how it can be affected. Prescriptive analytics guide alternatives using predictive and descriptive analytics, multicriteria problem solving, mathematical optimization or simulation techniques. The implementation of prescriptive analytics in practice is highly complicated, and most companies are still unwilling to use it in their regular tasks. The correct use of a prescription analytical approach can lead to effective and optimal decision-making. Many major corporations now use intelligent automation to optimize inventory and production. Some

of the key instances that prescriptive analytics enable companies to respond include:

a) What kind of offer should each end-user make?

b) What should be the shipping strategy for each major retailer?

c) Which commodity should be launched, and when?

10.3.1 Statistical Analysis

The research comprises essentially two forms of analyses: analytical and inferential. Historical records are operated in descriptive statistics to explain or outline the characteristic of a phenomenon using graphs or charts or numeric measurements. Inferential statistics are used to conclude the characteristics of concepts and to forecast their performance. The inconsistencies between descriptive and inferential studies are seen in Table 10.2. Both qualitative and quantitative approaches should be used to benefit from the methods and the best choices simultaneously. In the case of uncertainties, predictive analysis is used, for example in risk analysis, inventory and distribution. Statistical multivariate approaches are now used to track the supply chain to control material distribution efficiently and minimize the possibility of unexpected circumstances [20]. Because of the number, range, truthfulness and speed of BDA, the supply chain requires simple and robust research methods. Orthodox statistical approaches are not reactive anymore, since big data contribute to noise, variability etc. Proposing and introducing appropriate statistical

Table 10.2 Comparative Analysis of Descriptive and Inferential Statistics

Basis for comparison	Descriptive statistics	Inferential statistics
What it is used for	Organizing, analyzing and presenting data in meaningful way	Comparing, testing and predicting data
Form of final result	Charts, graphs and tables	Probability
Usage	To describe the current situation	To explain the chances of occurrence of an event
Function	It explains the data that are already known to summarize	It attempts to reach the conclusion to learn about the population that extends beyond the data availability

approaches are thus very critical, and this topic has recently gained great attention. For instance, a simultaneous statistical algorithm for an advanced statistical analysis of big data is presented in a study. This algorithm utilizes specific approaches such as normal least squares, gradient conjugation and Mann-Whitney U checking to model and compare the density and distributed squares of large data (Tiwari, Wee, Daryanto 2018).

10.3.2 Simulation

Industries require modelling techniques to enhance the process of product development and stimulate innovation, accelerate marketing activities, eliminate unnecessary costs and develop advancement. Simulation offers various proven sustenance for each and every phase of the design of the product and development process, such as the production of more quality products with improved productivity for the consumer and the creation of a better outcome for the them (Ranjan 2014). For instance, when consumer-goods giant Proctor & Gamble introduces new detergent liquids, predictive modelling and analytics are used to anticipate how moisture will evoke some scent particles such that the appropriate fragrances are set to release at the right moment during the washing-up process. Simulations and computational models must be used to develop the software of large-scale data, such as simulation-driven product design. The use of simulators to produce new products and services is identified as a challenge in today's competitive world, since manufacturing companies must constantly accelerate their operational excellence, predict customer preferences, require time-to-market products and meet expenses.

Modelling and simulation help developers conduct the "what if" analysis with a variety of device settings and complexities (Shao, Shin, Jain 2014). LLamasoft 2016 has established a simulation model to evaluate the vast data obtained from the backgrounds and shop floor setting of the modern production process. This paradigm strengthened the decision-making process in this manufacturing system. For instance, as a predictive method, simulation may allow firms to anticipate the need for equipment and support resources depending on customer-demand prediction and observations from several other past records such as time required, production and shipment performance. LLamasoft (Balaraj 2013) highlighted several instances about where the modelling of the distribution chain can be used as shown: forecasting the operation, checking the stock strategy, evaluating output competence, assessing efficiency of the resource and assessing the optimized outcome. SCA is implementing new approaches for the simulation issue with a huge data volume. Presently, there are many simulation tools that make it possible to test the efficiency of the protocol before it is developed. Enterprise dynamics (ED) is one of the best and most commonly used tools that practitioners and researchers employ to model SCM problems.

10.3.3 Optimization

The optimization method is an important technique for mining data in the supply chain (Slavakis, Giannakis, Mateos 2014). Optimization-based approaches may evaluate several goals, such as fulfilment of consumer demands and reduction in cost by the extraction of information and expertise from the massive amount of data produced by complex networks that have different variables or limitations such as routes and capability. Using supply-chain modelling strategies, multiuser teamwork, progress tracking and situation planning, companies can eventually accomplish their multiple targets. The use of optimization strategies helps to plan the supply chain while improving forecasting precision poses the big challenge of optimization (Wang, Gunasekaran, Ngai, Papadopoulos 2016). In order to analytically optimize, Panchmatia (2015) has used various computational learnings and signal-processing methods, key element analysis, subspace clustering, compressive sampling and dictionary learning. Souza (2014) discussed the possibilities of incorporating BDA in the SCM on the basis of the SCOR supply chain concept. The BDA is a vital part of the supply chain at organizational, operational and tactical levels. SCA is, for example, used in product development, networking and procurement at the strategic level. SCA can be used in manufacturing, supply planning, sourcing and stock at the tactical and operational stage, too.

10.4 Applications of BDA in SCM

A huge amount of data is produced in the manufacturing process through internal networks and external channels that consist of instrumentation or sensor networks on the shop floor. Big data is applied to enhance the evaluation and incorporation of these repositories; it will boost delivery and sales operation productivity and consistent operation and device tracking. Predictive techniques and big data are required for manufacturing companies to expand their manufacturing business. Predictive machinery servicing is an urgent industry primed for development in this area. The vast number of suppliers and the diversity of their appraisal and preference metrics make it impossible to identify the correct and appropriate provider for the distribution chain. The use of cloud technologies to choose vendors has a significant influence. With new device connectivity and data exposure, the intensity of APIs and convergence of advanced big data systems and analytics packages are more efficient and consumer oriented. A literature review reveals that BDA can be used in different SCM fields. A summary of BDA implementations in various fields of the supply chain is given in the following sections (Jin, Ji 2013).

10.4.1 BDA in Supplier Relationship Management

The management of supplier associations with each other includes regulations in strategic planning and the management of all contacts with suppliers in companies to mitigate the likelihood of loss and to amplify the importance of such collaborations.

Establishing close ties and growing coordination with the main suppliers is a significant factor in the development and discovery of new value and in reducing the possibility of SRM failure. The effectiveness of organizations that rely on partnership management and cooperation are strategic tools and SRM. Using BDA techniques, exact details can be given on corporate spending habits to better maintain relationships with suppliers (Wang, Gunasekaran, Ngai 2018). Big data will, for example, offer reliable data on investment returns (ROI) and an in-depth review of prospective suppliers. A research used the blurry synthetic assessment and analysis hierarchy (AHP) method to analyze and pick suppliers, considering the great ability of BDA as one of the aspects assessed (Prasad, Zakaria, Altay 2018). The goal is to pick out a supplier partner who can evolve from big data to the potential challenges.

10.4.2 BDA in Supply-Chain Network Design

The logistic network design is a business initiative that covers the acquisition of supply-chain suppliers and identifies organization strategies and initiatives to meet long-lasting planned goals. The supply-chain design initiative requires the grit of a physical structure of the logistic network that impacts most business divisions or functional areas of an organization. It is necessary to assess customer loyalty and supply-chain productivity in planning the supply-chain network. The objective of the supply-chain model is to create a web of participants capable of achieving the company's long-term strategic objectives. The following steps should be taken in the design of the supply chain: (1) define the long-lasting planned objectives; (2) state the complexity of the task; (3) decide on the type of analyses to be made; (4) define methods to be used and (5) ultimately complete the project with optimum design.

The organization can achieve a major competitive edge by choosing the best logistic network architecture and the necessary preparations. Afshari and Peng (2015) presented a nonlinear mixed-integer model for the delivery center using huge amounts of data in the model and generated random large datasets for the warehouse, consumer order and conveyance operations. They believed that the conduct data collection was analyzed using marketing analytics software. Their results suggest that BDA will provide all required details on the expense data of fines and the quality of service; hence, it is a very useful method for the dynamic architecture of delivery networks. Rfesearch explores the use of BDA in design initiatives such as supply-chain education, healthcare and disaster relief (Suh, Suh 2001). As humanitarian data has speed, precision, high volume and high diversity characteristics, these analytics can be implemented in the human-centered supply chain.

10.4.3 BDA in Product Development and Design

The important key issue of goods suppliers is that these goods adhere to the needs of their consumers. As tastes and prospects of consumers develop over the lifespan of the product, designers need tools to forecast and quantify those desires and expectations. In the product-design process, lack of adequate knowledge about consumer needs and desires is an important concern. If designers track customer behavior constantly and access to up-to-date consumer-choices information, they can create products that match consumer likings and desires. Constant consumer behavior analysis, product design and development processes have produced massive data and considered big data. The selection, management and application of new empirical approaches to obtain valuable knowledge and then apply it to judgements will minimize ambiguity (Mistree, Smith, Bras, Allen, Muster 1990). *Engineering design* is described as a process to turn consumer requirements into design requirements (Dym, Little 1999). Data science (DS) is characterized as a method for turning observable real-world data into understandable decision-making information (Martin, Ishii 2002).

While different approaches to product design are available (Labbi, Ouzizi, Douimi 2015; Khan, Christopher, Creazza 2012), all these strategies are popular for DS. Figure 10.2 provides a graphical view of the construction process. Big data can influence multiple sectors, and the design of goods is no different. This is partially because engineers are gradually converting their goods into sensors and networking technologies. Therefore, the product specificities of the business must be taken into account in the supply-chain planning process, and all stakeholders and supply-network restrictions have to be incorporated at design stage (Jin, Liu, Ji, Liu 2016). The commodity architecture of the supply chain offers a comparative edge and stability in the supply chain (Johanson, Belenki, Jalminger, Fant, Gjertz 2014). BDA methods for product design and production have recently been used to generate new products according to consumer tastes. The use of BDA in product design makes it possible for the manufacturer to be continuously aware of consumer needs and demands that contribute to the production of a product according to their specifications and preferences (Mistree, Smith, Bras, Allen, Muster 1990). Creators may use their online actions and buy data from consumers to forecast and appreciate consumer requirements (Shapiro 2005). The designers can define product characteristics and forecast potential product patterns by constant consumer-behavior analysis and information on the views and requirements of customers. The value of big data is extracted in the automotive industry from the automobile that has massive performance data and consumer requirements (Li, Thomas, Osei-Bryson 2016). The overall goal of industries that manufacture market profitability is to stay sustainable for as long as possible (Baraka 2014). This now enables the application of the (runtime) data-driven design concept. A new way to produce

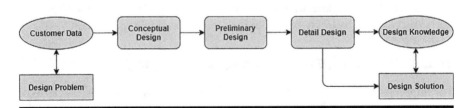

Figure 10.2 Design Process.

information for quality improvement and the accomplishment of their targets has been enabled by recent data-collection advances and use of data-analytics tools (Andrienko, Andrienko 2006). Product creators should, as one doctrine, better their goods and services indefinitely based on the use of real-life, function and failure results. While a significant number of data-analytical (software) methods and packages have been created to collect data relevant to products, data analytics and product enhancement tools are still being exploited prematurely (Chase 2013). Designers are also faced with many problems and many limits. Reportedly, it is not trivial for designers to select the most appropriate data analytics tools (DATs) and to use them in design engineering (Feng, Shanthikumar 2018).

Design engineering also has several other factors that can evolve as a consequence of big data:

- Informed product manufacturing: how can companies improve product-design strategies if they have no knowledge about how consumers use them but where they are posing challenges and what characteristics they ignore? This detail will be accessible to organizations shortly. Mechanical engineers have the chance to gain goods that have never before been feasible. With a computer integrated with technologies like the Internet of Things (IoT), products will pour data to engineers. Think of a fork capturing a utility cabinet or a force measurement conveying internal temperature readings.
- Stimulated engineering: in the tradition of creating competitive products, engineers depend on advertisers, consumer visits or their own guesses. However, big data could have accurate input volumes not provided by either of these networks. Items collect a lot of knowledge over their life cycles, and emerging trends for the IoT would provide producers much more information. A large volume of data is obtained and can be turned into consumable information properties from smart devices. Since products can speak to engineers, engineers can have a significant effect on the competitiveness of their products, as never before.
- Quicker product development: the more cloud-based data, the faster (and cheaper) knowledge can be secured relative to operating on company networks and individual systems. This will contribute to the early inclusion of more individuals and fields in the development cycle of product. The cloud computing architecture would allow for new approaches to the parallel device engineering and CAD (Computer-Aided Design) design concepts integrating software, electronics and mechanics in product creation.

In the end, the engineers will face many surprises and a few unexpected shocks as all these diverse disciplines are interconnected in obtaining big data and product design during distinct phases of the development process. The real goal is to overcome these minute challenges and create better products for a different stage in the overall product design.

10.4.4 BDA and Procurement Management

Procurement essentially includes investment and contractual processes. Big companies require sophisticated IT structures to handle their vast amounts of company data and facilitate their growth. In the past, companies spent much time documenting and disclosing their events. Companies now obtain vast volumes of data, whether internal information or information of some other organizations in real time. The SCA can efficiently control supplier output and supply-chain risk. In addition, databases are used to offer more productivity to the supply chain. Influencing the news on exchange-rate movement and phenomenon impacts supply chain. We should extend this method for handling supply-chain risks and risk-decision support and emergency readiness. Schlegel used massive data analytics in order to control risks in the supply chain.

10.4.5 BDA in Product Customization

Companies are expected obtain relevant knowledge and recognize trends with BDA, which will help them develop processes and make goods.

The supply chains and whole distribution process require full details in fine-grained in order to simplify the supply chain. By using this technique, suppliers can assess how well their supply chains operate successfully and decrease the risks. This is something productive that make businesses able to recognize bottlenecks in goods-and-services development. There has been a demand for personalized goods, so businesses have gone into mass manufacturing to feed this desire. There has been some investigation on BDA's application in the production market. In 2010, Zhong et al. applied RFID and big data to help logistic chain position supervision. He then applied the idea of using wireless technologies, IoT, RFID, and the concept of BDA to construct an intelligent shop-floor environment. Stich et al. also determined BDA methodology for forecasting need and output trends in manufacturing. Conversely, in the 1980s, early additive manufacturing was developed. New information technology and developments are shifting the supply-chain management constraints. 3D printing is an advanced technique that enables engineers to construct a tangible structure from a computer-assisted template. Considering the applications and consequences of predictive analytics and big data is needed because additive manufacturing (AM) is going to make conventional models obsolete.

10.4.6 BDA in Demand Planning

Several supply-chain officials are involved in using big data in market forecasts and short-term output planning. The effective demand forecasting has always been challenging in SCM. Market-purchase statistics can be calculated by the Broad-based Black Economic Empowerment Act. The biggest challenge these organizations face is the capacity to use modern technologies and computing architecture. The Broad-based Black Economic Empowerment Act, of course, helps people to consider consumer dynamics and identify root causes of issues. Data analytics can be used to forecast consumers' tastes and trends, which could then encourage and fuel market innovation. A model was used to forecast potential demand for electric vehicles based on weather and historical dynamics of real-world traffic. Thus, planners will schedule the charge by forecasting the market. Another research provides a blueprint for forecasting passenger demand for air passengers. Our findings suggest a prediction error of 5.3% (Levelling, Edelbrock, Otto 2014).

10.4.7 BDA in Inventory Administration

Stock management is the procedure of handling actual the material and facilities of the organization. One of the goals used in the inventory-management design is described in the following list:

- Inform the object specifics, amount and point of order.
- Make it easy for company owners to file trademarks.
- Automate quality management as part of controlled inventory.
- Minimize stock by analyzing the prior buying and usage habits of the company.
- Use the assistance of digital equipment for this mode of action to take place.
- Improve the inventory audit procedures as they are more successful.

Over the past decade, big data technology has significantly increased business performance. The following are some of the advantages of BDA in supply chains and some of the ways in which businesses are using the data surrounding big data to handle their physical inventories.

There are different ways big data monitor the inventory.

- To increase operating performance there is constant tracking and review of service results, thus eliminating bottlenecks and improving the efficiency of operations. BDA advantages will enhance the efficiency and quality of the entire supply chain.
- Managers will constantly track and analyze these real-time data to pinpoint and maximize the profit margins of their investment.
- These real-time data and access to these data will help maximize supply chain and consumer buying, which will boost customer loyalty. There are also a wide range of predictive approaches including studies to estimate consumer sales and product preparation at various periods.
- Companies should make the transition from on-premises to cloud systems since SaaS tech bundles. This capability can be used seamlessly with other current technologies.

There are only two publication from Perish research in the field of BDA. BDA allows companies to make greater use of recent technologies in order to achieve a competitive edge. Big data would be a critical aspect of the integrated inventory-control systems. Data-mining approaches can also be utilized for data analysis and to uncover and isolate essential relationships.

10.4.8 BDA and Logistics

With the increased production of vast quantities of devices and data, pollution issues, dynamic monitoring acts, evolving manufacturing models, talent constraints, infrastructure and the emergence of digital technologies, the logistics sector has undergone a profound transition. In this industry, it is important to standardize the structure and content of data exchanges to improve the connectivity and cooperation between various sectors such as shippers, businesses, logistics institutions, retailers and distributors in order to promote the development of new mutual enterprise processes. However, cost control by minimizing unnecessary and ongoing inventory, proactively adapting to incoming and outgoing incidents and exchanging assets in the new supply-chain climate have become important.

Today effective technologies are required for timely and quick research and real-time understanding to make reliable and timely decisions because of the huge amount of data produced from various sources such as RFID tags, scanners, sensors and GPS along with the convergence of market evaluation and the fusion of multiple data sources. With such a vast stream of data, large data sets and analytical approaches are needed for their administration and management. As high quantities of data, for instance, scale, destination, origin and weight, for huge numbers of consignments are produced daily, there exists tremendous competence for new industry development and improving consumer experience and operating efficiency. Companies have to use data systems and data-analytical techniques to get insight into businesses that are not fast, and for organizations it is a new issue. Infosys offers are planned to improve the vision of logistics organizations through a three-way strategy:

■ Limitless information: the customer, logistics and suppliers from the logistics industry have formed a strategic partnership, and logistic technology such as IoT devices, supply-chain execution systems, transport management systems (TMS) and warehouse management solutions (WMS) are used to exchange and reach all participants with the vast range of information provided by the industry. In the supply chain, a platform maintains and incorporates a large array of data derived by numerous internal and external systems and offers the necessary confirmation and management for enhancing the data's confidence and supplying business customers with the right data for self-service insight and analysis generation.

- Widespread analysis: an adaptive and open architecture is essential for smoothly incorporating and successfully applying the multiple insights of an enterprise.
- The rapid transition in industries and the advent of innovative data collection and measurement technology as well as the "boundaryless" model contribute to organizations abandoning conventional BI analytical approaches and governance systems and employing modern and emerging technologies. Organizations will become knowledge-based, leveraging a versatile horizontal framework and tools that are consistent with the corresponding protection, next-generation data sets and business semantics.

Many academic reports have highlighted the use of big data in the transport and supply-chain sectors. These analytics were employed to achieve comparative benefitss and offer new logistics services (Brouer, Karsten, Pisinger 2016). Maritime firms have also used analytical and prescriptive analytics to address their challenges in planning (Mehmood, Graham 2015). In one more report, they used large-scale data to share transport resources to increase the quality of urban healthcare (Lee 2004). It is clear that big data analytics will help all operations and processes of the supply chain and build agile supply chains.

10.4.9 BDA and Agile Supply Chains

Supply chains are generated by the most competitive organizations and will adapt to unpredictable market changes (Choi, Wallace, Wang 2018). Wamba, Gunasekaran, Dubey, et al. (2018) suggested that BDA provides an important influence on the activities of operations management. Gunasekaran et al. concluded that logistic network disturbances had detrimental consequences, and agile supply-chain vendors were increasingly used to deliver better competitive outcomes through big data and market analytics (Gunasekaran, Yusuf, Adeleye, Papadopoulos 2018; Srinivasan, Swink 2018). Swafford, Ghosh and Murthy (2008) further suggested that, while big data has made use of analytic technologies for organizational decisions of the supply chain to consider consumer intentions/behavior, it is not yet understood desirably. Gunasekaran et al. (Gunasekaran, Yusuf, Adeleye, Papadopoulos 2018) and Srinivasan and Swink (2018) suggest that predictive analytics and big data have beneficial consequences for the success of the organizational output and supply chain (Srinivasan, Swink 2018; Swafford, Ghosh, Murthy 2018). Swafford et al. suggested that SCA has a beneficial impact on IT capability (Gunasekaran, Yusuf, Adeleye, Papadopoulos 2017). Authors in Ghosh, Murthy (2008) also noted that the exposure of the supply network is a requirement for data analysis and vice versa. The usability of the BDA and the supply chain are compatible in that both technologies assist one another (Gunasekaran, Yusuf, Adeleye, Papadopoulos 2017; Srinivasan, Swink 2018). Visibility of the logistic network is a preferred operational power to reduce the possibility of delays in the supply chain (Giannakis, Louis 2016). Ghosh and Murthy (2008) claim that visibility chain developing companies are expected to be empowered by investing in BDA. Dubey et al. stated a constructive effect on the prospects of the supply chain on the SCA (Dubey, Altay, Gunasekaran, Blome, Papadopoulos, Childe 2018). Based on available data, companies can specifically forecast market trends to make this information more responsive, agile and effective.

Many other experiments have been carried out to research big data analytics promoting advanced agility in the supply chain (Bertsimas, Kallus, Hussain 2016). There has been extensive use of several processes and parts of BDA applications in the supply chain, but publications that talk about data analysis applications for the supply chain continue to be minimal. Many components and procedures have been extensively utilized in the supply-chain BDA, but publications involving data processing applications in strategic procurement and material management remain small. Professionals involved in this field must be capable of thinking according to the big data obtained and utilizing it in decision-making and planning, which is considered to be the big challenge. Big data SCA facilitate to improve decisiveness associating the approach of the company with procurement strategies and offering accurate views (Wang, Gunasekaran, Ngai, Papadopoulos 2016). In addition, BDA enhances inventory judgment by enhancing the perception of unpredictable consumer requirement (Brockhaus, Kersten, Knemeyer 2013).

10.4.10 BDA and Sustainable Supply Chain

Even though sustainable SCM has been debated for some time in industries, it has been difficult to actually enforce the phenomenon of sustainability in the extended supply chain (McWilliams, Siegel 2011). However, major companies see environmental initiatives as long-term investments for strategic capital building (Jelinek, Bergey 2013). Increasingly, corporations are involved in making use of BDA in their environmental initiatives, which offers them a competitive edge (Manyika, Sinclair, Dobbs, Strube, Rassey, Mischke 2012). According to a survey study from Mckinsey, 65% of customers who make repeat buys by shop alarms are able to anticipate BDA companies, and 75% of such consumers indicated that they probably opt to use the service again (Hazen, Skipper, Ezell, Boone 2016).

Many researchers consider sustainable development in business BDA implementations (social, environmental and financial) a budding field (Hsu 2013; Davenport 2006). BDA methods can then be employed across the logistic network in order to obtain maximum profits (Hsu 2014). As the decision-making process in organizations is focused on data, businesses must adjust their strategic capacities, which impact profitability. Since sustainability and BDA are increasing in value, these two fields must be combined by companies to gain a preservable competitive advantage (Davenport 2006; Keeso 2014). In spite of the immediate demand for data analyses to be combined with environmental management policies and supply-chain measures, there has been no progress so far (Garetti, Taisch 2012). Few researchers have discussed the topic of BDA and sustainability to achieve competitive and strategic benefits (Davenport 2006; Keeso 2014). In order to accomplish the three-dimensional natural, economic and social sustainability (Belaud, Negny, Dupros, Michéa, Vautrin 2014), today's organizations must use methodologies to evaluate vast quantities of data to obtain insights and information.

Many experiments have used large-scale data mining to mitigate and minimize the impacts of these environmental hazards (Bettencourt-Silva, Clark, Cooper, Mills, Rayward-Smith, De La Iglesia 2015) and forecast natural disasters. Huge data also was captured in satellite imagery, weather radar and terrestrial tracking systems for glaciers melting, forestation and extreme weather. These data were used to research changes in global climate thoroughly and assign clear causalities (Ranjan 2014). BDA is being utilized for the welfare and health of the population. For instance, in Europe and the USA, BDA has been used to recognize and forecast prostate cancer biomarkers for the proper timing of preventive action (Halamka 2014; Baek, Park 2015). Various other researchers used policy-based BDA to facilitate and strengthen sustainable development initiatives in separate operations. For example, to safeguard the environment and implement sustainability initiatives, computing platforms are employed to capture and exchange environmental data and use them, among other uses, for the government-led publication of risk reduction and to study medical records (Dubey, Gunasekaran, Childe, Wamba, Papadopoulos 2016). Literature on the BDA application to the sustainability of the supply chain was, however, much less discussed. Scholars thus understand the need for more study in this area ((Manyika, Sinclair, Dobbs, Strube, Rassey, Mischke 2012; Hsu 2013; Shen, Chan 2017; Nedelcu 2013). Furthermore, the possible threats disrupting processes must be defined and expected for the sustainable supply chain. The writers review the literature on the supply-chain risk assessment in the next section.

10.5 BDA Application in Diverse Areas of the Supply Chain

BDA activities have been widely published in recent years. One of the key reasons the data should be used to maximize efficiency is to include "fruitful and accurate information for the right user at the right time." This section gives a summary of BDA applications in various industries, including engineering, finance and medical services.

10.5.1 Applications of BDA in Manufacturing

While big data is relevant in the world today, many companies underestimate the significance of the use of massive data for their business results. BDA methods should be used correctly to monitor, assess and exchange employee success measurements. BDA methods are often used to classify workers with bad or good results and to identify difficult or dissatisfied employees. These strategies allow companies to continually track and analyze data in real time instead of only annual research focused on human memory. In today's world, innovative data-processing tools have to be exploited in the automotive sector in order to achieve comparative advantages and boost competitiveness in design, production, distribution and prompt product supply. In 2010 the packaging sector deposited nearly 2 exabytes of new data (Nedelcu 2013). Because different digital machines, electronic devices and sensors are employed in production lines and factories, a massive quantity of data is produced. These analytics can also be applied to construct a smart logistic framework for the shop floor in factories (Stich, Jordan, Birkmeier, Oflazgil, Reschke, Diews 2015; Zhong, Xu, Chen, Huang 2017). The design and production engineering method often produces a vast amount of data in the form of computer-aided engineering and computer-aided manufacturing models, process performances, CAD, product malfunction data, internet transaction etc. BDA tools can also be used to detect defects, quality of product and enhance product production operations (Wang, Alexander 2015).

Techniques in data mining can also be applied to forecast consumer requests and choices. One of the most renowned manufacturing companies, Raytheon Corp, built smart factories by providing strong capability to handle enormous data from a wide range of locations, involving equipment, CAD modelling, sensors, digital records, internet transactions and simulations that allow the organization to manage multiple development operations in real time (Noor 2013). Through continuous analysis and tracking of large amounts of data gathered from different sensors in produced goods, including in the jet engines, GE (General Electric) case, medical imagers, locomotives and gas turbines, GE establishes creative and effective servicing strategies (Davenport 2013). The German truck trailer and body manufacturer Schmitz Cargobull employs sensor data, BDA and telecommunications to examine freight temperatures and weight, roads, and trailer preservation to reduce their failure (Chick, Netessine, Huchzermeier 2014). The famous Toyota Connected was launched by Toyota Motor Corporation as its Big Data Business Unit to extensively enhance its data-processing capability. In addition, Toyota uses large-scale vehicle data obtained from the linked car network to generate new services and business such as security services, as well as accessibility services, traffic intelligence services and concept feedback (Toyota Motor Corporation 2016). BDA incorporation of production system architecture can be converted over a long period of time from a descriptive system model to a predictive output model using what-if analysis, simulation and cause-effect model (Cochran, Kinard, Bi 2016).

10.5.2 Applications of BDA in Finance

Maintenance of competitive edge and improving performance are two critical priorities for financial institutions. Such organizations must use BDA and effective computational tools in their market plans constantly to gain a feasible competitive edge and remain robust in industry. Big data and predictive methods have advanced significantly in recent years, and a lot of money has been made in them. Big data and predictive information and expertise are collected from banks and financial services companies, which can be used for constant in-house analysis of customer behavior in real time, anticipating consumer demands and preferences and delivering the appropriate services and resources for consumer requirements. Based on the outcomes of this concurrent data collection and assessment, it boosts total profitability and efficiency. Following the 2008 global financial crisis, big data and predictive technologies had to be used by financial firms to achieve strategic advantages [2]. Big data and computational tools are very important and necessary in most financial organizations such as insurance firms, wealth management, the stock market and the banks due to the great volume of finance transactions and activities. Organizations must be capable of handling the immense data and deriving the information or ideas found in the collected data and then including those in their market and decision-making processes. Bean estimated that 70% of the world's finance service company claimed that BDA was relevant, and 63% applied broad data in their administration (Bean 2016). According to Technavio, the expense of big data technology will rise 26% from 2015 to 2019, indicating the value of big data in this industry in the global financial sector (Technavio 2015). Through continued surveillance of customer behavior and data processing, BDA strategies offer valuable insights that strengthen consumer intelligence, such as consumer risk analysis, customer retention and client centricity. All financial-service transactions and operations, including anticipating and developing new goods and services, algorithmic analysis and trading, algorithmic exchange and analytics and business intelligence (for example employee collaboration) are protected by BDA. In addition, such analytics are also used to facilitate risk assessment and monitoring activities (Connors, Courbe, Waishampayan 2013). The chief financial officer (CFO) should use computational methods to evaluate and derive facts and observations from broad data and then use experience and information in the decision-making process. Consequently, a market research and intelligence platform should be used by the chief financial officer (CFO) to increase data precision, make smarter decisions and have greater value (Chen, Chiang, Storey 2012). Techniques used to measure stock volatility and quantify VPIN can also be used in financial markets (Wu, Bethel, Gu, Leinweber, Rübel 2013). Real-time decision-making and quantitative models can be used by financial firms to achieve a strategic edge on volatile financial markets (Peat 2013). The Barclays Financial Corporation uses big data extensively to sustain its activities and to build and retain its core strategic edge. BDA is used in numerous areas including financial crime, treasury, risk, finance and intelligence (Barclays 2015). The Deutsche Bank has also introduced big data to its clients. Deutsche Bank has established a data laboratory that facilitates other divisional and company functions with internal results, research consulting, business testing concepts and technical support (Bank 2014).

10.5.3 BDA Applications in Healthcare

In the health sector, a significant quantity of data is generated to regulate and manage the different care, safeguarding and maintaining procedures and regulatory standards and enforcement of patients. Big data in healthcare is important because of diverse forms of data, electronic health records including omics, sensors and imaging and text that are nuanced, high-dimensional, heterogeneous, poorly annotated and largely unstructured that have arisen in modern biomedicine. New and powerful methods are needed to process and interpret these data rapidly. In the insurance sector, "big data" contains all data about well-being and patient health. The US Congress report in August 2012 described *big data* as "large volumes of high-speed, complex, and variable data requiring advanced technologies that enable information to be recorded, stored, distributed, administered and analysed." BDA in healthcare include few broad features such as heterogeneity, variety, high-dimensionality, speed, generation and the like. Medical healthcare system use of computational methods includes vision identification, lesion detection, voice acceptance, facial recognition etc. Established computational methods can be used with huge quantities of patient-related clinical and medical records, currently unanalyzed, to achieve a better interpretation of findings that can then be used at the time of treatment. An immense diversity of healthcare data from personal medical records to radiology photographs, research instruments and patient's data is currently under development, and human heredities need comprehensive, modern protection and management systems. BDA lowers healthcare expenditure as well as increases healthcare systems' precision, efficiency, consistency and performance. Bort posted on influenza battling on the basis of the flu data almost instantly (Bort 2012). Several other Big Data projects were conducted to track the use of inhalers and lower the risk of cancer and asthma attacks (Nambiar, Bhardwaj, Sethi, Vargheese 2013). Big data also aid health insurers in detecting fraud and anomaly in the argument that the common transaction management system can hardly detect (Srinivasan, Arunasalam 2013). BDA comprises many healthcare principles, good care, proper life, fine creativity, the right supplier and the right value (Groves, Kayyali, Knott, Kuiken 2013). Big data will be seen in the future as a new use of massive data for population wellbeing and preventive care (Nambiar, Bhardwaj, Sethi, Vargheese 2013). While it's possible to use vast volumes of data in healthcare, there are many obstacles, such as enhancing the already-available platform to support the easy-to-use kit, data collection, menu drives and further real time. Other issues include data acquisition consistency, ownership, structured data and data cleaning in the healthcare sector (Raghupathi, Raghupathi 2014).

10.6 BDA in the Supply Chain

BDA develops various potential across the logistic network that increases data precision, analysis and transparency for networks and also generates better econtextual knowledge throughout the supply chains. Big data is a valuable method to address supply-chain challenges and push supply chains forward. For instance, BDA strategies have been used to analyze consumer behavior in retail supply chains by correctly projecting consumers' tastes and expectations. In order to thrive in today's dynamic environments, supply-chain decision-makers must constantly search for opportunities to leverage and handle data sources efficiently to achieve more value and driven edge. The appropriate and powerful use of big data methods and sources has contributed to major advances in supply-chain processes:

▪ To develop flexible or responsive supply chains by forecasting consumer dynamics and consumer needs and tastes and acquiring a deeper understanding. BDA will promote the real-time tracking and management of data to improve supply-chain decision speed, efficiency, precision and versatility. Using a wide variety of direct data feeds, news, social networks, weather and event data from various constant and complex data sources, it is possible to proactively forecast and schedule all supply-chain activities.

▪ Develop secure, smart supply chains through deep learning, IoT and profound learning strategies in each operation involved in supply chain. For starters, by tracking the supply chain in real time, IoT may be applied in production processes in order to deliver real-time telemetry data to reveal specifics. Machine learning algorithms equipped to interpret the knowledge will reliably foresee inevitable faults in the machine. Deep learning methods may also be used to forecast the desires and expectations of consumers reliably.

▪ Funding for environmental growth in SCM. BDA will certainly improve initiatives to improve social, environmental and financial results. Detailed preparation for timely distribution of the goods can be achieved, for instance, by the study of GPS real-time traffic data, which decreases greenhouse dioxide production and the expenditure on fuel utilization.

▪ Allow worldwide supply chains to take proactive steps toward supply-chain risk rather than reactive ones (e.g., loss of supply by natural disasters or engineered, contextual or organizational distractions). In a dynamic global supply chain, analytical strategies can assist logistic network management to respond and predict proactively in contradiction to external future incidents.

Nowadays, BDA is also used extensively in the supply-chain domain. For example, POS data provide real-time demand information with pricing information. It offers the indication for refilling, such as the inventory method operated by the seller. Sensor information comprises an automated refill indicator, automatic storage and receipt information and also contains automated checkout information that informs inventory status in real time. Data from suppliers provide valuable details on suppliers and purchasing procedures that can aid in supply risk control and improved communication with various stages in the supply process. Manufacturing data collected from sensors provide real-time tracking of production devices and recognise various unavoidable issues. The real-time position of the supplied inventory during the distribution period, helping find optimum path and decreasing the stock lead times and gear up the performance optimization (Row, Pournader 2017). In spite of the possible utilization of massive amounts of data, multiple logistic networks cannot use the ability of BDA technologies to produce valuable information and observations for their companies into available data. The underlying factors are the absence of sufficient methods for large data processing, which contribute to a substantial decrease in costs (Rowe, Pournader 2017). Another important aspect that considered to be essential is the efforts to enhance the potential of BDA in supply-chain management (Tiwari, Wee, Daryanto 2018).

10.7 Conclusion

In several fields such as SCM, BDA has become an important functional problem. There are several areas where effective analytical methods can be improved in this field. As mentioned in previous literature (Wang, Gunasekaran, Ngai, Papadopoulos 2016; Souza 2014; Trkman, McCormack, De Oliveira, Ladeira 2010), SCM has a number of techniques and simple applications (e.g., analytical, prescriptive). This aim of this chapter is to explain the most relevant and contemporary implementations of various BDAs within the supply chain and also to identify certain strategies that are crucial for managers in SCM. BDA has significant supply-chain implementations from one end to the other. BDA has various essential uses in the supply chain. This is applied, for example, in multiple SCM sectors, including sales-department demand data, manufacturer data, distribution data, production data and before-supplier data. BDA also conducts and facilitates product creation, supplier relationship management, growth, consumer-requirement forecasting, manufacturing, inventory, network design, sourcing and efficient and/or viable supply-chain operations. BDA can handle and coordinate a wide variety of data in a dynamic global supply chain. Several studies have employed diverse BDA approaches in various sectors like health, financing/banking and manufacturing. BDA strategies can also be used for other sectors including restaurants, technology, electricity and other services. Different BDA strategies are applied, based on the circumstances and strategic criteria of the organizations. The company's history, politics, climate and executive team are very important decision-making considerations, since the main obstacles for many of today's supply chains are ample tools with analytical capability. In the decision-making processes and operations, the supply chain must create continuous and strong relations among data experts and their business operations as well as apply suitable BDA approaches to address questions as to how data will enhance the performance of the supply chain. Mutual cooperation and communication among diverse supply-chain units therefore must be developed, BDA techniques used to associate them and the data and knowledge exchanged and accessed across the supply chain should be accessible.

References

Addo-Tenkorang R, Helo PT. Big data applications in operations/supplychain management: A literature review. *Computers and Industrial Engineering*. 2016; 101:528–543.

Afshari H, Peng Q. Using big data to minimize uncertainty effects in adaptable product design. In: *ASME 2015 International Design Engineering Technical Conferences and Computers and Information in Engineering Conference*. Boston, MA: American Society of Mechanical Engineers; 2015, pp. V004T05A052-V004T05A052.

Akter S, Wamba SF, GunAsekaran A, Dubey R, Childe SJ. How to improve firm performance using big data analytics capability and business strategy alignment? *International Journal of Production Economics*. 2016; 182:113–131.

Andrienko N, Andrienko G. Exploratory analysis of spatial and temporal data: A systematic approach. *Springer Science & Business Media*; 28 Mar 2006.

Baek H, Park SK. Sustainable development plan for Korea through expansion of green IT: Policy issues for the effective utilization of big data. *Sustainability*. 2015; 7(2):1308–1328.

Balaraj S. Optimization model for improving supply chain visibility. *Infosys Labs Briefings*. 2013; 11(1):9–19.

Bank D. Big Data: How it can become a differentiator. *Deutsche Bank White Paper. Interactive*; 2014. Available from: www.cib.db.com/insightsand-initiatives/flow/35187.htm

Baraka Z. *Opportunities to Manage Big Data Efficiently and Effectively* (Doctoral dissertation). Dublin Business School; 2014.

Barclays. *Big Data: Getting to Grips with a Rapidly Changing Landscape*; 2015. Available from: www.barclayscorporate.com/content/dam/corppublic/corporate/Documents/insight/BigData-report.pdf

Bean R. Just using big data isn't enough anymore. *Harvard Business Review*. 2016; 2:2016.

Belaud JP, Negny S, Dupros F, Michéa D, Vautrin B. Collaborative simulation and scientific big data analysis: Illustration for sustainability in natural hazards management and chemical process engineering. *Computers in Industry*. 2014; 65(3):521–535.

Bertsimas D, Kallus N, Hussain A. Inventory management in the era of big data. *Production and Operations Management*. 2016; 25(12):2006–2009.

Bettencourt-Silva JH, Clark J, Cooper CS, Mills R, Rayward-Smith VJ, De La Iglesia B. Building data-driven pathways from routinely collected hospital data: A case study on prostate cancer. *JMIR Medical Informatics*. 2015; 3(3):e26.

Bort J. *How the CDC is Using Big Data to Save You from the Flu*. Available from: www.businessinsider.com/the-cdc-is-using-big data-to-combatflu-2012-12

Brockhaus S, Kersten W, Knemeyer AM. Where do we go from here? Progressing sustainability implementation efforts across supply chains. *Journal of Business Logistics*. 2013; 34(2):167–182.

Brouer BD, Karsten CV, Pisinger D. Big data optimization in maritime logistics. In: *Big Data Optimization: Recent Developments and Challenges*. Cham: Springer; 2016, pp. 319–344.

Chase CW Jr. Using big data to enhance demand-driven forecasting and planning. *The Journal of Business Forecasting*. 2013; 32(2):27.

Chen H, Chiang RH, Storey VC. Business intelligence and analytics: From big data to big impact. *MIS Quarterly*. 2012; 36(4).

Chick S, Netessine S, Huchzermeier A. *When Big Data Meets Manufacturing*. France: Insead Knowledge; 2014.

Choi TM, Wallace SW, Wang Y. Big data analytics in operations management. *Production and Operations Management*. 2018; 27(10):1868–1883.

Cochran DS, Kinard D, Bi Z. Manufacturing system design meets big data analytics for continuous improvement. *Procedia CIRP*. 2016; 50:647–652.

Connors S, Courbe J, Waishampayan V. Where have you been all my life? How the financial services industry can unlock the value in Big Data. *PwC Financial Services Viewpoint*; 2013.

Davenport TH. Competing on analytics. *Harvard Business Review*. 2006; 84(1):98.

Davenport TH. The future of the manufacturing workforce. *Report One: Technology and the Manufacturing Workforce: An Overview*. Milwaukee; 2013.

Dubey R, Altay N, GunAsekaran A, Blome C, Papadopoulos T, Childe SJ. Supply chain agility, adaptability and alignment: Empirical evidence from the Indian auto components industry. *International Journal of Operations & Production Management*. 2018; 38(1):129–148.

Dubey R, Gunasekaran A, Childe SJ, Wamba SF, Papadopoulos T. The impact of big data on world-class sustainable manufacturing. *The International Journal of Advanced Manufacturing Technology*. 2016; 84(1–4):631–645.

Dym CL, Little P. *Engineering Design: A Project-Based Introduction*. John Wiley and Sons; 1999.

Feng Q, Shanthikumar JG. How research in production and operations management may evolve in the era of big data. *Production and Operations Management*. 2018; 27(9):1670–1684.

Garetti M, Taisch M. Sustainable manufacturing: Trends and research challenges. *Production Planning and Control*. 2012; 23(2–3):83–104.

Giannakis M, Louis M. A multiagent based system with big data processing for enhanced supply chain agility. *Journal of Enterprise Information Management*. 2016; 29(5):706–727.

Groves P, Kayyali B, Knott D, Kuiken SV. The 'Big Data' Revolution in Healthcare: Accelerating Value and Innovation. 2013.

Gunasekaran A, Yusuf YY, Adeleye EO, Papadopoulos T. Agile manufacturing practices: The role of big data and business analytics with multiple case studies. *International Journal of Production Research*. 2017; 56(1–2):385–397.

Gupta S, Altay N, Luo Z. Big data in humanitarian supply chain management: A review and further research directions. *Annals of Operations Research*. 2017:1–21.

Halamka JD. Early experiences with big data at an academic medical center. *Health Affairs*. 2014; 33(7):1132–1138.

Hazen BT, Skipper JB, Ezell JD, Boone CA. Big data and predictive analytics for supply chain sustainability: A theory-driven research agenda. *Computers and Industrial Engineering*. 2016; 101:592–598.

Hsu J. *Big Business, Big Data, Big Sustainability*. Carbontrust.com; Oct 2013.

Hsu J. Why big data will have an impact on sustainability. *The Guardian*; 2014. <www.theguardian.com/sustainable-business/big dataimpact-sustainable-business> [Accessed: 31 January 2014].

Jelinek M, Bergey P. Innovation as the strategic driver of sustainability: Big data knowledge for profit and survival. *IEEE Engineering Management Review*. 2013; 41(2):14–22.

Jin J, Liu Y, Ji P, Liu H. Understanding big consumer opinion data for market-driven product design. *International Journal of Production Research*. 2016; 54(10):3019–3041.

Jin Y, Ji S. Partner choice of supply chain based on 3d printing and big data. *Information Technology Journal*. 2013; 12(22):6822.

Johanson M, Belenki S, Jalminger J, Fant M, Gjertz M. Big automotive data: Leveraging large volumes of data for knowledge-driven product development. In: *2014 IEEE International Conference on Big Data (Big Data)*. Washington, DC: IEEE; 2014, pp. 736–741.

Kaisler S, Armour F, Espinosa JA, Money W. Big data: Issues and challenges moving forward. In: *2013 46th Hawaii International Conference on System Sciences*. Maui, HI: IEEE; 7 Jan 2013, pp. 995–1004.

Keeso A. Big data and environmental sustainability: A conversation starter. *Smith School of Enterprise and the Environment. Working Paper Series, Working Paper 14–04*; Dec 2014, https://alankeeso.medium.com/big-data-and-environmental-sustainability-a-conversation-starter-in-brief-4052d0b2f0ae

Khan O, Christopher M, Creazza A. Aligning product design with the supply chain: A case study. *Supply Chain Management: An International Journal*. 2012; 17(3):323–336.

Labbi O, Ouzizi L, Douimi M. Simultaneous design of a product and its supply chain integrating reverse logistic operations: An optimization model. *Xème Conférence Internationale: Conception et Production Intégrées*; 2015. Available from: https://www.semanticscholar.org/paper/Simultaneous-design-of-a-product-and-its-supply-%3A-Labbi-Ouzizi/32cae0ee9ced1baa30368eaa95668ff032a0a65a

Lee HL. The triple-a supply chain. *Harvard Business Review*. 2004; 82(10):102–113.

Levelling J, Edelbrock M, Otto B. Big data analytics for supply chain management. In: *2014 IEEE International Conference on Industrial Engineering and Engineering Management*. Selangor, Malaysia: IEEE; 9 Dec 2014, pp. 918–922.

Li Y, Thomas MA, Osei- Bryson KM. A snail shell process model for knowledge discovery via data analytics. *Decision Support Systems*. 2016; 91:1–2.

LLamasoft. Supply chain simulation: why its time has come. *LLamasoft White Paper*; 14 Aug 2016. Available from: www.llamasoft.com/supplychain-simulation-time-come-whitepaper/

Manyika J, Sinclair J, Dobbs R, Strube G, Rassey L, Mischke J, et al. *Manufacturing the Future: The Next Era of Global Growth and Innovation*. McKinsey Global Institute; 2012. Available from: https:// www.mckinsey.com/businessfunctions/operations/our-insights/the-future-of-manufacturing

Martin MV, Ishii K. Design for variety: Developing standardized and modularized product platform architectures. *Research in Engineering Design*. 2002; 13(4):213–235.

McWilliams A, Siegel DS. Creating and capturing value: Strategic corporate social responsibility, resource-based theory, and sustainable competitive advantage. *Journal of Management*. 2011; 37(5):1480–1495.

Mehmood R, Graham G. Big data logistics: A health-care transport capacity sharing model. *Procedia Computer Science*. 2015; 64:1107–1114.

Mistree F, Smith WF, Bras B, Allen JK, Muster D. Decision-based design: A contemporary paradigm for ship design. *Transactions, Society of Naval Architects and Marine Engineers*. 1990; 98:565–597.

Nambiar R, Bhardwaj R, Sethi A, Vargheese R. A look at challenges and opportunities of big data analytics in healthcare. In: *2013 IEEE International Conference on Big Data*. Santa Clara, CA: IEEE; 6 Oct 2013, pp. 17–22.

Nedelcu B. About big data and its challenges and benefits in manufacturing. *Database Systems Journal*. 2013; 4(3):10–19.

Noor A. Putting big data to work. *Mechanical Engineering*. 2013; 135(10):32–37.

Peat M. Big data in finance. *In Finance: The Magazine for Finsia Members*. 2013; 127(1):34.

Prasad S, Zakaria R, Altay N. Big data in humanitarian supply chain networks: A resource dependence perspective. *Annals of Operations Research*. 2018; 270(1–2):383–413.

Raghupathi W, Raghupathi V. Big data analytics in healthcare: Promise and potential. *Health Information Science and Systems*. 2014; 2(1):3.

Ranjan R. Modeling and simulation in performance optimization of big data processing frameworks. *IEEE Cloud Computing*. 2014; 1(4):14–19.

Rowe S, Pournader M. Supply Chain Big Data Series Part 1. *KPMG Australia*. Available from: https://assets.kpmg.com/content/dam/kpmg/au/pdf/2017/big data analytics-supplychainperformance.pdf.2017

Shao G, Shin SJ, Jain S. Data analytics using simulation for smart manufacturing. In: *Proceedings of the Winter Simulation Conference*. Savannah, Georgia: IEEE; 7 Dec 2014, pp. 2192–2203.

Shapiro N. Competition and aggregate demand. *Journal of Post Keynesian Economics*. 2005; 27(3):541–549.

Shen B, Chan HL. Forecast information sharing for managing supply chains in the big data era: Recent development and future Research. *Asia-Pacific Journal of Operational Research*. 2017; 34(01):1740001.

Slavakis K, Giannakis GB, Mateos G. Modeling and optimization for big data analytics:(statistical) learning tools for our era of data deluge. *IEEE Signal Processing Magazine*. 2014; 31(5):18–31.

Song ML, Fisher R, Wang JL, Cui LB. Environmental performance evaluation with big data: Theories and methods. *Annals of Operations Research*. 2018; 270(1–2):459–472.

Souza GC. Supply chain analytics. *Business Horizons*. 2014; 57(5):595–605.

Srinivasan R, Swink M. An investigation of visibility and flexibility as complements to supply chain analytics: An organizational information processing theory perspective. *Production and Operations Management*. 2018; 27(10):1849–1867.

Srinivasan U, Arunasalam B. Leveraging big data analytics to reduce healthcare costs. IT Professional. 2013; 15(6):21–28.

Stich V, Jordan F, Birkmeier M, Oflazgil K, Reschke J, Diews A. Big data technology for resilient failure management in production systems. In: *IFIP International Conference on Advances in Production Management Systems*. Cham: Springer; 2015, pp. 447–454.

Suh NP, Suh NP. *Axiomatic Design: Advances and Applications*. New York: Oxford University Press; 2001.

Swafford PM, Ghosh S, Murthy N. Achieving supply chain agility through IT integration and flexibility. *International Journal of Production Economics*. 2008; 116(2):288–297.

Technavio. *Global Big Data IT Spending in Financial Sector—Market Research 2015–2019*. Available from: www.technavio.com/report/global-big data-it-spending-infinancialsector marketresearch-2015–2019.

Tiwari S, Wee HM, Daryanto Y. Big data analytics in supply chain management between 2010 and 2016: Insights to industries. *Computers and Industrial Engineering*. 2018; 115:319–330.

Toyota Motor Corporation. *Toyota's Connected Strategy Briefing*; 2016. Available from: http://newsroom.toyota. co.jp/en/detail/14129306/

Trkman P, McCormack K, De Oliveira MP, Ladeira MB. The impact of business analytics on supply chain performance. *Decision Support Systems*. 2010; 49(3):318–327.

Wamba, SF, Gunasekaran, A, Dubey, R. et al. Big data analytics in operations and supply chain management. *Annals of Operations Research* 2018; 270(1–4). https://doi.org/10.1007/s10479-018-3024-7

Wang G, Gunasekaran A, Ngai EW. Distribution network design with big data: Model and analysis. *Annals of Operations Research*. 2018; 270(1–2):539–551.

Wang G, Gunasekaran A, Ngai EW, Papadopoulos T. Big data analytics in logistics and supply chain management: Certain investigations for research and applications. *International Journal of Production Economics*. 2016; 176:98–110.

Wang L, Alexander CA. Big data in design and manufacturing Engineering. *American Journal of Engineering and Applied Sciences*. 2015; 8(2):223.

White M. Digital workplaces: Vision and reality. *Business Information Review*. 2012; 29(4):205–214.

Wu K, Bethel E, Gu M, Leinweber D, Rübel O. A big data approach to analyzing market volatility. *Algorithmic Finance*. 2013; 2(3–4):241–267.

Zhong RY, Newman ST, Huang GQ, Lan S. Big data for supply chain management in the service and manufacturing sectors: Challenges, opportunities, and future perspectives. *Computers & Industrial Engineering*. 2016; 101:572–591.

Zhong RY, Xu C, Chen C, Huang GQ. Big data analytics for physical internet based intelligent manufacturing shop floors. *International Journal of Production Research*. 2017; 55(9):2610–2621.

Chapter 11

Evaluation Study of Churn Prediction Models for Business Intelligence

Shoaib Amin Banday and Samiya Khan

Contents

11.1 Introduction

The concept of *churn* quantifies the susceptibility of a customer who is in a business relationship with a company to terminate the same in a given time [1]. Its initial usage is credited to customer relationship management (CRM) systems [2]. However, in due course of time, the relevance of churn analysis for various other business domains was realized. Understanding if a customer will cease his or her relationship with the company is a relevant business problem considering the fact that retained customers form a major chunk of revenue for companies when compared to newly targeted customers [3].

DOI: 10.1201/9781003175711-11

Moreover, the success of marketing campaigns run for customer retention is better than those for new customer acquisition [4]. Churn analysis enables companies to improve their customer retention rate, which eventually adds value to company's business. Many business domains have explored the applicability of churn analysis for disparate service sectors. Most of these studies focus on development of a model that uses different parameters for predicting if a customer will 'churn'. As mentioned previously, the use of churn in businesses was initiated for determining customer status in the CRM.

CRMs have evolved from operational functionalities to also support analytical capabilities. The former solely focused on improving the operational efficiency of business processes such as sales, retail and customer service, in addition to many others [2]. The growing need for studying customer characteristics and behavior brought in the idea of analytical CRMs [5, 6, 7], starting with using customer parameters to personalize offerings and evolving to application of computational techniques to other domains such as banking [8] and telecom [9]. In conclusion, churn analysis has risen to become the most critical computational technique for customer management and service personalization [10, 11, 12].

Existing literature on churn analysis is domain specific and covers specialized fields such as banking [13], insurance [14], telecom [15] and retail [16]. Besides this, there exist some survey papers that investigate the use of churn analysis in different business domains [17] and computational techniques employed for churn prediction [18]. However, none of the available literature provides a comprehensive qualitative and quantitative analysis of the computational techniques that are used for churn prediction in businesses. This chapter discusses the concept of churn analysis and its relevance to diverse business domains, also providing a comparative experimental analysis of different machine and deep learning algorithms. Therefore, this research shall be helpful for researchers in moving their research forward in this field and facilitating modeling technique selection for the dataset.

The rest of the chapter is organized in the following manner: section 11.2 explains the concept of churn and its relevance for businesses. Section 11.3 illustrates the use of churn analysis in disparate business domains and associated applications. Section 11.4 investigates existing literature for available predictive models and techniques used for churn analysis, particularly for businesses. Section 11.5 provides a qualitative evaluation of some machine learning and deep learning algorithms for churn prediction. Besides this, it also provides quantitative evaluation of the aforementioned computational techniques on multiple datasets. Lastly, section 11.6 synopsizes the chapter providing a sketch of drawn conclusions and identified future research directions.

11.2 Churn: Definition and Background

There are many existing definitions of the term 'churn'. The most accepted definition of churn describes it as prolonged inactivity [19]. With that said, the quantifications of the terms 'prolonged' and 'activity' vary on the basis of business domain and industry concerned. Typically, there are two types of churn, namely, contractual and noncontractual churn [20]. When the contract for a customer has expired and the customer has not shown any willingness to extend the contract, the resultant churn is called contractual churn.

With the advent of the internet and increasing popularity of ecommerce, churns have been observed because of the low costs involved in switching between providers [21]. In contractual churn, it is witnessed that customers lost interest in a service to such an extent that they decided to terminate the business relationship [4, 22]. Such customers will, in all probability, not return. Customers closing a bank account or terminating a phone contract are typical examples of contractual churn. This type of churn is more commonly observed in flat-rate services.

On the other hand, there are no time constraints associated with noncontractual churn. Such type of churn is detected when the customer crosses the churn criterion set by the service provider. This criterion is typically associated with change of behavior in terms of inactivity and is called 'time window' [23]. The objective of churn analysis is to identify the window of time within which the customer's trust can be regained so that business outcomes can be predicted and transformed. In consideration of the time aspect of churn analysis, three churn observation criteria are observed. These are binary, daily and monthly. The daily and monthly observation criteria are typically associated with status update of the customer in the company's database. On the basis of database entries, binary churn observation is determined.

For example, on the basis of the contract status of a customer, binary churn observation is determined for contractual churn. On the contrary, for noncontractual settings, binary churn is computed on the basis of the inactivity features described by the company for churn analysis. The objective of performing churn analysis at a periodic level is to identify customers who are expected to churn and then alter marketing strategies in such a manner that such customers are tempted not to churn. Incentives and special offers are possible and tested interventions [3, 4].

11.3 Churn Analysis for Businesses

As mentioned previously, a major chunk of the work performed on churn analysis was done for CRMs [7, 21]. All problems associated with churning such as identification of customers that are expected to churn, coming up with strategies to prevent customer churn, retention strategies for churning customers and customer development planning are comprehensively covered in the CRM use case. Typically, log data is used for churn analysis, particularly for applications that are internet-based services. Ahn et al. [20] identified 14 business fields that make extensive use of churn analysis, which are illustrated in Figure 11.1.

The majority of the previous studies in churn analysis are focused on the telecommunications industry [4, 24–26]. The second-most impacted industries in this case

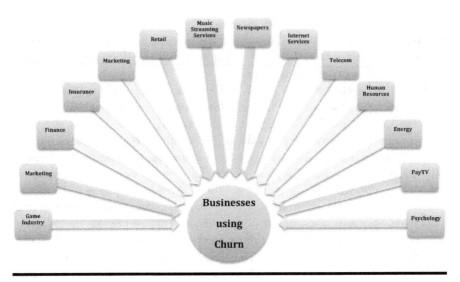

Figure 11.1 Businesses using Churn Analysis [20].

are the finance [27–28] and insurance sectors [29]. Some more recent studies in churn analysis are centered on the gaming industry [4, 30, 31]. There have also been specific studies for sectors such as psychology [32], internet services, music streaming and newspapers [33], human resources [34] and energy [35], in addition to several others.

Evidently, churn analysis is a concept that continues to remain relevant across disparate business domains. Moreover, churn analysis has evolved from its traditional form of log data analysis to use of advanced artificial intelligence techniques on complex, heterogeneous data in the recent past. Considering the diverse applicability of the concept to applications for business intelligence, development of computational techniques to provide advanced business intelligence (BI) solutions for specific business domains is deemed appropriate.

11.4 Churn Prediction Models

Existing literature demonstrates the use of four analytical domains for churn analysis, namely, statistics, graph theory, machine learning and deep learning. However, literature also supports the use of hybrid techniques that incorporate multiple aspects of these four core domains [36–38]. Since the scope of this chapter is restricted to machine and deep learning techniques for churn prediction, the rest of this section shall focus on existing literature that specifically discusses this component of churn analysis. Machine and deep learning techniques are known to be used for non-contractual churn analysis.

Its efficacy is considered better than statistical methods for the reason that it can handle nonlinear interfeature relationships and can be rather effective when learning patterns are heterogeneous and arising from a diverse set of features. Research on the use of deep learning for churn prediction has also found decent ground in the recent past. Traditional machine learning techniques like association rule mining [39], random forest [40], boosting [41], Classification And Regression Trees [10], decision trees [15, 42, 43], Support Vector Machine (SVM) [35, 44] and eXtreme Gradient Boosting (XGB) [45] have been used for churn prediction. Lee et al. [46] proposed a deep learning model for game churn prediction analysis, which is attributed as one of the first dedicated studies in this area.

It was deduced that the unified use of machine learning and deep learning architectures could substantially improve churn predictability. Several other comparative studies have been performed for specific industry sectors such as insurance [29], which also proposed the use of deep shallow learning for churn prediction and is considered a breakthrough algorithm for this domain of study. However, none of the existing comparative studies provide a comprehensive and cumulative standpoint on the use of these techniques for churn prediction. Moreover, existing literature confirms that the choice of modeling technique depends on the business field and application.

Since deep learning techniques require dense and large amounts of data to train the model, they are relatively successful for fields such as telecom and gaming where log data is available or else the models end up with the problem of overfitting. On the other hand, sectors like finance and insurance do not evidently have a lot of data available. Thus, a combination of statistical and machine learning techniques or conventional survival analysis methods can be considered for use. However, with the growing digitization and integration of heterogeneous data sources, amount of data required for model training may no longer be a problem, which makes the prospect of using machine and deep learning techniques for churn prediction bright.

11.5 Evaluation of ML/DL Models for Churn Prediction

The use case chosen for this evaluation study is bank churn prediction. The problem statement evaluates the dataset and proposes churn models for predicting if a bank customer will churn or not. Evidently, it is a binary classification problem. In order to evaluate the performance of different machine and deep learning models for churn prediction, the Kaggle dataset[1] for bank churn analysis is used. The dataset has 10,000 entries and 14 attributes. From preliminary exploratory analysis, it was determined that the dataset is imbalanced as 20.4% of the customers within

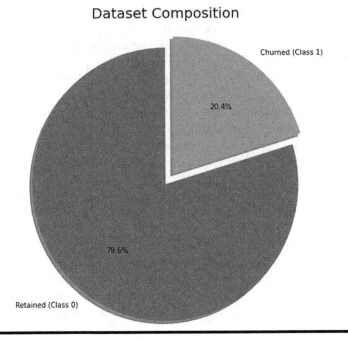

Figure 11.2 Composition of Dataset.

the dataset churned while 79.6% of the customers were retained, as illustrated in Figure 11.2.

It is noteworthy that the objective of this predictive model is to accurately predict churning and not retention because a bank would be interested in knowing the customers that churned more accurately. In the experiments, five machine learning techniques, namely, logistic regression, SVM with Radial Basis Function or RBF Kernel, SVM with polynomial kernel, random forest classifier and XGB classifier were used. Besides this, Artificial Neural Network (ANN) was used as the deep learning method for churn prediction. Existing literature suggests the use of advanced deep learning techniques such as Recurrent Neural Network and Convolutional Neural Network for churn prediction as well. However, these models shall be explored in future work.

For all modeling techniques, the percentages of training data and test data are 80% and 20%, respectively. Data preparation included dropping of irrelevant features and one-hot encoding of categorical features. The parametric settings used for experimentation are described in Table 11.1. All the experiments were performed on a 10th Gen Intel Core i7 processor. A summary of the performance evaluation metrics determined for all the techniques is provided in Table 11.2.

Table 11.1 Paraetric Settings for Different Modeling Techniques

Class	Modeling technique	Variant	Parametric settings
Machine learning	Logistic regression	-	C=100, max_iter=250, multi_class='multinomial', tol=1e-05
	SVM	RBF Kernel	C=100, gamma=0.1, probability=True
		Polynomial Kernel	C=100, degree=2, gamma=0.1, kernel='poly', probability=True
	Random Forest Classifier	-	max_depth=8, max_features=6, min_samples_split=3, n_estimators=50
	Extreme Gradient Boosting Classifier	-	base_score=0.5, booster='gbtree', colsample_bylevel=1, colsample_bynode=1, colsample_bytree=1, gamma=0.01, gpu_id=-1, importance_type='gain', interaction_constraints=", learning_rate=0.1, max_delta_step=0, max_depth=7, min_child_weight=5, missing=None, monotone_constraints='()', n_estimators=20, n_jobs=1, nthread=1, num_parallel_tree=1, random_state=0, reg_alpha=0, reg_lambda=1, scale_pos_weight=1, seed=0, silent=True, subsample=1, tree_method='exact', validate_parameters=1, verbosity=None
Deep Learning	ANN	-	Model—Sequential, Number of hidden layers=6, Optimizer=Adam, Loss=Binary Cross-entropy Batch size=10, Epochs=2000

As mentioned previously, the aim of this modeling is to predict if a customer will churn. Therefore, the precision, recall and F1 scores of 1's are more important to the analysis than the ones determined for 0's. Moreover, the evaluation metrics are determined for test data to evaluate the performance of the data on previously unseen data. Table 11.2 provides the metrics generated during experimentation for the different modeling techniques.

Table 11.2 Summary of Experiments Performed

Class	Technique	Variant	Precision	Recall	F1 score	Accuracy	ROC AUC score
Machine learning	Logistic regression	-	0.73	0.02	0.04	81%	0.51
	SVM	RBF Kernel	0.26	0.67	0.38	56%	0.61
		Polynomial Kernel	0.26	0.66	0.38	57%	0.61
	Random forest classifier	-	0.8	0.39	0.52	86%	0.68
	Extreme gradient boosting classifier	-	0.76	0.46	0.46	87%	0.71
Deep learning	ANN	-	0.77	0.51	0.61	87%	0.73

It is important to note that 20.4% of the customer data had churns. Therefore, even if a recall of more than this baseline is achieved, it is certainly an improvement. However, this value should be as high as possible. In addition, the targeted solution must also have high precision so that the bank can focus efforts and resources in the right direction without worrying about false positives. Therefore, accuracy is not the only parameter of concern for the problem. Other parameters are equally important and shall need to be taken into consideration.

Area under the curve (AUC) of receiver operating characteristic (ROC) is the most generically used characteristic for evaluating the performance of churn prediction models. Moreover, ROC AUC score is an important parameter for evaluating classifier performance with respect to its ability of distinguishing between the two classes. The ROC curves with the respective scores for the different predictive models are illustrated in Figure 11.3 and Figure 11.4.

From Table 11.2, Figure 11.3 and Figure 11.4, it can be deduced that random forest classifier is the best machine learning technique for churn prediction. With that said, its evaluation with respect to ANN shows comparable results with random forest classifier fairing better at the ROC AUC curve. Therefore, deep learning as a modeling technique shows considerable prospect for churn prediction modeling. Advanced deep learning techniques can be explored in the future to test if results can be better for this and other applications.

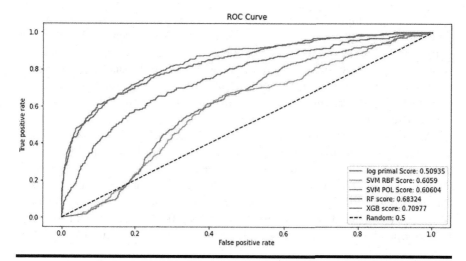

Figure 11.3 ROC Curve for Machine Learning Algorithms.

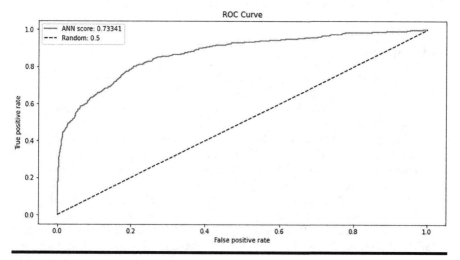

Figure 11.4 ROC Curve for ANN.

11.6 Conclusion

Churn prediction holds significant value for businesses in view of the fact that identification of customers who are expected to terminate their services with a company can be further used to tweak marketing strategies and support such customers to drive customer retention. Several statistical, graph theory-based and machine or deep learning computational techniques have been put to use for modeling the problem of churn prediction. This chapter discusses the concept of churn, its relevance for businesses and existing churn prediction models, at length. Besides this, it also provides an evaluation of five machine-learning techniques (logistic regression, SVM with RBF, SVM with polynomial kernel, random forest classifier and extreme boosting gradient classifier) and one deep learning technique (ANN) for churn prediction.

ANN shows considerably improved performance in comparison to random forest, which performed best amongst the machine learning techniques used. However, there are certain limitations of this work. The size of the dataset is limited with churned customers forming a small fraction of the same. Therefore, bigger datasets can be used for future analyses. Besides this, literature has indicated that choice of modeling technique can be application-dependent. Therefore, similar analyses can be performed for other use cases to evaluate this assertion in the future.

Note

1. www.kaggle.com/adammaus/predicting-churn-for-bank-customers

References

[1] Chandar, M., Laha, A. and Krishna, P., 2006, March. Modeling churn behavior of bank customers using predictive data mining techniques. In *National Conference on Soft Computing Techniques for Engineering Applications (SCT-2006)* (pp. 24–26). Rourkela, India.

[2] Parvatiyar, A. and Sheth, J.N., 2001. Customer relationship management: Emerging practice, process, and discipline. *Journal of Economic & Social Research*, 3(2).

[3] Frederick, F.R. and Sasser, W.E., 1990. Zero defections: Quality comes to services. *Harvard Business Review*, 68(5), p. 105.

[4] Mozer, M.C., Wolniewicz, R., Grimes, D.B., Johnson, E. and Kaushansky, H., 2000. Predicting subscriber dissatisfaction and improving retention in the wireless telecommunications industry. *IEEE Transactions on Neural Networks*, 11(3), pp. 690–696.

[5] He, Z., Xu, X., Huang, J.Z. and Deng, S., 2004. Mining class outliers: Concepts, algorithms and applications in CRM. *Expert Systems with Applications*, 27(4), pp. 681–697.

[6] Teo, T.S., Devadoss, P. and Pan, S.L., 2006. Towards a holistic perspective of customer relationship management (CRM) implementation: A case study of the Housing and Development Board, Singapore. *Decision Support Systems*, 42(3), pp. 1613–1627.

[7] Ngai, E.W., Xiu, L. and Chau, D.C., 2009. Application of data mining techniques in customer relationship management: A literature review and classification. *Expert Systems with Applications*, 36(2), pp. 2592–2602.

[8] Prasad, U.D. and Madhavi, S., 2012. Prediction of churn behavior of bank customers using data mining tools. *Business Intelligence Journal*, 5(1), pp. 96–101.

[9] Yan, L., Wolniewicz, R.H. and Dodier, R., 2004. Predicting customer behavior in telecommunications. *IEEE Intelligent Systems*, 19(2), pp. 50–58.

[10] Tamaddoni Jahromi, A., Sepehri, M.M., Teimourpour, B. and Choobdar, S., 2010. Modeling customer churn in a non-contractual setting: The case of telecommunications service providers. *Journal of Strategic Marketing*, 18(7), pp. 587–598.

[11] Bose, R., 2002. Customer relationship management: Key components for IT success. *Industrial Management & Data Systems*, 102(2), pp. 89–97. https://doi.org/10.1108/02635570210419636

[12] Ngai, E.W., 2005. Customer relationship management research (1992–2002): An academic literature review and classification. *Marketing Intelligence & Planning*, 23(6), pp. 582–605. https://doi.org/10.1108/02634500510624147

[13] Karvana, K.G.M., Yazid, S., Syalim, A. and Mursanto, P., 2019, October. Customer churn analysis and prediction using data mining models in banking industry. In *2019 International Workshop on Big Data and Information Security (IWBIS)* (pp. 33–38). Indonesia, IEEE.

[14] Günther, C.C., Tvete, I.F., Aas, K., Sandnes, G.I. and Borgan, Ø., 2014. Modelling and predicting customer churn from an insurance company. *Scandinavian Actuarial Journal*, 2014(1), pp. 58–71.

[15] Dahiya, K. and Bhatia, S., 2015, September. Customer churn analysis in telecom industry. In *2015 4th International Conference on Reliability, Infocom Technologies and Optimization (ICRITO)(Trends and Future Directions)* (pp. 1–6). Noida, India, IEEE.

[16] Ficano, C.C., 2013. Business churn and the retail giant: establishment birth and death from W al-M art's entry. *Social Science Quarterly*, 94(1), pp. 263–291.

[17] García, D.L., Nebot, À. and Vellido, A., 2017. Intelligent data analysis approaches to churn as a business problem: A survey. *Knowledge and Information Systems*, 51(3), pp. 719–774.

[18] Jain, H., Yadav, G. and Manoov, R., 2021. Churn prediction and retention in banking, telecom and IT sectors using machine learning techniques. In *Advances in Machine Learning and Computational Intelligence* (pp. 137–156). Springer, Singapore.

[19] Periáñez, Á., Saas, A., Guitart, A. and Magne, C., 2016, October. Churn prediction in mobile social games: Towards a complete assessment using survival ensembles. In *2016 IEEE International Conference on Data Science and Advanced Analytics (DSAA)* (pp. 564–573). Montreal, Canada, IEEE.

[20] Ahn, J., Hwang, J., Kim, D., Choi, H. and Kang, S., 2020. A survey on churn analysis in various business domains. *IEEE Access*, 8, pp. 220816–220839.

[21] Lejeune, M.A., 2001. Measuring the impact of data mining on churn management. *Internet Research*, 11(5), pp. 375–387. https://doi.org/10.1108/10662240110410183

[22] Chen, Y., Xie, X., Lin, S.D. and Chiu, A., 2018, February. Wsdm cup 2018: Music recommendation and churn prediction. In *Proceedings of the Eleventh ACM International Conference on Web Search and Data Mining* (pp. 8–9). New York, NY, Association for Computing Machinery.

[23] Buckinx, W. and Van den Poel, D., 2005. Customer base analysis: Partial defection of behaviourally loyal clients in a non-contractual FMCG retail setting. *European Journal of Operational Research*, 164(1), pp. 252–268.

[24] Hung, S.Y., Yen, D.C. and Wang, H.Y. (2006). Applying data mining to telecom churn management. *Expert Systems with Applications*, 31(3), pp. 515–524.

[25] Ahn, J.H., Han, S.P. and Lee, Y.S., 2006. Customer churn analysis: Churn determinants and mediation effects of partial defection in the Korean mobile telecommunications service industry. *Telecommunications Policy*, 30(10–11), pp. 552–568.

[26] Au, W.H., Chan, K.C. and Yao, X., 2003. A novel evolutionary data mining algorithm with applications to churn prediction. *IEEE Transactions on Evolutionary Computation*, 7(6), pp. 532–545.

[27] Chiang, D.A., Wang, Y.F., Lee, S.L. and Lin, C.J., 2003. Goal-oriented sequential pattern for network banking churn analysis. *Expert Systems with Applications*, 25(3), pp. 293–302.

[28] Mavri, M. and Ioannou, G., 2008. Customer switching behaviour in Greek banking services using survival analysis. *Managerial Finance*, 34(3), pp. 186–197. https://doi.org/10.1108/03074350810848063

[29] Zhang, R., Li, W., Tan, W. and Mo, T., 2017, June. Deep and shallow model for insurance churn prediction service. In *2017 IEEE International Conference on Services Computing (SCC)* (pp. 346–353). Honolulu, HI, IEEE.

[30] Viljanen, M., Airola, A., Pahikkala, T. and Heikkonen, J., 2016, September. Modelling user retention in mobile games. In *2016 IEEE Conference on Computational Intelligence and Games (CIG)* (pp. 1–8). Santorini, Greece, IEEE.

[31] Milošević, M., Živić, N. and Andjelković, I., 2017. Early churn prediction with personalized targeting in mobile social games. *Expert Systems with Applications*, 83, pp. 326–332.

[32] Borbora, Z., Srivastava, J., Hsu, K.W. and Williams, D., 2011, October. Churn prediction in mmorpgs using player motivation theories and an ensemble approach. In *2011 IEEE Third International Conference on Privacy, Security, Risk and Trust and 2011 IEEE Third International Conference on Social Computing* (pp. 157–164). Boston, MA, IEEE.

[33] Dechant, A., Spann, M. and Becker, J.U., 2019. Positive customer churn: An application to online dating. *Journal of Service Research*, 22(1), pp. 90–100.

[34] Glady, N., Baesens, B. and Croux, C., 2009. Modeling churn using customer lifetime value. *European Journal of Operational Research*, 197(1), pp. 402–411.

[35] Moeyersoms, J. and Martens, D., 2015. Including high-cardinality attributes in predictive models: A case study in churn prediction in the energy sector. *Decision Support Systems*, 72, pp. 72–81.

[36] Breiman, L., 2001. Statistical modeling: The two cultures (with comments and a rejoinder by the author). *Statistical Science*, 16(3), pp. 199–231.

[37] Stewart, M., 2019. The actual difference between statistics and machine learning. *Towards Data Science*. https://towardsdatascience.com/the-actual-difference-between-statistics-and-machine-learning-64b49f07ea3

[38] Bzdok, D., Krzywinski, M. and Altman, N., 2018. Machine learning: Supervised methods. *Nat Methods*, 15, pp. 5–6. https://doi.org/10.1038/nmeth.4551

[39] Chiang, D.A., Wang, Y.F., Lee, S.L. and Lin, C.J., 2003. Goal-oriented sequential pattern for network banking churn analysis. *Expert Systems with Applications*, 25(3), pp. 293–302.

[40] Coussement, K. and De Bock, K.W., 2013. Customer churn prediction in the online gambling industry: The beneficial effect of ensemble learning. *Journal of Business Research*, 66(9), pp. 1629–1636.

[41] Clemente, M., Giner-Bosch, V. and San Matías, S., 2010. Assessing classification methods for churn prediction by composite indicators. *Manuscript, Dept. of Applied Statistics, OR & Quality, UniversitatPolitècnica de València*, Camino de Vera s/n, 46022.

[42] Wei, C.P. and Chiu, I.T., 2002. Turning telecommunications call details to churn prediction: A data mining approach. *Expert Systems with Applications*, 23(2), pp. 103–112.

[43] Bahnsen, A.C., Aouada, D. and Ottersten, B., 2015. A novel cost-sensitive framework for customer churn predictive modeling. *Decision Analytics*, 2(1), pp. 1–15.

[44] Vafeiadis, T., Diamantaras, K.I., Sarigiannidis, G. and Chatzisavvas, K.C., 2015. A comparison of machine learning techniques for customer churn prediction. *Simulation Modelling Practice and Theory*, 55, pp. 1–9.

[45] Hadiji, F., Sifa, R., Drachen, A., Thurau, C., Kersting, K. and Bauckhage, C., 2014, August. Predicting player churn in the wild. In *2014 IEEE Conference on Computational Intelligence and Games* (pp. 1–8). Dortmund, Germany, IEEE.

[46] Lee, E., Jang, Y., Yoon, D., Jeon, J., Yang, S.I., Lee, S.K., Kim, D.W., Chen, P.P., Guitart, A., Bertens, P. and Perianez, A., 2018. Game data mining competition on churn prediction and survival analysis using commercial game log data. *arXiv* pre-print arXiv:1802.02301.

Chapter 12

Big Data Analytics for Marketing Intelligence

Tripti Paul and Sandip Rakshit

Contents

DOI: 10.1201/9781003175711-12

12.1 Introduction

Marketing intelligence can help organizations improve their efficiency by finding new opportunities, highlighting emerging risks, discovering new market insights, and enhancing decision-making processes. Organizations use surveys of customer satisfaction to learn more about their customers' attitudes. Critical variables for strategic marketing decisions, such as consumer opinions toward a product, service, or business, can be automatically tracked using big data analytic technologies (Saritha et al., 2021).

Twenty-five percent of the world's stored information was digital in 2000. Today, over 98% of all stored information is digital. The complexity of this digital disruption has the potential for significant business problems, with the shockwave at the forefront of marketing. The biggest challenge for every organization in the marketing area is how to turn big data into business insights for improved customer relationships (Buhalis and Volchek, 2021).

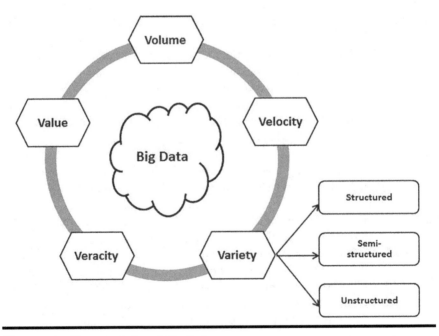

Figure 12.1 Characteristics of Big Data.

Big data is a phrase that refers to massive (terabytes–exabytes), unorganized, and dynamic (ranging from genome-analysis to social science, sensor, social networks, or mobile apps data to web gadgets data) data sets that require advanced and specific techniques to store, process, interpret, and visualize (Krishnan, 2013). With five V's, big data can be characterized (Figure 12.1). The five V's include volume, velocity, variety, veracity, and value (Ishwarappa and Anuradha, 2015).

(i) **Volume:** refers to the amount of data produced from internal and external organizations, growing every year. Usually, consider big data to be data in work over one petabyte.

(ii) **Velocity:** represents the unparalleled speed at which online users, smartphone users, social media users, and others generate data. For extracting useful and relevant information, data is produced and processed quickly. Big data is complex and can be analyzed in real-time.

(iii) **Variety:** refers to the data forms, as big data can come from various sources and in multiple formats (e.g., audio, images, logos, text, videos, etc.). Big data is often not organized, and putting it into a relational database is not always possible. The category in which big data falls is also an essential fact for data analysts to consider. The difficulty of storing and analyzing big data is typically increased when dealing with a variety of structured, semi-structured, and unstructured data. Ninety percent of ample information is unstructured.

    a) **Structured data:** refers to data types that are specified explicitly within a framework. Structured data is basically in relational databases, which come in tables with rows and columns. For example, structured query language (SQL) files.

    b) **Semistructured data:** is in the middle of the structured and unstructured data spectrum. The majority of the time, this corresponds to unstructured data with metadata. For example comma-separated values, JavaScript Object Notation, and extensible markup language files.

    c) **Unstructured data:** in most cases, unstructured data is saved in its original format. Unstructured data does not belong in any defined data structure, like structured data, which is standardized and easy to access in relational databases—for example, audio files, video files, images, etc.

(iv) **Veracity:** refers to the information's authenticity or whether it comes from a credible, trustworthy, authentic, and responsive source. It alludes to contradictions in the consistency of various big data sources. Likely, the information is not entirely right.

(v) **Value:** the essential component of big data. It is the objective of big data analytics. It is the method of finding hidden deals in massive datasets. It represents the value extracted from the analysis of the existing data. There is no point in handling and maintaining data if individuals cannot derive any competitive advantages.

12.2 Literature Review

Since the advent of the internet, the essential phenomenon to attract the digital computing industry's interest has been "big data". Doug Laney of Gartner popularized the foundation concept in a paper on the topic by McKinsey & Co. The primary explanation for the current popularity of "big data" is that the technology platforms that have accompanied it now enable users to process data in various formats and structures without the limitations that conventional systems and database platforms impose.

12.2.1 Big Data

Data is the simplest and most basic type of information or knowledge. According to a series of studies conducted by Carnegie Mellon University, *information* or *data processing* refers to arranging, collecting, storing, retrieving, and handling data. Big data is defined as large quantities of data with varying degrees of complexity, produced at various speeds and varying degrees of ambiguity, which cannot be processed using conventional analytics techniques (Krishnan, 2013).

It was not until 2011 that the term "big data" was introduced. In an academic article, Berry (2011) first suggested the importance of "big data" to management. Manyika et al. (2011) also discussed how "big data" technology and networks have become a critical factor in increasing a firm's efficiency and competitiveness. Following these two landmark works, the publishing of "big data" has exploded. *Big data analytics* is the process of examining a large amount of data (Ishwarappa and Anuradha, 2015).

12.2.2 Type of Big Data Analytics

There are mainly four types of big data analytics: (i) descriptive big data analytics, (ii) diagnostic big data analytics, (iii) predictive big data analytics, and (iv) prescriptive big data analytics (Mikalef et al., 2020) (Figure 12.2).

Descriptive Big Data Analytics

Descriptive big data analytics is used to explain what happened in the past based on data presented through graphics or reports, but it does not suggest why or what will happen in the future.

Thus, descriptive big data analytics summarizes past data into clear and understandable formats. Clustering, summary statistics, and segmentation procedures are used in this analytics. The primary objective of descriptive analytics is to dig into the details of what happened. With more recent data, this can sometimes be time sensitive, as it is easier to do a descriptive analysis.

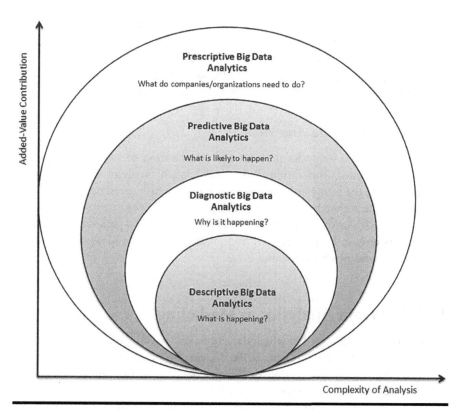

Figure 12.2 Type of Big Data Analytics.

Diagnostic Big Data Analytics

Diagnostic big data analytics is closely linked to descriptive analysis to understand why any given event occurred in the past. Therefore, diagnostic analysis techniques would allow an analyst to drill down and thus isolate the root cause of a problem after reviewing the descriptive data.

Well-designed business information dashboards integrating time-series data reading (i.e., data over many successive points in time), filters, and drill-down capabilities allow such analysis to be carried out.

Predictive Big Data Analytics

Predictive big data analytics is all about forecasting. This analytics is most useful for organizations to go through data to predict what could happen. These are all achieved by predictive models, whether it is the probability of an activity occurring in the future, projecting a quantifiable quantity, or estimating a point in time at which this might happen.

Typically, predictive models use several variable data to render the forecast. The variability of the component data will be linked to what is likely to be predicted. Then these data are combined into a score or prediction together.

Prescriptive Big Data Analytics

Prescriptive big data analytics provides an interpretation of what has happened, why it has happened, and various "what-may-happen" analyses to help the consumer to decide the best course of action to take. Typically, prescriptive analysis is not only a single action, but it is also a host of other activities.

Therefore, this analytics prescribes a solution to a specific problem. Perspective analytics operates in both descriptive and predictive analysis. Most of the time, it focuses on AI and machine learning.

12.3 Big Data Analytics in Marketing

Marketing science is a field in which data and data analytics play a critical role in decision-making (Liang and Liu, 2018). Market and customer insights provide recommendations for marketing decision-makers, and they must be handled regularly due to the dynamism of today's market climate (Amado et al., 2018). As part of their marketing plan, organizations and decision-makers must consider data generated by customers and markets. For marketing decision-making, data must be used as a critical component of the marketing strategy (Fan et al., 2015).

Organizations are now applying big data analytics to understand their customers better and achieve optimum customer engagement. Big data are, however, not a solution but just raw material. The challenge remains to transform the data into knowledge that managers can use to solve challenges and achieve improved performance (Erevelles et al., 2016). Therefore, big data analysis has become necessary for obtaining useful insights into data to benefit significantly in the global market (Xu et al., 2016).

12.4 Big Data Analytics Tools

Some popular big data analytics tools are as follows:

Dataiku DSS: is a web framework for collaborative data science. It also aids in the creation, prototyping, and exploration of a team's ideas. However, it is more effective in delivering its data items.

Google Fusion Tables: is a fantastic platform for data collection, mapping, and visualization of large datasets. Google Fusion Tables can also be added to the list of market analytics resources. It is also one of the most successful big data analytics programs.

Hadoop: is a big data storage and management system that uses distributed storage and parallel processing. It is the most widely used program for dealing with large amounts of data.

KNIME: through visual programming, KNIME aids in the visualization, analysis, and modeling of data. It is used to link various data-mining and machine-learning devices.

NodeXL: is a program for visualizing and analyzing relationships and networks. NodeXL conducts accurate measurements. It is an open-source (exclude professional version) network analysis and visualization program. One of the best statistical methods for data processing is NodeXL. Advanced network metrics are included. This tool also includes data importers and automation to access social media networks (Kauffmann et al., 2019).

OpenRefine: this data-cleaning app is also known as GoogleRefine. Since it aids in preparing data for the study, it works with a single row of data. Cells should be placed under columns, equivalent to relational database tables.

RapidMiner: is a tool that is able to perform machine learning techniques. Data visualization, processing, mathematical modeling, and predictive analytics are all part of data mining. RapidMiner, a Java-based big data analytics platform, is quickly gaining traction.

Spark: is used to process and analyze vast volumes of data in real-time.

12.5 Traditional Marketing Analytics vs. Big Data Analytics

Organizations have several different ways (social media data, transactional data, survey data, sensor network data, etc.) to gather data from several knowledge sources for traditional marketing intelligence activities such as consumer opinion mining. Different techniques may be used to discover marketing intelligence depending on the characteristics of the data obtained. Estimation methods based on a single data source can only include a limited collection of insights, potentially resulting in distorted business decisions. On the other hand, the combination of heterogeneous data from multiple sources gives a comprehensive view of the market and creates more precise marketing intelligence.

Most traditional marketing relies on analytics with restricted analytical platforms and deployment capability that deal with small data sets (megabytes or gigabytes or kilobytes). Such fixed-scale data sets are typically accessible from the administrator or researcher's machine, where the analysis occurs locally. This analysis is not readily replicable, and the central body coordinates decision-making.

However, recent developments in marketing and information technology have a large scale, versatility, flexible solution for strategic activities and new products' success. For example, Netflix analyzes millions of data points generated by its viewers in real-time, thereby deciding if a series would become a popular web series (Jabbar et al., 2020).

In marketing, big data analysis varies primarily from conventional marketing analysis in the revolution instead of in the evolution of communications systems. Big data analysis is used by businesses to track the information flow and analyze large data volumes in real-time. In contrast, traditional marketing analytics primarily concentrate on enhancing key performance metrics for additional insight into advertisement, promotion, customer relationship management, and new product development.

Big data analytics differs from traditional marketing analytics in five the V's of data: volume, velocity, variety, veracity, and value, and in that big data analytics can enhance business decision-making for better success. The changing speed of technology includes rapid market research that can be done by traditional market analytics. Big data analytics could provide the requisite real-time speed for this challenge to be met.

12.6 Big Data Analytics' Position in Rising Business Value through Marketing Intelligence

Market intelligence is not only about sales and keeping ahead of the next player, but it is also about discovering and using knowledge to make an organization grow smoother from top to bottom. Big data analytics can help organizations make better use of data mining (Figure 12.3) to enhance brand awareness, control supply chain risks (Paul and Mondal, 2019), produce competitive intelligence, and provide real-time market insights to help make crucial decisions (Ram et al., 2016). Whenever a retailer uses big data correctly, it can raise earnings growth by 60% by gaining market share over competitors and leveraging accurate customer data (Xu et al., 2016).

The main benefits of big data analytics are as follows:

i) Big data analytics provides reliability by making relevant data widely visible.
ii) By collecting accurate performance data, big data analytics promotes performance improvement and variability exposure.
iii) By segmenting the population, big data analytics assists in better serving the real needs of consumers.
iv) Big data analytics enhances decision-making with automated algorithms by presenting useful insights.
v) Big data analytics creates new business models, concepts, goods, and services.
vi) Information development, new management concepts for production, and the economy based on this are the most popular aspects of big data analytics.

Figure 12.3 The Parameters of Marketing Intelligence Taken from Big Data.

Therefore, big data analytics can enhance marketing intelligence in many ways, including distribution network efficiency, demand planning, inventory tracking, financial assessment, market information, and real-time personalized service.

12.7 Application of Big Data in Marketing Intelligence

Various big data applications in the customer service domain are demonstrating the enormous potential for enhancing marketing impact. The following examples illustrate the different applications.

12.7.1 "Next Best Action" to Involve Customers

The next best action marketing is a customer-centric marketing strategy that evaluates all possible deals for each customer in real-time and then selects the best one. The customer's demands and expectations and the marketing organization's business goals, strategies, and regulations decide the next best action deal. It is in stark contrast to conventional marketing strategies, including creating a product or service offer and then locating interested and qualified prospects.

The use of real-time processing technology, which uses customer service data, transaction records, customer details, and a collection of business rules to decide the one or more deals that the customer is qualified for at the time of contact, enables the customer to take the next best step. These are prioritized and tailored to provide the consumer with the best deal possible.

An algorithm blends advanced analytics (which calculates the customer's willingness to accept the offer) and complex business rules to assess priorities (determining the treatment logic). Furthermore, big data sources, including social media (Sivarajah et al., 2020) and click-stream, can significantly improve analytical models' predictability.

12.7.2 Personalization of Online Shopping

The retail industry changed dramatically with the introduction of online retailers using the internet to extend their market scope while lowering inventory, staff, and operating costs. It now takes shopping to the next level by turning it into a customized experience by gathering and processing massive quantities of data that are distinguished by volume, variety, velocity, and value (Elhoseny et al., 2020).

User attitudes, searching and brand preference, product characteristics, geographical region of sales, inventory levels, successful promotions, campaigns, etc. that can be digitally tracked are all gathered by online retailers using big data analytics. Intelligent machine-learning algorithms transform these data sources, which develop by several terabytes each day, into knowledge and insights, identifying consumer preferences and product affinities, tracing geographic peculiarities, and identifying seasonal effects, among other things, to predict customers' present and future needs (Saidali et al., 2019).

This analysis is then used to provide consumers with a customized experience by illustrating things of interest, suggesting the most likely deals, and assisting customers in finding what they want, when they want it, at the best possible price. Customers save time on personalized pages, which improves their loyalty and the bottom line of online retailers. In the world of online shopping, big data has affected the paradigm (Hallikainen et al., 2020).

12.7.3 Big Data Monetization for Dynamic Advertising

Organizations (with large amounts of data) use data-monetization to generate new revenue streams by leveraging previously untapped or underutilized data. Several factors are coming together to establish ideal conditions for data monetization.

The amount and variety of data now available to mobile providers—whether in the form of purchases, inquiries, text messages, tweets, GPS coordinates, or live video feeds—provides a veritable goldmine of insights and applications. Now mobile phones have become the primary source of information for users, and those same devices have begun to encourage new types of information, such as extremely accurate, real-time geolocation data (Elia et al., 2020).

Telecom companies, which have access to vast customer data quantities, have the unique ability to monetize the information they collect. They are likely to provide the most reliable and full customer details due to their direct interactions with consumers. They can create a 360-degree view of the customer by generating analytics-driven behavioral insights based on mobile interaction, venue, and demographic data.

Such observations will help outdoor marketers assess outdoor advertising units' efficacy and validate specific ad campaigns' influence and scope. Outdoor advertising agencies may gain insight into the preferences of the people they want to target and the best locations to reach them. Data enables marketers to transform every billboard into a targeted object that comes to the right viewer at the right time in the right place, giving considered "dead boards" new life (Wang and Wang, 2020).

12.7.4 Machine-To-Machine Analytics and Improved Product Life Cycle

The sensor technology used in computers, cars, mobile devices, power grids, and enterprise networks has advanced dramatically. As a result, machine-to-machine data is being generated at an unprecedented rate and in real-time. Companies can evaluate and increase manufacturing processes' efficiency, predict system failures, and determine the best time to up-sell new products to customers using data emitted by sensors from various applications. Furthermore, the data can provide insights for product creation, customer service, and sales staff, enhancing product functionality, boosting revenue, and cutting costs.

Big data exhaust from sensors in devices is a goldmine for data scientists looking to uncover hidden trends and provide deep insights that can help companies, governments, and society as a whole. Companies analyze sensor data, provide real-time information on event correlations and root cause analysis, forecast future threats, and visualize alternative scenarios using advanced statistical modeling techniques.

Large enterprise networks can analyze system log data from multiple network devices in real-time, predict the network devices that are more likely to malfunction, and detect possible network outages ahead of time, allowing for proactive remediation to improve customer service standards. Another useful application is to monitor consumer use of devices and goods and send proactive reminders and triggers to the sales team when it is time to notify the customer about a product update or refresh. It is an excellent way to develop a one-on-one relationship with a customer and help with cross-selling and up-selling.

12.8 Challenges of Big Data Analytics in the Context of Marketing Intelligence

Although big data analytics can support businesses in gaining a competitive edge over their competitors in various ways, it still faces a range of challenges (Hamilton and Sodeman, 2019).

The main challenge of big data analytics is the lack of resourceful significant data sources, the lack of accessible real-time analytics capabilities, the unavailability of adequate network infrastructure for running applications, the need to extend peer-to-peer networks, data privacy and security concerns, data integration issues and decentralized data, and the unavailability of cost-effective storage (Wang et al., 2020).

Besides, the application of big data analytics for marketing intelligence is complicated because of the need for expensive software and significant computing infrastructure to perform the analysis (Mikalef et al., 2020).

The other challenge is that big data remains a priority for hackers because it involves storing large amounts of aggregated heterogeneous data from many sources.

Regulation for legal standards, especially data privacy laws, has become a significant concern. Furthermore, since big data analytics is still in its early stages, there are no specific rules for safeguarding and protecting privacy, which could jeopardize public interest in big data storage and analytics (Xiang and Xu, 2020).

The challenge is to set guidelines for establishing contractual restrictions on exposing and disclosing data to unauthorized persons, restricting data copying, establishing staff background checks for those who have access to the data, and setting contractual restrictions on the use of unique project data (Zhang et al., 2020).

12.9 Summary and Conclusion

Digital customers are interconnected through mobile phones and tablets, laptops, online video game consoles, services, and platforms that can be accessed through these devices. They create various consumer touch-points through different mediums as they switch between platforms and devices, software, third-party, network devices, social networks, location-based, and mobile (Liu et al., 2021). This knowledge provides advertisers with a fantastic opportunity to better target their customers. Advanced analytics, such as optimization techniques, has been used by retailers to offer customized online recommendations to their customers.

12.9.1 Data in a New Way around Customers

To a significant extent, big data refers to the ever-increasing deluge of data that is created in today's digital ecosystem in terms of volume, variety, velocity, and complexity. Customers create big data sets based on online transactions, page views, social media interactions, digitally connected devices, geolocation, and other factors. These big data platforms allow for fast and cost-effective data ingestion and real-time data analysis (Lytras et al., 2020).

12.9.2 Big Data Analytics and Big Opportunity

Undoubtedly, taking advantage of big data's potential is on chief marketing officers' agenda in almost every major organization. When and how are they supposed to tap into big data sets, and what should they do with it? What is the best way to know the benefits? What are the prospects, the challenges? Marketing executives, in particular, want to know how to monetize big data (Rust, 2020).

Advanced and powerful analytics tools for big data create potential approaches to resolving some of the core marketing imperatives and producing impressive results. These strategies can change conventional marketing roles and enhance the performance of essential marketing functions. Marketers gather data from several real-time consumer touch-points to provide a full picture of each customer's behavior. The analysis of this high level of information in motion allows marketers to refine customer segmentation models and use their experience to create customer involvement strategies and increase customer interactions (Blanka and Traunmüller, 2020).

Marketing literature suggests that they offer a personalized experience across all platforms as the number of consumer channels grows. Both of these activities contribute to a personalized service while still enhancing the marketing investment's return. In the long run, marketers can use these unique, real-time insights to affect production processes and pricing by incorporating them back into the organization (Maroufkhani et al., 2020).

12.9.3 Big Data Analysis Key Considerations

Big data analytics is a path that allows organizations to overcome the most challenging real-world problems through the transformation of data into insights that affect strategic decisions. When organizations continue to take advantage of the big data chance, they do not have to confront the different obstacles ahead (Iqbal et al., 2020).

To get the most out of their big data project, marketing leaders will need to start by asking a few key questions:

i) What should be the big data analytics strategy to achieve target marketing goals?

ii) What market results would we like to change by using big data in the context of consumers?

iii) What features and capabilities should we build to gain a competitive edge using big data?

iv) What will technological solutions be available to embark organization's big data analytics journey?

v) Does the company have the requisite in-house expertise and tools to continue on a big data journey?

Big data analysis' benefits are many, and they will be primarily dependent on the organization's senior managers' visionary leadership. Senior managers can promote a culture of innovation and learning by using big data to drive critical pilots and communication points (Ranjan and Foropon, 2021). These successes would open the way for large-scale implementation of big data methods in marketing, making it more intelligent and useful to consumers, based on the achievements.

References

Amado, A., et al. (2018) 'Research trends on Big Data in marketing: A text mining and topic modeling based literature analysis', *European Research on Management and Business Economics*. European Academy of Management and Business Economics, 24(1), pp. 1–7. https://doi.org/10.1016/j.iedeen.2017.06.002.

Berry, D. (2011) 'The computational turn: Thinking about thedigital humanities', *Culture Machine*, 12, ISSN 1465-4121. https://pdfs.semanticscholar.org/7f61/f59bddbfaacdcb4078acbb52d539bf2a0cbe.pdf?_ga=2.116959046.1925915430.1632046326-1062652003.1632046326

Blanka, C. and Traunmüller, V. (2020) 'Blind date? Intermediaries as matchmakers on the way to start-up—industry coopetition', *Industrial Marketing Management*. Elsevier Inc., 90, pp. 1–13. https://doi.org/10.1016/j.indmarman.2020.05.031.

Buhalis, D. and Volchek, K. (2021) 'Bridging marketing theory and big data analytics: The taxonomy of marketing attribution', *International Journal of Information Management*. Elsevier Ltd, 56, p. 102253. https://doi.org/10.1016/j.ijinfomgt.2020.102253.

Elhoseny, M., Kabir Hassan, M. and Kumar Singh, A. (2020) 'Special issue on cognitive big data analytics for business intelligence applications: Towards performance improvement', *International Journal of Information Management*, 50(4), pp. 413–415. https://doi.org/10.1016/j.ijinfomgt.2019.08.004.

Elia, G., et al. (2020) 'A multi-dimension framework for value creation through Big Data', *Industrial Marketing Management*. Elsevier Inc., 90, pp. 617–632. https://doi.org/10.1016/j.indmarman.2020.03.015.

Erevelles, S., Fukawa, N. and Swayne, L. (2016) 'Big Data consumer analytics and the transformation of marketing', *Journal of Business Research*. Elsevier Inc., 69(2), pp. 897–904. https://doi.org/10.1016/j.jbusres.2015.07.001.

Fan, S., Lau, R. Y. K. and Zhao, J. L. (2015) 'Demystifying Big Data analytics for business intelligence through the lens of marketing mix', *Big Data Research*. Elsevier Inc., 2(1), pp. 28–32. https://doi.org/10.1016/j.bdr.2015.02.006.

Hallikainen, H., Savimäki, E. and Laukkanen, T. (2020) 'Fostering B2B sales with customer big data analytics', *Industrial Marketing Management*. Elsevier Inc., 86, pp. 90–98. https://doi.org/10.1016/j.indmarman.2019.12.005.

Hamilton, R. H. and Sodeman, W. A. (2019) 'The questions we ask: Opportunities and challenges for using big data analytics to strategically manage human capital resources', *Business Horizons*. Elsevier Ltd, 63(1), pp. 85–95. https://doi.org/10.1016/j.bushor.2019.10.001.

Iqbal, R., et al. (2020) 'Big data analytics: Computational intelligence techniques and application areas', *Technological Forecasting and Social Change*. Elsevier, 153(December 2017), pp. 0–1. https://doi.org/10.1016/j.techfore.2018.03.024.

Ishwarappa and Anuradha, J. (2015) 'A brief introduction on big data 5Vs characteristics and hadoop technology', *Procedia Computer Science*. Elsevier B.V., 48, pp. 319–324. https://doi.org/10.1016/j.procs.2015.04.188.

Jabbar, A., Akhtar, P. and Dani, S. (2020) 'Real-time big data processing for instantaneous marketing decisions: A problematization approach', *Industrial Marketing Management*. Elsevier Inc., 90, pp. 558–569. https://doi.org/10.1016/j.indmarman.2019.09.001.

Kauffmann, E., et al. (2019) 'A framework for big data analytics in commercial social networks: A case study on sentiment analysis and fake review detection for marketing decision-making', *Industrial Marketing Management*. Elsevier Inc., 90, pp. 523–537. https://doi.org/10.1016/j.indmarman.2019.08.003.

Krishnan, K. (2013) 'Introduction to Big Data', *Data Warehousing in the Age of Big Data*. Elsevier, pp. 3–14. https://doi.org/10.1016/b978-0-12-405891-0.00001-5.

Liang, T. P. and Liu, Y. H. (2018) 'Research landscape of business intelligence and Big Data analytics: A bibliometrics study', *Expert Systems with Applications*. Elsevier Ltd, 111(128), pp. 2–10. https://doi.org/10.1016/j.eswa.2018.05.018.

Liu, X., Shin, H. and Burns, A. C. (2021) 'Examining the impact of luxury brand's social media marketing on customer engagement: Using big data analytics and natural language processing', *Journal of Business Research*. Elsevier Inc., 125, pp. 815–826. https://doi.org/10.1016/j.jbusres.2019.04.042.

Lytras, M., et al. (2020) 'Cognitive computing, Big Data analytics and data driven industrial marketing', *Industrial Marketing Management*. Elsevier Inc., 90, pp. 663–666. https://doi.org/10.1016/j.indmarman.2020.03.024.

Manyika, J., Chui, M., Brown, B., Bughin, J., Dobbs, R. and Roxburgh, C. (2011) *Big Data: The Next Frontier for Innovation, Competition, and Productivity*. Seattle: McKinsey Global Global Institute.

Maroufkhani, P., et al. (2020) 'Big data analytics adoption: Determinants and performances among small to medium-sized enterprises', *International Journal of Information Management*. Elsevier Ltd, 54, p. 102190. https://doi.org/10.1016/j.ijinfomgt.2020.102190.

Mikalef, P., et al. (2020) 'Exploring the relationship between big data analytics capability and competitive performance: The mediating roles of dynamic and operational capabilities', *Information and Management*. Elsevier B.V., 57(2), p. 103169. https://doi.org/10.1016/j.im.2019.05.004.

Paul, T. and Mondal, S. (2019) 'A strategic analysis of tea leaves supply chain before manufacturing—a case in Assam', *Benchmarking: An International Journal*, 26(1), pp. 246–270. https://doi.org/10.1108/BIJ-01-2018-0007.

Ram, J., Zhang, C. and Koronios, A. (2016) 'The implications of Big Data analytics on business intelligence: A qualitative study in China', *Procedia Computer Science*. The Author(s), 87, pp. 221–226. https://doi.org/10.1016/j.procs.2016.05.152.

Ranjan, J. and Foropon, C. (2021) 'Big Data analytics in building the competitive intelligence of organizations', *International Journal of Information Management*. Elsevier Ltd, 56(February 2020), p. 102231. https://doi.org/10.1016/j.ijinfomgt.2020.102231.

Rust, R. T. (2020) 'The future of marketing', *International Journal of Research in Marketing*. Elsevier B.V., 37(1), pp. 15–26. https://doi.org/10.1016/j.ijresmar.2019.08.002.

Saidali, J., et al. (2019) 'The combination between Big Data and Marketing Strategies to gain valuable Business Insights for better Production Success', *Procedia Manufacturing*. Elsevier B.V., 32, pp. 1017–1023. https://doi.org/10.1016/j.promfg.2019.02.316.

Saritha, B., Bonagiri, R. and Deepika, R. (2021) 'Open source technologies in data science and big data analytics', *Materials Today: Proceedings*. Elsevier. https://doi.org/10.1016/j.matpr.2021.01.610.

Sivarajah, U., et al. (2020) 'Role of big data and social media analytics for business to business sustainability: A participatory web context', *Industrial Marketing Management*. Elsevier, 86(July 2018), pp. 163–179. https://doi.org/10.1016/j.indmarman.2019.04.005.

Wang, S.-C., Tsai, Y.-T. and Ciou, Y.-S. (2020) 'A hybrid big data analytical approach for analyzing customer patterns through an integrated supply chain network', *Journal of Industrial Information Integration*. Elsevier BV, 20, p. 100177. https://doi.org/10.1016/j.jii.2020.100177.

Wang, W. Y. C. and Wang, Y. (2020) 'Analytics in the era of big data: The digital transformations and value creation in industrial marketing', *Industrial Marketing Management*. Elsevier Inc., pp. 12–15. https://doi.org/10.1016/j.indmarman.2020.01.005.

Xiang, Z. and Xu, M. (2020) 'Dynamic game strategies of a two-stage remanufacturing closed-loop supply chain considering Big Data marketing, technological innovation and overconfidence', *Computers and Industrial Engineering*. Elsevier Ltd, 145, p. 106538. https://doi.org/10.1016/j.cie.2020.106538.

Xu, Z., Frankwick, G. L. and Ramirez, E. (2016) 'Effects of big data analytics and traditional marketing analytics on new product success: A knowledge fusion perspective', *Journal of Business Research*. Elsevier B.V., 69(5), pp. 1562–1566. https://doi.org/10.1016/j.jbusres.2015.10.017.

Zhang, C., et al. (2020) 'Linking big data analytical intelligence to customer relationship management performance', *Industrial Marketing Management*. Elsevier Inc., 91, pp. 483–494. https://doi.org/10.1016/j.indmarman.2020.10.012.

Chapter 13

Demystifying the Cult of Data Analytics for Consumer Behavior: From Insights to Applications

Suzanee Malhotra

Contents

DOI: 10.1201/9781003175711-13

13.1 Consumer Behavior: Overview

The puzzle of understanding consumer needs and expectations is multiplex. The study of consumer behavior provides a path to solve and understand the mysteries of the puzzle, layer by layer, and treat the consumers better. Consumer behavior is a subset of human behavior exhibited in context of markets and involves the search, purchase, usage and disposal of goods and services for satisfaction of their needs and wants (Chaudhary and Kumar 2016), which further impacts their behavior and indeed the society at large (Kotler and Keller 2016; Schiffman, Wisenblit and Kumar 2016).

The origination of consumer behavior is marketing's definition, since its whole focus is on the satisfaction of consumer needs and wants (Kotler and Keller 2016; Schiffman, Wisenblit and Kumar 2016). It is an adapted science from mother sciences like biology, chemistry and economics and social sciences like psychology, sociology and anthropology (Schiffman, Wisenblit and Kumar 2016). Study of consumer behavior in action context involves the study of its various facets and their consequential impacts, which are essential for the business firms and marketers in decision-making.

13.1.1 Importance of Consumer Behavior

The study of consumer behavior offers bundles of possibilities to the marketers in gearing their decision-making and planning (Kotler and Keller 2016; Schiffman, Wisenblit and Kumar 2016). The importance of consumer behavior is given Table 13.1. Some of the key important aspects are highlighted as follows:

Table 13.1 Importance of Consumer Behavior

Insightful knowledge	The understanding of consumer behavior provides insights into the factors (personal, cultural, social or psychological) that affect the buying behavior of consumers and their feelings regarding the varied brand choices.
Analyzing trends	The study of consumer behavior helps in knowing which products follow the latest trends, which have become obsolete and what can be done to fill a gap if present in meeting the consumer needs and paving a way for rolling out of new products/services.
Actionable strategies	The understanding of consumer behavior is a deciding factor for planning actionable marketing strategies. For example, considerable attention is devoted towards the analysis of consumer behavior while designing the 4Ps mix.
Fructifying loyalty	Study of consumer buying behavior can aid the marketer in fructifying the intentional loyalty into actional loyalty.
Segmentation basis	Study of consumer behavior and its layers is also a key basis for market segmentation and differentiation.

13.1.2 Types of Consumer Behavior

The consumer buying behavior varies for a range of goods and services. It changes from a mere simple process into a complex one depending on the extent of buyer involvement, differences in brands, contemplations and significant others' involvement in the buying behavior. Broadly there are four types of buying behaviors discussed as follows:

13.1.2.1 Habitual Buying Behavior

Buying behavior with respect to brands with little perceptual differences and commanding very little involvement on the part of the consumers is known as *habitual buying behavior* (Kotler and Armstrong 2016). Such type of behavior doesn't require extensive brand information search or active evaluation and comparison. It is more passive in nature developed out of routinized actions and strengthened by repetitive media exposure (though short in nature) creating a brand familiarity. Buying of *daily needs groceries* is a typical example of this type of consumer behavior.

13.1.2.2 Dissonance-Reducing Buying Behavior

The behavior where consumers are decidedly involved in making a decision with respect to an unusually high-priced or risky product/service with little perceptual brand differences is known as *dissonance-reducing buying behavior* (Kotler and Armstrong 2016). With little perceptual brand differences, the consumers rely broadly on price and the purchase convenience when making a choice. Even after purchase a consumer may constantly seek others' approval for the choice made. The 'dissonance' here refers to the feeling of regret that a consumer may experience if his/her choices go wrong or the outcome doesn't turn out as expected. It is in this type of behavior where after-sales support and assurances can help marketers in reducing the consumers' annoyance by making them happy regarding their brand choice. Buying of consumer electronics durables like air-conditioners, televisions, washing machines and others are characterized by this type of behavior.

13.1.2.3 Complex Buying Behavior

This is the behavior where consumers are decidedly involved in making a decision with respect to an unusual, high-priced, risky and self-expressive product/service, with the understanding that significant perceptual brand differences exist (Kotler and Armstrong 2016). Here the buyer undergoes a learning process about brands, where the typical 'belief-attitude-action' process sets in. The marketers thus must try to influence and reach out to the consumers in the various stages of information seeking and evaluation of alternatives so that their brand gets a firm place in the 'consideration set' decision by the consumer. The more the marketer devotes itself to creating knowledge of its brands and features offered by their products, the more the likelihood of the brand being a consumer's choice. Buying a car involves a know-how of mileage, engine and safety features, or buying a laptop involves know-how of the processor, operating system, RAM, and resolution, and both are characterized by this type of buying behavior.

13.1.2.4 Variety Seeking Behavior

The behavior commanding low consumer involvement but involving brands with significant perceptual brand differences is referred to as *variety seeking behavior* (Kotler and Armstrong 2016). This type of behavior is marked by considerable brand switching, not owing to dissatisfaction, but owing to the mere human need to enjoy variety in life. Here the market leader and market challenger use different marketing tactics to woo the consumers. While the former relies on frequent advertising reminders, the latter lures the consumers by offering them discounts, coupons, free samples or special deals. Buying biscuits or perfume sprays are characterized by this type of behavior.

13.1.3 Factors Influencing Consumer Behavior

A range of factors influence the consumer behavior, the understanding of which is a must for every marketer to gauge the patterns and trends guiding consumer behavior. The broad categorical factors are discussed in Table 13.2:

Table 13.2 Factors Influencing Consumer Behavior

Personal factors These include the factors characterizing a consumer like age, income, occupation, personality and lifestyle (Kotler and Armstrong 2016; Kotler and Keller 2016). For example, a consumer aged 35 years, earning a 6-figure salary per month as a corporate lawyer can easily maintain a luxury car. Similarly, a student with minimalist lifestyle and volunteering personality would be content with a yarn bag rather than a branded designer brand.
Cultural factors These factors comprise the value system, beliefs, language, social structure and stratification, customs, arts etc. to which a person is exposed (Kotler and Armstrong 2016; Kotler and Keller 2016). For example, a consumer being brought up in the United States would prefer individual freedom as opposed to one being brought up in Japan where group belongingness is a base for individual decisions also. Similarly, a society may be classified by the presence of various social classes like one set of consumers having a fine preference for ultraluxury products as opposed to others who seek more value for money in their purchases.
Social factors A person's family, reference groups, opinion leaders and changing roles comprise the social factors influencing consumer behavior (Kotler and Armstrong 2016; Kotler and Keller 2016). For example, a decision to buy a smart television for living room may be initiated, influenced and decided by taking into consideration all the family members preferences. Similarly, a person's place of work and peers have an open or tacit influence on the brand choices made by them.
Psychological factors The attitudes, beliefs, perceptions, learning and motivations of a consumer also impact their behavior (Kotler and Armstrong 2016; Kotler and Keller 2016). For example, a consumer with a good personal usage experience with a Dell laptop may develop a strong loyalty to it. Also, brands like Cartier, Prada and Louis Vuitton are perceived as high-end luxury brands.

However, in this era of digital boom, adding customers to your pie and delivering them what they want with value cannot be accomplished without using the worth of data analytics and its components to your leverage. The sections that follow will add on the knowledge and applicability of how having the power of data analytics at hand can help in marketing and understanding of the consumer behavior at length. Getting an initial understanding regarding the meaning of insights will shed light on demand drivers and models expressing it. We then move on to market segmentation and targeting discussion regarding popular techniques for the same, finally discussing the data analytics role in the consumer buying behavior at the end.

13.2 Insights

A managerial head plans for strategy execution, organizes a team for accomplishing goals, guides and leads them through the journey and plays a key role in strategic decisions. But here is pertinent thought: how does the managerial head arrive at the decision made, how do they gear the decision execution with respect to the turbulent business environment, are the material facts guiding such decision-making always available, or are the decisions solely determined by the material facts? The key function of business analytics is to render *insights* guiding managerial decision-making. But what is the meaning of insights, what are the key characteristics of insights and how are they put to use in studying consumer behavior? This is discussed in the following section.

13.2.1 Meaning of Insights

In the world of big data (Shakil and Alam 2016) and analytics (Khan et al. 2017; Khan, Shakil and Alam 2018), marketers are required to look beyond the mere observations, suggestions or comments offered by the consumers (Grigsby 2018). The intriguing set of knowledge set apart from traditional domains is what is referred to as *insights*. *Insights* can be defined as critical pieces of information that offer novel knowledge establishing causation relationships and yielding quantifiable benefits that are a source of competitive edge over other players and demand execution (Grigsby 2018). Let's look at the key features of insights as stated in the definition.

13.2.2 Features of Insights

The key features of insights forming a crucial part of the definition are discussed as follows:

13.2.2.1 Insights Offer Novel Knowledge

For any set of information to be characterised as an insight it must offer the business some novel, critical and original knowledge guiding the decision-making (Grigsby 2018). It must cross the line of being a mere observation, thought or comment and must be capable of being potentially exploited by the business people for their benefit.

13.2.2.2 Insights Provide Causation Relationship

Insights provide important cause and effect relationships (Grigsby 2018) for different business phenomena like demand, supply, cost of production and marketing mix among many others helping them to time and tackle various business strategies after taking into account their consequences.

13.2.2.3 Insights Add Competitive Edge

Insights lend the business a substantial and crucial competitive edge over other players in the market (Grigsby 2018). They are characterised as critical pieces of information, a substantial business asset that adds advantage to a firm over its competitors.

13.2.2.4 Insights Yield Quantifiable Results

Insights offer information that has a bearing on the decision-making in quantifiable terms (Grigsby 2018). It could be in terms of having a bearing on the sales, cost, profit margin or risk of undertaking a specific plan (Monika and Chaudhary 2014). Thus, the businesses must extract both the qualitative and quantitative juices from the information for it to be characterised as an insight.

13.2.2.5 Insights Demand Execution

Whatever insights are characterized as, ultimately they need to be put into action (Grigsby 2018), or the entire significance of such information is reduced to zero. Thus, a business analyst must deduce meaningful strategies from all relevant insights and make it a point to execute them. The features of insights are given Figure 13.1.

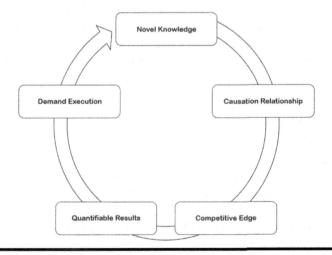

Figure 13.1 Features of Insights.

13.2.3 Putting Insights into Action for Consumer Behavior Study

If an insight is of such significance to the business on the whole, then ultimately the insights become very essential to marketing in getting a grasp of consumer behavior. The ultimate aim of marketing is to meet consumer satisfaction and earn loyalty (Chaudhary and Singh 2018). Combining insights with marketing plans can be rewarding for a business firm.

For example, The 2016 Reebok ad campaign, '25,915 Days' reminding people of the average number of days every human gets to live, was based on the insight where people tend to complain about their busy and hectic lives as a major reason for not being able to exercise regularly. The ad depicted the life journey of a women in reverse pattern, highlighting her dedicated passion for keeping her body fit, in a way urging people to make the most of their limited life span and keep up their exercise regime regularly to honor their health. By doing so the brand not only created the buzz for fitness but also earned a due share of recognition for its products.

Thus, putting essential insights into strategizing the marketing plans and tactics can aid the marketer in attracting the consumer's attention for their brands, generate revenue for the business firms and potentially also garner brand loyalty in the long run. Now let's have a look the demand-driving factors and how a marketer can express the demand in amenable models for data analytical use.

13.3 Demand

The task of marketers is to provide goods or services to the consumer, which provide satisfaction to the consumers (Kotler and Keller 2016). The share of sales a marketer is able to account for in the total market pie depends on the demand generated for its goods or services in particular. So, this section discusses the key drivers of demand, the deterministic vs. probabilistic demand equations and demand elasticity modelling.

13.3.1 Drivers of Demand

The key drivers of demand as found in microeconomics are price of the product/service, price of the associated substitute or complementary products/services, income or purchasing power capacity of consumers, likeability or preference for product/service and future price-level expectations for the product/service (Mankiw 2011). Besides these microeconomic drivers, the marketing drivers of consumer demand comprise promotional campaigns and appeals, ancillary product features and benefits, easy reach of the product/service within the consumer's vicinity and unforgettable consumer experience provided.

13.3.2 Deterministic vs. Probabilistic Demand Equations

The two most widely used models for expression are discussed in the following sections:

13.3.2.1 Deterministic Demand Equation

A deterministic demand equation, also known as an *algebraic equation*, is a simple linear equation where the left-hand side of an equation equates with the right-hand side (Grigsby 2018). Suppose there is a Firm Zeal, with both domestic and international presence. To calculate its domestic demand, the firm formulizes a deterministic equation as follows:

Domestic Demand = Total Demand – International Demand

If the firm knows about the total demand figure and the international demand figure, then it can easily determine the domestic demand figure. Thus, in deterministic-type equations, with the knowledge of any two quantities of an equation, one can compute the third one easily.

13.3.2.2 Probabilistic Demand Equation

In the real business world one seldom deals with such simple and straightforward models as dealt with in deterministic models, for the mere reason that the business environment is influenced by an influx of uncertainties constantly. Thus, businesses use the probabilistic models, also known as probabilistic regression models, where due consideration is ascertained to the uncertainty or randomness (known as 'random error'). A typical probabilistic equation is in the form:

$$Y = a + bx + e$$

where Y = dependent variable (to be determined)
    a = intercept (does not impact dependent variable)
    b = coefficient of independent variable (also known as slope)
    x = independent variable (known quantity)
    e = random error (due to uncertainty)

The presence of this random error or uncertainty adds the element of the probability that this model gets its name from (Grigsby 2018). Continuing from our previous example, now the domestic demand (dependent variable) of Firm Zeal will not be impacted by the foreign demand figures (intercept). But the price charged (independent variable) for the product and its elasticity (slope) in the domestic market are major factors impacting the domestic demand. After taking into account the random or uncertain factors (random error), the probabilistic demand equation for domestic demand estimation of Firm Zeal so formulated will be:

Domestic Demand = International Demand - coefficient of elasticity * Price + Random error
(where (–) minus sign indicates the inverse relationship between price and demand).

In statistics the dependent and interdependent (or interrelationship) are two popular modes of data analysis (Grigsby 2018). In the dependent type data analysis, use of expressed equations (either deterministic or probabilistic) is made to arrive at conclusions. In the interdependent or interrelationship type data analysis, use of factor variances and covariances (as found in factor analysis or discriminant analysis) is made.

13.3.3 Demand-Price Elasticity Modelling

In general parlance *elasticity* is defined as "a microeconomic calculation that shows the per cent change in response given a per cent change in stimulus" (Grigsby 2018, 45). In simple terms, elasticity is a barometer reflecting a proportionate change in one quantity because of proportionate change in another quantity. The demand-price elasticity is the proportionate change in demand attributable due to proportionate change in price and is denoted by a negative sign (because price and demand vary inversely). For example, if a 10% change in price brings about a 20% change in demand, then the resultant demand-price elasticity is (-) 2 being proportionate change in demand divided by proportionate change in price. One must never forget that demand-price elasticity is a unitless barometer. Demand-price elasticity is said to be elastic, that is numerically greater than 1, when the proportionate change in demand is greater than the proportionate change in price. On the other hand it is said to be inelastic, that is numerically less than 1, when the former is lesser then the latter. It is generally seen that for discretionary purchases there exists elastic demand, while for staples it is inelastic.

One can use the regression equations for computing the demand-price elasticity, where the coefficient of price is the barometer of demand elasticity. Using the simple regression equation

$$X = a + bY,\ \text{for estimation of demand-price elasticity where}$$

X = demand (in units)
b = demand-price elasticity
Y = price (in Rupees)

When one is given the details about the regression equation parameters other than demand, one can estimate the value of demand using them. For example, where

a = 53.76
b = – 0.14
Y = 24

then X (demand) = 50.4 units and demand-price elasticity is (–) 0.14. It is a case of inelastic demand.

One may use a multiple regression equation, which will provide a lot more information than mere demand-price elasticity, like demand-advertisement expenses elasticity, demand-income elasticity and others (Grigsby 2018). For example,

$$X = a + b1 * Price + b2 * Advertisement\ expenses + b3 * Income$$

where b1, b2 and b3 respectively define demand-price elasticity, demand-advertisement expenses elasticity and demand-income elasticity.

After getting a fair bit of understanding regarding the importance of insights and demand and its drivers, now let's focus our understanding on the next big leap for a marketer, which is the crucial decision regarding the segmentation and the data analytical technique to be used for the same.

13.4 Market Segmentation

Segmentation (also known as 'partitioning') is a one of the critical 4 P's for market strategy and involves segregating the market into identifiable, substantial, accessible, stable and responsive subsegments that are homogeneous within the internal boundaries of a segment and heterogeneous externally (Grigsby 2018; Kotler and Keller 2016). Actionable and profitable market strategies require the marketers to segregate the market into smaller groups and then go for segment-wise targeting or positioning (Kotler and Keller 2016). With the rapid advancement in data analytical tools have come novel techniques of segmentation that will be discussed in the sections ahead. The popular techniques used in market segmentation is shown in Figure 13.2.

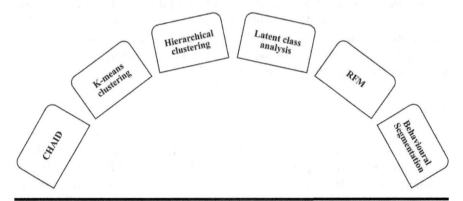

Figure 13.2 Popular Techniques Used in Market Segmentation.

13.4.1 Popular Techniques Used in Market Segmentation

13.4.1.1 CHAID

Chi-squared Automatic Interaction Detection, popularly shortened to CHAID, refers to a descriptive technique used to track relationship between a categorical dependent barometer and an independent barometer (independent barometer can be either continuous or categorical) (Grigsby 2018). In simple words, it helps us in understanding the pattern of splits emerging in the data and in making further decisions. In this technique first the dependent variable is considered, then one by one after screening out all the independent variables the one best independent variable that throws light on the classification of the dependent variable is known (Díaz-Pérez and Bethencourt-Cejas 2016). This process keeps on repeating until all the insights about the dependent variable are known sufficiently. It is widely used in market segmentation (McCarty and Hastak 2007). For example, a CHAID analysis run on a specific market to gauge their price sensitivity with respect to income levels would reveal the price sensitivity patterns that can be used by the marketer to segregate the market into appropriate income-based segments on the basis of the findings and undertake marketing plans accordingly. Owning to the simplicity and imaging results, it is very popular (Díaz-Pérez and Bethencourt-Cejas 2016; Díaz-Pérez et al. 2020). But it is advisable to supplement this with other techniques, for it just provides a segment classification and lacks in other insightful analysis.

13.4.1.2 K-Means Clustering

K-means clustering is one of the simplest (Alam, Shakil and Sethi 2016) and time-tested mathematical techniques for segmentation (Grigsby 2018). The 'k' in the name of the technique refers to the number of clusters/segments that one wishes to extract out of the data (Alam and Sadaf 2015a), and 'means' refers to the average nearest distance of data items from the clusters (Kim and Ahn 2008). In this technique one is to prestate the number of clusters that one wants to extract (which is a limitation of this technique also). The benefits of this technique lie in the ease of execution (Shakil and Alam 2014) and visual results, making it still a highly recommended technique for segmentation (Grigsby 2018). But the arbitrariness added due to self-specifying of the needed clusters number and the lack of a control mechanism are major limitations of this technique.

13.4.1.3 Hierarchical Clustering

Hierarchical clustering, or hierarchical cluster analysis, is an interdependent mathematical technique used to classify similar items in groups called clusters, which are unique from each other but the same within (Malik and Tuckfield 2019). In this technique the data items closely resembling each other are first identified (Alam and Sadaf 2015b), followed by their grouping into a cluster (Grigsby 2018). This process keeps on going until exhaustion is reached. It provides substantial findings regarding market segmentation by returning analysis results run on a market in terms of various segments or clusters segregated. In this method one does not need to prestate the clusters required manually, as needed in k-means clustering. The ease of usage coupled with graphical results make it an attractive technique, but it lacks in comparison to latent class analysis (Grigsby 2018).

13.4.1.4 Latent Class Analysis

Latent class analysis, popularly known as LCA, is a statistical technique used to understand the categorization of data items into particular segments. It is a technique that is statistically and analytically better than other techniques discussed until now and works well with both categorical and continuous variables (Hallikainen, Alamäki and Laukkane 2019). Grigsby has referred to it as "the state of the art in segmentation" (Grigsby 2018, 142). It uses the responses of the respondents for creation of segments or groups contrasting with other techniques where data items led to creation of clusters (Lukac, Doerflinger and Pulignano 2019). Thus, it is also considered a factor analysis technique. The ability to treat all types of data variables and missing items and its superiority over other techniques makes it a potentially strong technique for segmentation (Grigsby 2018). However, the additional training and proper handling of the data adds to its complexity in usage.

13.4.1.5 RFM

RFM analysis, an acronym for recency, frequency and monetary, is used as a marketing segmentation technique for finding the best pool of consumers (Kotler and Keller 2016). The three parameters for filtering consumers are recent timing of their purchases, recurrence of the purchases and the money value of the purchases (Grigsby 2018; Kotler and Keller 2016). It is based on the Pareto principle of economics, which states that focused attention on 20% of key areas achieves 80% of the desired performance (Koch 2013). It is widely used in directing email marketing strategies, building rapport with consumers and targeting repeated advertising appeals (McCarty and Hastak 2007). The simplicity of application and understanding has led to its extensive execution by firms over years. However, this technique offers no analytical reasoning behind choosing a particular pool of consumers or their purchase reasons (Grigsby 2018).

13.4.1.6 Behavioral Segmentation

Courtesy of the limitations faced in the RFM analysis, a new and enveloping technique called behavioral segmentation emerged for segmentation and in-depth consumer analytics (Grigsby 2018). Behavioral segmentation looks beyond consumer classification into the consumer behavior patterns, the key reasons triggering those patterns, the mixed needs and motivations of the consumers and other evolving behaviors (Mackellar 2009). Thus, one may refer to it as a marketing segmentation technique that supersedes other techniques discussed so far. It offers substantial and sustainable analytical findings regarding consumer behavior and guides much marketing strategy planning (Grigsby 2018). But with the depth of findings offered it is also characterized as the most complex technique requiring extensive marketing knowledge and mastering analytical skills.

Consumer segmenting is one way of getting the full frame market picture into focussed domain, but it is the tool of targeting that lets the marketer zoom and narrow down the consumers. The following section will discuss the meaning of consumer targeting and also highlight popular analytical techniques used for the same.

13.5 Consumer Targeting

While segmenting involves segregating the market into uniform segments, it is the task of targeting that involves actionable strategic moves to earmark potential buyers. Targeting aims to assess who is going to buy the market offering after responding to the targeting appeals (Kotler and Keller 2016). This section aims to introduce a few techniques applied in consumer targeting.

13.5.1 Popular Techniques Used in Consumer Targeting

13.5.1.1 Maximum Likelihood

The application of the maximum likelihood technique in targeting provides a projection regarding what parameters generate the maximum response out of the pooled data (Grigsby 2018). When a marketer applies this estimation technique for a set of targeting appeals on a sample of consumers, the results bring out the critical appeals, which can bring the maximum response out of the pooled consumers. Thus, its application tends to provide an assurance to the marketer regarding planned targeting appeals and their likelihood of success for a consumer segment (Gordini and Veglio 2017). One can use this method in the form of either regression equations (logistic) or in the manner of factor analysis structures (Grigsby 2018).

13.5.1.2 Lift Charts

Lift Charts are a visual predictive technique to market targeting, which helps the marketer to get access to a larger but relevant pool of consumers relevant enough for success of a particular program run (Duran, Pamukcu and Bozkurt 2014). With the use of machine language codes, this technique renders the data as to who are the consumers more probable to respond, alongside stating their probable estimated values. They are popularly used by small firms and operational employees while carving out targets to be predecided for running of marketing campaigns and programs. Popular types of lift charts used are the decile lift chart, cumulative lift charts and double lift charts (Ayetiran and Adeyemo 2012; Duran, Pamukcu and Bozkurt 2014; Grigsby 2018).

13.5.1.3 Survival Analysis

Survival analysis, created by Sir David Cox (Cox 1972), offers diagnostic solutions with respect to the most critical information of consumer action, that is, 'the timing' (Grigsby 2018). It is very critical to know when is a consumer is most likely to plan for a purchase or when he/she is likely to make a purchase and when a consumer is most likely to get the exposure to the marketing appeals and programs (Drye, Wetherill and Pinnock 2001). In the fast and competitive marketing era where 'time is money', timing is very crucial to tap consumers; thus survival analysis has become very important and effective for marketers. But with its increased importance comes added complications in its application and execution, thus properly taught and experienced staff is needed.

Now with this fair bit of understanding of the key stages used by the marketers in understanding the consumers and their behaviors, finally we are in position to relay the understanding of the consumer buying process stages and how can we use the discussed data analytical tools in the different stages of the process.

13.6 Consumer Buying Process and Analytics

Consumer buying behavior is marked by 4 prominent stages, viz., prepurchase, purchase, post purchase and post consumption (Schiffman, Wisenblit and Kumar 2016). Each stage is characterised by unique peculiarities to which a marketer must pay due attention in planning. With the added advantage offered by the power of data analytics, the route to consumer satisfaction generation as well as marketers' profitability has become very refined. This section discusses the stages of consumer buying behavior and correlates the findings derived from of each stage with the data analytics techniques discussed in the previous sections for marketing strategy planning and execution.

13.6.1 Prepurchase Stage

The essential identification of the need is the first step of this stage. In the very first step an uneasy feeling or sort of deprivation triggers the further course of buyer action (Schiffman, Wisenblit and Kumar 2016). Some needs are explicitly aroused while others need to have special emphasis due to their implicit nature (Kotler and Armstrong 2016). It is via the consumers' needs and their identification with such needs that the marketer is able to get hold of intriguing insights leading to new product development or tweaking of the marketing strategies. For example, witnessing people struggling to get their 'selfies' clicked with the back cameras made the marketers think of providing a front-camera in the smartphones. It was the insightful gap found in the smartphone development trajectory that has now revolutionized many social media platforms and their advancement also.

The second step of the first stage involves consumer search for options available to meet the need identified (Schiffman, Wisenblit and Kumar 2016). When a consumer relies on personal information and experience for an option search it is called *primary search*, while relying on others' suggestions and experiences is called *secondary search* (Kotler and Armstrong 2016). A marketer can put to use various segmentation techniques like CHAID, k-means or hierarchal clustering or latent class analysis to identify the distinct segments so that the consumer seeking information can get the needed information from their own primary efforts or from the peers of the same segment.

The final step of the first stage is evaluation of various options identified and searched for (Schiffman, Wisenblit and Kumar 2016). After successful weighing of all the options, the consumer arrives at some short-listed options, known as the 'consideration set'(Kotler and Keller 2016). Here the maximum likelihood approach comes to aid the marketer in knowing what factors or drivers are more likely to be converted from a likeable and probable choice to a sure and preferred choice.

13.6.2 Purchase Stage

With the identification of the 'consideration set', now the consumer decides the key W's: when (timing of purchase), where (location of purchase) and from whom to buy (seller-specific details like independent dealer or mall) and H's: how (mode of payment) and how much (quantity of purchase) characterizing the purchase. The survival analysis can be exploited by the marketers to time the purchase action of the consumers. Also, in the stage of purchase, pricing plays a key role, which can be understood by the marketers by using the demand-price elasticity modelling.

13.6.3 Post Purchase Stage

This stage is characterised by the discomfort or unease that a consumer goes through before consumption of the good/service after purchasing it (Kotler and Keller 2016). The discomfort is known as 'cognitive dissonance' and is marked by the highest levels in this stage (Schiffman, Wisenblit and Kumar 2016). Well, the post purchase stage may be an event of discomfort for the consumers, but the data pertaining to the post purchase, can be successfully put to use by the marketer in running the RFM analysis, which can lead to better segmenting and targeting prospects in the future also.

13.6.4 Post Consumption Stage

Once the consumption good/service is done, the outcome is essential to be known by the marketers for further action planning (Kotler and Keller 2016). Gauging satisfaction experienced in case of self-use goods/services is easy vis-à-vis goods/services meant to please others or seeking approvals of others (Chaudhary 2018). The marketers must analytically put to use all the data from the first stage to the post consumption stage under the behavioral segmentation technique for diagnosing long-term viable findings. Also, the application of lift-charts on the data set can give indications to the marketers as to where they hold good chances to successful targeting in future.

References

Alam, Mansaf, and Kishwar Sadaf. 2015a. "Labelling of Web Search Result Clusters Using Heuristic Search and Frequent Itemset." *Procedia Computer Science* 46, 216–222.

Alam, Mansaf, and Kishwar Sadaf. 2015b. "Relevance Feedback Versus Web Search Document Clustering." *2015 2nd International Conference on Computing for Sustainable Global Development (INDIACom)*. New Delhi, India: IEEE, 1665–1669.

Alam, Mansaf, Kashish Ara Shakil, and Shuchi Sethi. 2016. "Analysis and Clustering of Workload in Google Cluster Trace Based on Resource Usage." *19th IEEE International Conference on Computational Science and Engineering (CSE 2016)*. Paris, France: IEEE, 740–747.

Ayetiran, Eniafe Festus, and Adesesan Barnabas Adeyemo. 2012. "A Data Mining-based Response Model for Target Selection in Direct Marketing." *I.J. Information Technology and Computer Science* 1, 9–18.

Chaudhary, Kiran. 2018. "Impact of Emotional State of E-Buyers on E-Satisfaction: An Empirical Study." *SHANLAX International Journals of Management* 5, no. 2, 83–88.

Chaudhary, Kiran, and Suneel Kumar. 2016. "Customer Satisfaction Towards Flipkart and Amazon: A Comparative Study." *International Journal of Academic Research & Development JAR&D* 2, no. 1, 35–42.

Chaudhary, Kiran, and Narender Singh. 2018. "Factors Determining Customer Satisfaction, Customer Trust and Customer Loyalty in Online Retailing: An Empirical Study." *International Journal in Multidisciplinary and Academic Research (SSIJMAR)* 7, no. 1, 1–13.

Cox, David R. 1972. "Regression Models and Life-tables." *Journal of the Royal Statistical Society: Series B (Methodological)* 34, no. 2, 187–202.

Díaz-Pérez, Flora M., and M. Bethencourt-Cejas. 2016. "CHAID Algorithm as an Appropriate Analytical Method for Tourism Market Segmentation." *Journal of Destination Marketing & Management* 5, no. 3, 275–282.

Díaz-Pérez, Flora M., Alan Fyall, Xiaoxiao Fu, Carlos Gustavo García-González, and Gary Deel. 2020. "Florida State Parks: A CHAID Approach to Market Segmentation." *Anatolia*, 1–16.

Drye, Tim, Graham Wetherill, and Alison Pinnock. 2001. "When Are Customers in the Market? Applying Survival Analysis to Marketing Challenges." *Journal of Targeting, Measurement and Analysis for Marketing* 10, no. 2, 179–188.

Duran, Esra Akdeniz, Ayça Pamukcu, and Hazal Bozkurt. 2014. "Comparison of Data Mining Techniques for Direct Marketing Campaigns." *Sigma Journal of Engineering and Natural Sciences* 32, 142–152.

Gordini, Niccolò, and Valerio Veglio. 2017. "Customers Churn Prediction and Marketing Retention Strategies. An Application of Support Vector Machines Based on the AUC Parameter-selection Technique in B2B E-commerce Industry." *Industrial Marketing Management* 62, 100–107.

Grigsby, Mike. 2018. *Marketing Analytics: A Practical Guide to Improving Consumer Insights Using Data Techniques*. London: Kogan Page.

Hallikainen, Heli, Ari Alamäki, and Tommi Laukkane. 2019. "Individual Preferences of Digital Touchpoints: A Latent Class Analysis." *Journal of Retailing and Consumer Services* 50, 386–393.

Khan, Samiya, Xiufeng Liu, Kashish Ara Shakil, and Mansaf Alam. 2017. "A Survey on Scholarly Data: From Big Data Perspective." *Information Processing & Management* 53, no. 4, 923–944.

Khan, Samiya, Kashish Ara Shakil, and Mansaf Alam. 2018. "Cloud-Based Big Data Analytics—A Survey of Current Research and Future Directions." In: V. B. Aggarwal, Vasudha Bhatnagar, and Durgesh Kumar Mishra (eds.), *Big Data Analytics. Advances in Intelligent Systems and Computing 654*. Singapore: Springer. https://doi.org/10.1007/978-981-10-6620-7_57

Kim, Kyoung Jae, and Hyun Chul Ahn. 2008. "A Recommender System Using GA K-means Clustering in an Online Shopping Market." *Expert Systems with Applications* 34, no. 2, 1200–1209.

Koch, Richard. 2013. *The 80/20 Manager: The Secret to Working Less and Achieving More*. London: Little, Brown.

Kotler, Philip, and Gary Armstrong. 2016. *Principles of Marketing*. 16th ed. Harlow: Pearson.

Kotler, Philip, and Kevin Lane Keller. 2016. *Marketing Management*. Harlow: Pearson.

Lukac, Martin, Najda Doerflinger, and Valeria Pulignano. 2019. "Developing a Cross-national Comparative Framework for Studying Labour Market Segmentation: Measurement Equivalence with Latent Clas Analysis." *Social Indicators Research* 145, no. 1, 233–255.

Mackellar, Joanne. 2009. "Dabblers, Fans and Fanatics: Exploring Behavioural Segmentation at a Special-interest Event." *Journal of Vacation Marketing* 15, no. 1, 5–24.

Malik, Alok, and Bradford Tuckfield. 2019. *Applied Unsupervised Learning with R: Uncover Hidden Relationships and Patterns with K-means Clustering, Hierarchical Clustering, and PCA*. Birmingham: Packt.

Mankiw, N. Gregory. 2011. *Principles of Microeconomics*. 6th ed. Mason, OH: Cengage.

McCarty, John A., and Manoj Hastak. 2007. "Segmentation Approaches in Data-mining: A Comparison of RFM, CHAID, and Logistic Regression." *Journal of Business Research* 60, no. 6, 656–662.

Monika, and Kiran Chaudhary. 2014. "Global Marketing—A Comparison of Domestic and International Marketing." *International Journal of Management Research* 2, no. 4, 34–45.

Schiffman, Leon G., Joe Wisenblit, and S. Ramesh Kumar. 2016. *Consumer Behavior*. 11th ed. London: Pearson.

Shakil, Kashish Ara, and Mansaf Alam. 2014. "Data Management in Cloud Based Environment Using k-Median Clustering Technique." *International Journal of Computer Applications* 3, 8–13.

Shakil, Kashish Ara, and Mansaf Alam. 2016. "Recent Developments in Cloud Based Systems: State of Art." *International Journal of Computer Science and Information Security (IJCSIS)* 14, no. 12, 242–258.

Index

Printed in the United States
by Baker & Taylor Publisher Services